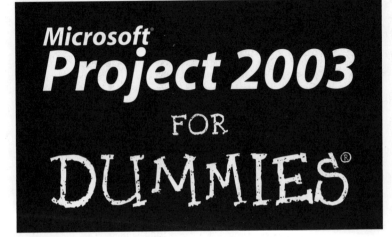

Microsoft® Project 2003 FOR DUMMIES®

by Nancy Stevenson

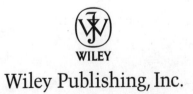

WILEY

Wiley Publishing, Inc.

Microsoft® Project 2003 For Dummies®

Published by
Wiley Publishing, Inc.
111 River Street
Hoboken, NJ 07030-5774

About the Author

Nancy Stevenson (Port Townsend, WA) is the author of over 40 books on technology and business topics ranging from motivating people to e-commerce and wireless technology. She co-authored the *Microsoft Project 98 Bible* and a project-management textbook for college students. As a manager in the software, publishing, and video industries, Ms. Stevenson has first-hand experience in managing a variety of projects. In addition, she has taught workshops on project management and project management software to Fortune 500 companies.

Dedication

To Bryn and Earl who keep the home fires burning.

Author's Acknowledgments

Thanks to Terry Varveris of Wiley for her support and patience, and to Christine Berman and Barry Childs-Helton for pulling it all together. Thanks also to Vickey Quinn for keeping me technically honest, one more time.

Publisher's Acknowledgments

We're proud of this book; please send us your comments through our online registration form located at www.dummies.com/register/.

Some of the people who helped bring this book to market include the following:

Acquisitions, Editorial, and Media Development

Project Editor: Christine Berman

Acquisitions Editor: Terri Varveris

Senior Copy Editor: Barry Childs-Helton

Technical Editor: Vickey Quinn

Editorial Manager: Leah Cameron

Media Development Manager: Laura VanWinkle

Media Development Supervisor: Richard Graves

Editorial Assistant: Amanda Foxworth

Cartoons: Rich Tennant, www.the5thwave.com

Production

Project Coordinator: Erin Smith

Layout and Graphics: Seth Conley, Joyce Haughey

Proofreaders: Susan Moritz; TECHBOOKS Production Services

Indexer: TECHBOOKS Production Services

Special Help
Kristie Rees

Publishing and Editorial for Technology Dummies

Richard Swadley, Vice President and Executive Group Publisher

Andy Cummings, Vice President and Publisher

Mary C. Corder, Editorial Director

Publishing for Consumer Dummies

Diane Graves Steele, Vice President and Publisher

Joyce Pepple, Acquisitions Director

Composition Services

Gerry Fahey, Vice President of Production Services

Debbie Stailey, Director of Composition Services

Contents at a Glance

Table of Contents

Introduction

Project management probably started back when a few cave dwellers got together and figured out how to work as a team to bag a wooly mammoth for their Sunday dinner. Some fellow — we'll call him Ogg — probably took the lead, so he was the very first project manager. He drew things in the dirt with a stick to help his team members understand the strategy of the hunt and communicated with them in ughs and grunts. Unlike you, he had no boss to report to, no budget, and no deadlines (lucky Ogg), but the fundamental spirit of a project was there.

Over the years, project management has evolved as a discipline that involves sophisticated analysis, projections, tracking of time and money, and reporting. Project-management software — which has, let's face it, been around only about a dozen years or so — has brought a new face and functionality to project management that would have left our friend Ogg ughless.

About This Book

Microsoft Project 2003, the most recent incarnation of the world's most popular project-management software, offers a tremendous wealth of functionality to users. However, it's probably not like any other software you've ever used, so mastering it can seem a daunting process. One trick is to understand how its features relate to what you do every day as a project manager. Another is to get someone like me to tell you all about its features and how to use them.

In *Microsoft Project 2003 For Dummies,* my goal is to help you explore all that Project offers, providing information on relevant project management concepts while also offering specific procedures to build and track your Project plans. But more importantly, I offer advice on how to make all these features and procedures mesh with what you already know as a project manager to make the transition easier.

Foolish Assumptions

I've made some assumptions about you, gentle reader. I figure that you are computer-literate and know how to use a mouse, a keyboard, software menus, and toolbars. I assume you know how to use most common Windows functions such as the Clipboard, and many basic software functions such as selecting text and dragging and dropping things with your mouse.

I do not assume that you've used Project or any other project-management software before. If you're new to Project, you'll find what you need to get up to speed, including information on how Project works, finding your way around, and building your first Project plan. If you've used an earlier version of Project, you'll find out about Project 2003 and all the new features it provides.

Conventions Used in This Book

I should explain a few odds and ends to make using this book easier:

- ✔ All project and task names are *italicized* to make them easier to identify.
- ✔ Web site addresses, known as URLs, are highlighted like this: www. microsoft.com.
- ✔ Menu commands are given in the order in which you select them, for example, "Choose Tools ➪ Resource Sharing ➪ Share Resources."
- ✔ Options in dialog boxes use initial caps even if they aren't capitalized on your screen to make it easier to identify them in sentences. (For example, what appears as Show summary tasks in the Options dialog box will appear as Show Summary Tasks in this book.)

How This Book Is Organized

This book is designed to help you begin to use Microsoft Project 2003 to plan, build, and track progress on projects, keeping in mind tried-and-true project-management practices and principles. I divided the book into logical parts that follow the process of building and tracking a typical project plan.

Part I: Setting the Stage for Project

Part I explains what Project 2003 can do for you, and what types of input you have to provide to use it successfully on your projects. You'll get your first glimpse of Project views, and master ways to navigate around them. You'll begin to build Project plans by making calendar settings, building a task outline, and then enter timing and timing relationships for those tasks.

Part II: People Who Need People

Part II is the Project resources section: You discover all you need to know about creating and assigning resources and material costs to tasks in a project.

This is also the place to explore the features of Project that help you incorporate several smaller projects into a master project, and how to share resources among projects.

Part III: Well, It Looks Good on Paper

Up to now, you've been mapping out your project plan. Now it's time to see whether that plan meets your needs in terms of budget and timing. Project offers a whole toolbox of tools that help you modify resource assignments and task timing to trim your costs and meet your deadlines so you can finalize your plan. You also get briefed on how to modify formatting of items in your project to make your plan look as polished as possible, both on-screen and in print.

Part IV: Avoiding Disaster: Staying On Track

As any experienced project manager knows, projects just about never happen the way you thought they would. In this part, you save a picture of your plan called a *baseline* and then begin to track actual activity against your plan. You'll also take a look at methods of reporting your progress, and how to get back on track when you find yourself derailed. In the final chapter, I provide advice on how to use what you learn in your projects to make better planning choices going forward.

Part V: Working with Enterprise Projects

With all that Project Professional has to offer the enterprise via its Project Server functionality and SharePoint online services, you can share documents online with your project team, have your human resources report their work time, and even integrate Project information with Outlook. This part shows you the basics of what Project Server can do, how to set it up, and how to work with it.

Part VI: The Part of Tens

Ten seems to be a handy number of items for humans to put into lists, so this part gives you two such lists: Ten Golden Rules of Project Management, and Ten Project-Management Software Products to Explore. The first of these chapters tells you about some dos and don'ts that can save you a lot of grief when you're using Project for the first time (or the fifth time, for that matter). The second offers a look at some add-on products and complementary software products that bring even more functionality to Microsoft Project.

Part VII: Appendixes

This book is accompanied by a handy CD filled with project-management goodies, including project-management add-on software and Microsoft Project templates. Appendix A is where I explain how to work with the CD and exactly what you can find there.

Earned value? Budgeted cost of work performed? Work breakdown structure? I'm telling you, project management has more terminology than video games. That's why I've provided a Glossary (Appendix B) that contains a lot of terms, some from the discipline of project management and some Project-specific. Definitions of key terms are included throughout this book, but when you need a refresher course, look here.

What You're Not to Read

First, you don't have to read this book from front to back (but if it's not in Japanese, don't read it from back to front). If you want to just get information about a certain topic, you can open this book to any chapter and get the information you need.

That said, I have structured the book to move from some basic concepts that equip you to understand how Project works through the steps involved in building a typical project. If you have an overpowering need to find out the whole shebang, you can start at the beginning and work your way through the book to build your first Project plan.

Icons Used in This Book

One picture is worth . . . well, you know. That's why *For Dummies* books use icons to give you a visual clue as to what's going on. Essentially, icons call your attention to bits of special information that might very well make your life easier. Following are the icons used in this book.

Remember icons signal either a pertinent fact that relates to what you're reading at the time (but is also mentioned elsewhere in the book), or a reiteration of a particularly important piece of information that's — well — worth repeating.

Tips are the Ann Landers of computer books: They offer sage advice, a bit more information about a topic under discussion that might be of interest, or ways to do things a bit more efficiently.

Warning icons spell trouble with a capital *T:* When you see a Warning, read it, because it's trying to tell you that if you're not careful you might do something at this point that could cause disaster.

Where to Go from Here

Time to take what you've learned in the project management school of hard knocks and jump into the world of Microsoft Project 2003. When you do, you'll be rewarded with a wealth of tools and information that help you to manage your projects much more efficiently.

Here's where you step out of the world of cave-dweller project management and into the brave, new world of Microsoft Project 2003.

Part I
Setting the Stage for Project

The 5th Wave   By Rich Tennant

"I did this report with the help of a satellite view atmospheric map from the National Weather Service, research text from the Jet Propulsion Laboratory, and a sound file from 'The Barfing Lungworms' new CD."

In this part . . .

Part I explains the types of input you have to give Project to make the best use of its capabilities. You get a briefing on using Project views, using calendar settings to build Project plans, creating task outlines, and then specifying the timing and relationships that organize your project's tasks.

Chapter 1

Project Management: What Is It, and Why Should I Care?

*W*elcome to the world of computerized project management with Microsoft Project. If you've never used project management software before, you're entering a brave, new world. It will be like walking from an office of twenty years ago — with no fax, voicemail, or e-mail — into the office of today with its wealth of high-tech devices.

Everything you used to do with handwritten to-do lists and word processors and spreadsheets all come magically together in Project. But this transition won't come in a moment, and it will take some basic understanding of exactly what project management software can do to get up to speed. If you've used Project before, this little overview will help you refresh your memory, and ease you into a few of the new features of Project 2003.

So, even if you're a seasoned project manager, take a minute to review this chapter — it provides the foundation for how you'll work with Project from here on.

The ABCs of Project Management

You probably handle projects day in and day out. Some are obvious just because your boss named them so that any fool would know they're projects:

The Acme Drilling Project, or the Network Expansion IT Project, for example. Others are less obvious, such as that speech thing you have to do on Saturday for your professional association or washing the dog.

Project management is simply the process of managing all the elements of a project, whether that project is large or small. Do you need to organize a company holiday party? It's a project. Have you been handed a three-year earth-exploration initiative to find oil in Iowa, coordinating subcontractors and government permits and working with a team of 300 people? That's definitely a project. Yes, even that speech thing is a project, because it has certain characteristics that need managing.

Understanding what your projects, large or small, have in common is the basis of understanding what Project can do for you. All projects have

- An overall goal
- A project manager
- Individual tasks to be performed
- Timing for those tasks to be completed (such as three hours, three days, or three months)
- Timing relationships between those tasks (for example, you can't begin using a new manufacturing process until you've trained people in the process)
- Resources (people, equipment, facilities, supplies, and so on) to do the work
- A budget (the costs associated with people, equipment, facilities, supplies, and so on)

Three Ts: Tasks, timing, dependencies (well, two Ts and a D)

As Lewis Carroll said, "If you don't know where you're going, any road will get you there." So first things first: You have to understand the goal of your project so you can begin to build the *tasks* that have to be performed to get you there.

A *task* is pretty much one of those items you used to scribble on your handwritten to-do lists, such as *Write Final Report* or *Apply for Permits*. Tasks are typically organized into *phases* (appropriate stages) in Project, arranged in an outline-like structure (as you can see in the project shown in Figure 1-1).

Figure 1-1:
The outline-like Gantt Chart view, in which you spend the most time when you work in Project.

Task master

A task can be as broad or as detailed as you like. For example, you can create a single task to research your competition, or you can create a project phase that consists of a *summary task* and *subtasks* below it. The summary task might be (for example) *Competitive Research,* for which the subtasks might include *Researching online business databases, Assembling company annual reports,* and *Reviewing competitive product lines.*

Adding tasks to a Project file doesn't cost you a thing (except a nanobit of memory), so remember that a project can have as many tasks and as many phases as you like. You simply use the outlining structure in Project to indent various levels of tasks. The more deeply indented in an outline a task is, the more detailed.

One handy thing about this outlining structure is that you can roll up all the timing and cost data from the subtasks within your phases into summary-level tasks. So three sequential subtasks, each taking a day to complete and costing you $200 apiece, result in a summary task that spans three days and costs $600. You can view your project at various levels of detail or get automatic tallies of timing and costs if you prefer to simply view the summary level of tasks.

For more about defining and creating tasks, check out Chapter 4.

It's all in the timing

They say timing is everything: Rome wasn't built in a day, a stitch in time saves nine, and don't even ask me about selling short in the stock market. The importance of timing applies to Project tasks, as well. Almost all tasks have timing, which is referred to as duration. A task's *duration* is the amount of time it will take to complete the task.

The only tasks without duration are milestones. A *milestone* is a task of zero duration; in essence it simply marks a moment in time that must be reflected in your Project outline. Typical milestones are the approval of a brochure design or an assembly line startup.

Project doesn't provide magic formulas for duration: Duration is assigned based on your own experience and judgment. Does designing a product package take three days or three weeks? Will obtaining a building permit happen in a day or a month? (Remember, you're dealing with City Hall, so think before you answer!) Project isn't an oracle: You have to provide facts, figures, and educated guesses to build your Project schedule. But after that information is entered, Project can do some weird and wonderful things with it that help you maintain and monitor your progress.

Task codependencies

The final piece in the puzzle of how long your project will take is something called dependencies. *Dependencies* are the timing relationships among tasks. If you have a schedule that includes ten tasks that all begin at the same moment in time, your entire project would take as long as the longest task (see Figure 1-2).

After you define and implement timing relationships, your schedule can stretch out over time like a long rubber band. One task might begin only after another is finished. Another task can start halfway through the preceding task. The second task can only start a week after the first task is over. Only after you've started to assign these relationships can you can begin to see a project's timing as related not just to each task's duration, but also to the specific ways that the tasks relate to each other.

Here are some examples of dependencies:

- ✔ You can't begin to use a new piece of equipment until you install it.
- ✔ You must wait for a freshly poured concrete foundation to dry before you can begin to build on it.
- ✔ You can't start to ship a new drug product until the FDA has approved it.

Figure 1-2:
This
schedule
includes
tasks with
timing but
no depen-
dencies.

One other brief note about the timing of tasks: In addition to applying dependencies to tasks, you can apply *constraints.* For example, let's say you don't want to start shipping your new ice-cream flavor until you get the ad for it in your Christmas catalog. So you set a dependency between those two events. But you can also set a constraint that says you must start producing the ice cream no later than November 3. In this case, if you don't make the catalog deadline, the product will still ship on November 3; that task will not be allowed to slip its constraint because of a dependency relationship.

You can find out more about the fine art of managing dependencies and constraints in Chapter 6.

Lining up your resources

When people first use Project, some get a bit confused about the topic of resources. Resources aren't just people. A *resource* could be a piece of equipment you rent or a meeting room that you have to pay an hourly fee to use. It could be a box of nails or a software program you have to buy.

There are two kinds of resources: work resources and material resources. *Work resources* are charged by how many hours or days the resource (often human) works on a task. *Material resources,* such as sewing supplies or steel, are charged by a per-use cost or by unit of measurement (such as square yard or linear foot or ton).

Some resources, such as people, perform their work according to a working calendar. If a person works an 8-hour day, and you assign him to a task that takes 24 hours to complete, that person would have to put in three workdays to complete the task. Someone with a 12-hour workday would take only two days to complete the same task.

In addition, you can set working and nonworking days for your human resources, which accommodates variations such as four-day weeks or shift work.

You can set different rates for resources, such as a standard hourly rate and an overtime rate. Project applies the appropriate rate based on each resource's calendar and work assigned.

Several views in Project let you see information about resources and how their assignment to tasks has an impact on project costs. Figure 1-3 is the Resource sheet, which shows columns of information about resources and their costs.

		Resource Name	Type	Material Label	Initials	Group	Max. Units	Std. Rate	Ovt. Rate	Cost/Use
	1	Corporate manageme	Work		C	Mgmt	100%	$0.00/hr	$0.00/hr	$0.00
	2	Project Office coord	Work		P		100%	$25.00/hr	$35.00/hr	$0.00
	3	Analyst	Work		A	Mktg	100%	$75.00/hr	$75.00/hr	$0.00
	4	Developer	Work		D		100%	$80.00/hr	$120.00/hr	$0.00
	5	Project Office staff	Work		P		100%	$20.00/hr	$30.00/hr	$0.00
	6	Steel	Material	STL	S			$0.00		$250.00
	7	Trips to plant	Material	PLANT	T			$0.00		$0.00
	8	Mohammed Durah	Work		M	Mgmt	100%	$100.00/hr	$100.00/hr	$0.00
	9	Penelope Marshall	Work		P	Eng.	100%	$50.00/hr	$75.00/hr	$0.00

Figure 1-3:
Resources charged at a rate per hour are the basis of how Project tallies costs.

One other important thing you should know about resources: They tend to have conflicts. No, I'm not talking about conference-room brawls (though there is that, too). These conflicts have to do with assigned resources that become overallocated for their available work time. If you assign one poor soul to three eight-hour tasks that must all happen on the same day, in the same eight hours, Project has features that do everything but jump up on your desk and turn on an alarm to warn you of the conflict. (Luckily, Project also provides tools that help you *resolve* those conflicts.)

You can also assign *fixed* costs to a task. For example, if your company charges a flat $2,000 for a new product's package design, no matter how many resources work on it, you could enter a fixed cost of $2,000 for the task of package design. (For more about resources and costs, see Chapter 7.)

Spreading the news

I am one of those people who need instant gratification. So one of the first things I ask about learning any new software product is, what's in it for me? Up to now, I've been telling you about the type of information you have to put into Project: information about tasks, task dependencies, and resources. But isn't it about time you got something back from Project? Of course it is.

You've finally reached one of the big payoffs for inputting all that information: reporting. After you've entered your information, Project offers a wealth of reporting options to help you view your project and communicate your progress to your project team, clients, and management.

You can generate pre-designed reports based on information in your schedule, or simply print any of the views that you can display in Project. Figures 1-4 and 1-5 show you just two of the reporting options available in Project.

Planning to keep things on track

Projects aren't frozen in amber like some organizational mosquito: They go through more changes than a politician in a campaign year. That's where Project's capability to make changes to your project data comes in handy.

After you've built all your tasks, given them durations and dependencies, and assigned all your resources and costs, you set a baseline. A *baseline* is like a snapshot of your project at the moment you feel it's ready to go. After you set a baseline, you will record some activity on your tasks. Then you can compare that actual activity to your baseline.

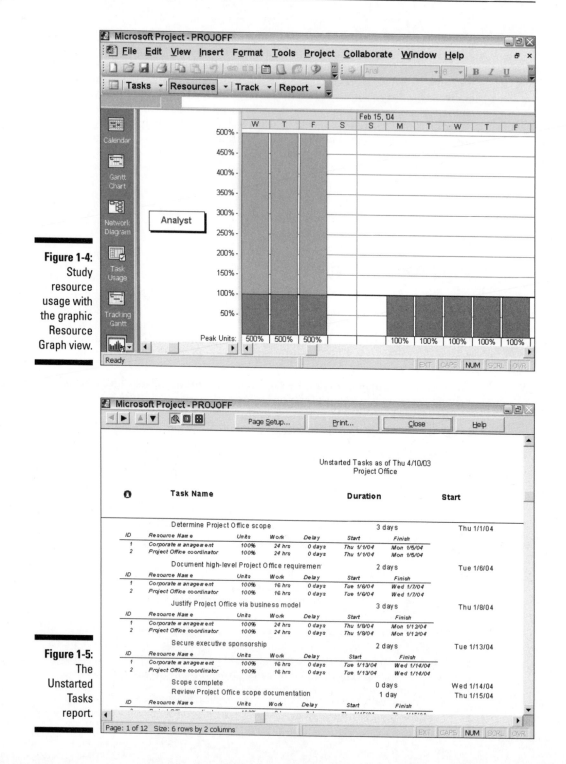

Figure 1-4:
Study resource usage with the graphic Resource Graph view.

Figure 1-5:
The Unstarted Tasks report.

Tracking activity on your project involves recording the actual timing of tasks and recording the time that your resources have put in on those tasks, as well as any actual costs you've accrued. You can then display Project views that show you how far off you are at any point in time (compared to your baseline) in terms of the actual timing of tasks and cost of your project.

Whether you have good news or bad, you can use reports to show your boss how things are going compared to how you thought they would go. Then, after you peel your boss off the ceiling, you can use a lot more Project tools to make adjustments to get everything back on track.

The Role of the Project Manager

Although it's not always easy to understand the role (let alone the usefulness) of some managers, it's always easy to spot the value of a *project* manager. This is the person who creates the master plan for a project and tries to ensure it gets implemented successfully. Along the way, this key person will use some skills and methods that have evolved over time, always seeking to manage how things get done and generally keeping them on track.

What exactly does a project manager do?

A project manager isn't always the highest authority in a project; often that role belongs to whoever manages the project manager, up to and including members of senior management. The project manager is the person on the front lines, making sure the parts of the project come together and assuming hands-on responsibility for successes as well as failures.

In project-management parlance, the person who champions (and has the ultimate responsibility for) a project is called the project *sponsor*.

A project manager manages these essential pieces of a project:

- ✔ **The project plan.** This is what you create with Microsoft Project. It includes the estimated steps and associated timing and costs involved in reaching the project goal.

- ✔ **Resources.** Managing resources involves resolving resource conflicts and building consensus, as well as assigning resources and tracking their activities on the project. This part of the job also involves managing nonhuman resources such as materials or equipment.

- ✔ **Communicating with the project team, management, and customers.** Communicating the project's status to everyone who has a legitimate stake in its success is a key responsibility.

Though a project manager may work for a project sponsor, there is often also a *customer* for whom the end product is being produced. That customer may be outside the project manager's own company, or within.

Understanding the dreaded triple constraint

You've seen the signs at the copy store or the auto repair place: You can have it fast, cheap, or right; pick two. That, my friend, is the triple constraint of project management in a nutshell.

In a project you have timing, resources (which are essentially costs), and quality of the product or service you end up with at the end of the project. Microsoft Project helps you manage the resources and timing of your project. The quality of your project is often affected directly by how well you manage them. If you add time, it costs more because resources are working longer hours at a certain wage. If you take away resources, it can affect quality . . . and so on.

Coming to a logical balance of time, money, and quality is at the core of what a good project manager does throughout the life of a project.

Tried-and-true methodologies

Microsoft Project incorporates some scheduling and tracking tools that have resulted from many years of developing project-management methods. A few of these are worth noting here:

The **Gantt Chart** (shown in Figure 1-6), which is the main view of Project, shows you a spreadsheet with columns of data along with a graphical representation of the tasks in the project arranged along a horizontal timeline. Using the data in the columns (such as task name, start date, finish date, and resources assigned to tasks), you can understand the parameters of each task, as well as see it's timing in the graphical area. Being able to view all of this information on one page helps you understand what's happening in your project in terms of time and costs.

The **Network Diagram** view in Project, shown in Figure 1-7, is essentially Microsoft's version of something called a PERT chart. PERT (Program Evaluation and Review Technique) was developed during the construction of the Polaris submarine in the 1950s. It is a mostly graphical representation of the tasks in your project reflecting the flow of work in your project rather than the literal timing of tasks. This view helps you to see how one task flows into another, and to get a sense of where you are, not so much in time, but in terms of the work you have to accomplish.

Figure 1-6:
The Gantt Chart method of project scheduling as it appears in Microsoft Project.

Figure 1-7:
A kissing cousin to the original PERT chart, the Network Diagram focuses on work, not time.

Risk management is a central part of project management because, frankly, projects are chock-full of risk. There's the risk that your resources won't perform, the risk that materials will arrive late, the risk that your customer will change all the parameters of the project halfway through — well, you get the picture.

Risk management is the art of anticipating risks, ranking them from most to least likely, and determining strategies to prevent the most likely ones from occurring. Project helps you with risk management by allowing you to try out *what-if scenarios:* You can change the start date or length of a task or phase of tasks (for example) and see just what that does to your schedule, such as the delays, cost overruns, and resource conflicts that might occur in such a scenario, down to the last hour and penny. Having this kind of information at your fingertips makes risk management easier and (almost) painless.

Finally, **resource management** consists of using resources wisely. A good project manager will find the right resource for the job, assign that person a reasonable workload, stay alert for shifts in schedule that cause that resource to be overbooked, and make adjustments during the life of the project that keep all resources most productive. In Project, tools are available such as a resource histogram or the *resource usage chart*, reflecting resource workload, as shown in Figure 1-8.

Figure 1-8:
A resource usage chart helps you spot resource-scheduling problems; notice how overbooked this resource is on this date.

The figure also shows *resource leveling* (a calculation that automatically reschedules resources to resolve overbooking), which can enable you to manage resources much more effectively.

You can even use codes for resources that designate skill level or abilities so that finding the right resource for each job is as simple as performing a search.

From To-Do List to Hard Drive

By now you're probably shaking your head and saying, "Boy, handwritten to-do lists look pretty good right now. Beats creating hundreds of tasks, assigning them durations, establishing dependencies among them, creating resources, entering resource calendar and rate information, assigning resources and costs to tasks, entering activity performed on tasks . . ." and so on.

Well, you're right *and* wrong about that. You do have to enter a lot into Project to get the benefit of its features. But you can also get a lot out of Project.

Getting up to speed with Project

Take a moment to review some of the wonderful things Project can do for you. This is why you (or your company) bought it and why you're investing the time to read this book.

With Project, you'll enjoy the following benefits:

✔ Project automatically calculates costs and timing for you based on your input. You can quickly recalculate what-if scenarios to solve resource conflicts, get your costs within budget, or meet your final deadline.

✔ Project offers views and reports that make a wealth of information available to you and those you report to with the click of a button. No more running up a report on total-costs-to-date to meet a last-minute request from your boss. If she wants to know total-costs-to-date, you can just print your Tracking Gantt view with the Tracking table displayed.

✔ You can use built-in templates to get a head start on your project. Templates are prebuilt plans for typical business projects such as commercial construction, engineering projects, a new product rollout, software development, and an office move.

✔ It's likely that you do similar types of projects all the time. After you create one project, use it as a template for future projects.

✔ You can create resources for your project according to information you've already created in your Outlook address book. You can even create one set of company resources, and give every project manager in the company access to them.

✔ A number of tools in Project employ complex algorithms (that you couldn't even begin to figure out) to do things such as leveling resource assignments to solve resource conflicts, filtering tasks by various criteria, modeling what-if scenarios, and calculating the value of work performed to-date in dollars.

Here's where the Internet comes in

You can also take advantage of all the Internet has to offer by using Project features to collaborate with others. Project allows you to request updates on a task's progress from team members by using e-mail. You can even publish your project on the Web.

The Professional version of Project includes a feature called Project Server that enhances workgroup collaboration. You can take advantage of an online project center with areas for discussions, tracking progress, exchanging data, and more.

Part V of this book looks at how to take advantage of the enterprise-wide features of Project Server and SharePoint.

Getting Started

As Shakespeare said, "In delay there lies no plenty." I don't know about you, but I need all the plenty I can get, so it's time to jump in and start using Project.

You have a few choices here. You can use a template to create a project or build one from scratch. In either case, you start by telling Project something about your project.

First, enter some project information

When you open Project 2003, you see a blank project file show up on-screen along with the Getting Started task pane (which includes links to open an existing project or create a new project).

What's Project Guide?

Project Guide is like some of those wizards you see in Microsoft products — it walks you through a series of steps, asking you to enter some information and automating a process for you. However, in many ways Project Guide is like no wizard you've ever seen.

First, it has four different sections (Tasks, Resources, Track, and Report). Within each of those categories may be ten or so links for you to click to initiate an action. When you do so, there may be a variety of sub-actions you can choose (depending on your particular project). Also, the sections of Project Guide span the entire life of your project, from the time you first enter task information to the time you generate your final report.

If you've never used project-management software (or Project itself), it can be very helpful to run through Project Guide to set up your first schedule, enter resources, track activities on tasks, or generate reports. However, in order to know how to work through Project Guide and make intelligent choices, you'll have to have some basic understanding of how a project is built. My advice is to walk through many of these steps with me in this book, and *then* use Project Guide to practice building your first project. Then you can see whether its structure works the way your mind works — or not.

If you click Create a New Project in the Getting Started task pane, it changes to the New Project task pane. Here you can click Blank Project, and the task pane changes to the Tasks pane — the first of four phases of a feature called Project Guide. You can use Project Guide to walk you through the logical sequence of steps for creating a new project.

With the blank project open, a first logical step would be to input some general project information. To do so, you choose Project ➪ Project Information. The Project Information dialog box appears, as shown in Figure 1-9.

Here's what you can do in this dialog box:

- ✔ **Set the start date for the project.** If you're not sure when it will start, set the start date about a month or so ahead. Then, when you've built some tasks and have a better handle on the entire length of your project, you can come back here and set a new start date. Project will automatically recalculate all dates when you do.

- ✔ **Set the finish date for the project.** Especially if you have a *drop-dead date* (now *there's* an attention-getting term!) beyond which the project cannot wander and still reach completion, you can set the finish date. In such a case, be sure to look at the *next* setting in this list — and change it accordingly.

Figure 1-9:
The Project
Information
dialog box is
used for
some basic
project
settings.

✔ **Schedule from the start or finish of the project.** Most projects go from
the start forward. However, if you have an absolute drop-dead date for
the end of your project (for example, if you're organizing an event that
will occur on New Year's Day next year), you might want to set the finish
date and then work backward to fit all your tasks into the time allotted.
If you change this setting to Project Finish Date, the Finish Date box
becomes available.

✔ **Set the current date.** You may fill in the current date according to your
computer calendar, but you can choose another date if you like.

✔ **Set a status date.** You use a *status date* when you're tracking the progress
of your project at regular intervals. If you set a status date, your computer assumes that any activity you record in your project is being
tracked as of this date. You can find out more about this feature in
Chapters 12, 13, and 14.

✔ **Set the working calendar for your project.** You have three choices:
Standard, Night Shift, and 24 Hours. Base your choice on the working
habits of your organization. For example, if your company uses resources
in three shifts a day — a total 24 hours of straight working time — and
all those shifts would put in work on your project, then choose 24
Hours. If you use a day shift and a night shift, choose Standard. (Most
projects use a standard calendar with a typical eight-hour workday.)

Calendars can get a little confusing. A project calendar that you set in this dialog box indicates what the usual workday is like in your company, but you can also set up individual calendars for each resource you create. This helps you accommodate both shift workers and nine-to-fivers in the same schedule. See Chapter 3 for more about resource calendars.

✔ **Assign a priority to your project.** Doing so can be especially useful if (for example) you're using the same resources across several projects. With priorities set on all projects, Project tools can automatically reallocate resources according to your set priorities.

You can also create custom project information fields for your organization in the Enterprise Custom section of this dialog box. For example, you might want a field that explains which department in the company is running the project.

If you click the Statistics button in this dialog box, you get an overview of your project, as shown in Figure 1-10.

Starting from scratch

When you make settings in the Project Information dialog box and click OK, you are faced with a blank Project schedule, as shown in Figure 1-11. As a writer, I can tell you that nothing is as daunting — or inspiring — as facing a blank page. It's the canvas on which you create your Project plan.

What you're presented with is the Gantt Chart view. You can discover more about various views in Chapter 2. For now, note the following:

✔ The bar of icons along the left, called the *View Bar,* allows you to click and go to different views.

✔ To the right is a task pane currently displaying the *Project Guide,* an informational area with step-by-step guidance on how to build your project.

✔ In the middle of the view is the *sheet* section. This is a spreadsheet interface that you can use to enter, edit, and view information about your project.

✔ Finally, the *chart* area reflects your task information graphically after you begin to add tasks. *Taskbars* in this area indicate the duration and timing of tasks, as well as the progress you record on them. The indications of time increments across the top of the chart area, called the *timescale,* help you interpret the timing of each taskbar and can be adjusted to show your project in larger or smaller increments of time.

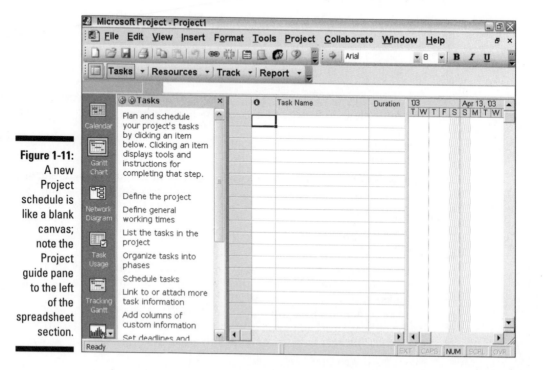

Figure 1-10:
You can
review
a summary
of the
information
you entered.

You start building a project by entering tasks. Simply click a cell in the Task Name column and then type the name. You can enter and edit details of a task by double-clicking the task name in the sheet to access the Task Information dialog box (see Figure 1-12) or by entering information directly into various columns, which you can display in many views.

Figure 1-11:
A new
Project
schedule is
like a blank
canvas;
note the
Project
guide pane
to the left
of the
spreadsheet
section.

Task Information ✕

| General | Predecessors | Resources | Advanced | Notes | Custom Fields |

Name: [Document high-level Project Office requ.] Duration: [2d] ☐ Estimated

Percent complete: [0%] Priority: [500]

Dates

Start: [Tue 1/6/04 ▾] Finish: [Wed 1/7/04 ▾]

☐ Hide task bar
☐ Roll up Gantt bar to summary

[Help] [OK] [Cancel]

Figure 1-12:
The various tabs in this dialog box hold a wealth of information about a single task in your project.

Using templates

Reinventing the wheel has never been one of my favorite sports, so I'm grateful that Microsoft has provided some convenient project templates. These include projects by type, for example an engineering project or an office move. Templates already have many tasks appropriate to the task type created for you.

After opening a template be sure to check its Project Information (choose Project ➪ Project Information) to make sure that the Start Date and Calendar options are set as you want.

Figure 1-13 shows the Project Office template. Templates typically contain sample tasks broken into logical phases, with task durations and dependencies in place. The templates from Microsoft often include resources, but you can create your own resources as well as use, edit, or delete the ones provided.

You can open a template from the New Project task pane. To do so, follow these steps:

1. **Choose File ➪ New.**

    The New Project task pane appears, as shown in Figure 1-14.

2. **Select On My Computer.**

    You can also use the On My Web Sites or Templates Home Page template to access online templates.

3. **Click the Project Templates tab, which is shown in Figure 1-15.**

Figure 1-13: Templates provide a great head start in building common business projects.

Figure 1-14: Here's the New Project task pane.

Figure 1-15:
Business
and
personal
templates,
such as
Home
Move, are
included
here.

Templates

General | Project Templates

Commercial Construction	Engineering	Home Move	Infrastructure Deployment
Microsoft Active Directory Dep...	Microsoft Exchange 20...	Microsoft Office XP Corporate...	Microsoft SharePoint...
Microsoft Windows ...	MSF Application...	New Business	New Product

Preview

Preview not available.

Templates on Office Online   OK   Cancel

4. **Click a template to display a preview.**

5. **When you find the template you want to use, click OK.**

   The template opens in Project document format (.MPP). You can then delete tasks, move them around, or add tasks as necessary for your project.

If you modify a template and think that you might use that set of tasks again for future projects, consider saving the file as a custom template before you begin to add specific project details. Just choose File ➪ Save As, and then select Template in the Save As Type list.

Saving a project for posterity

Saving Project files works just as saving does in most other software you've used. Here's a reminder.

To save a Project file that you haven't saved before, follow these steps:

1. **Choose File ➪ Save As.**

2. **Use the Save In list to locate the folder where you want to save the file, and then click to select it.**

3. **In the File Name text box, type a name for the project.**

4. **Click Save.**

It's a good idea to create a folder for your project where you save not only your Project files but also supporting documents, e-mails, and so on for your project. You can create a new folder from the Save As dialog box by clicking the Create New Folder button.

Getting help from Project

If you can get to work without mishap and turn a computer on, you probably know how to use a help system in software, too. But Table 1-1 offers a rundown of the type of help you'll find in Project 2003.

Table 1-1	Project Help Features
Help Option	*How to Use It*
Microsoft Project Help	Depending on whether you've activated the Office Assistant, this option displays the Assistant or opens the full Help feature with contents, the Answer Wizard, and topics listed in an index, along with the What's New listing of Project features.
Show the Office Assistant	Displays the annoying little icon that asks you to enter your question in a natural-language style (that is, a sentence) and offers topics to try to address your questions.
Contents and Index	Displays the same thing as Microsoft Project Help. Go figure.
Reference	Provides reference information such as a comprehensive list of all fields in Project, a glossary, and a table of mouse and keyboard shortcuts.
Getting Started	A side menu for this Help menu option offers a tutorial and project map. The tutorial provides a set of topics explaining Project from the basics of what is project management through creating a plan. The project map is another take on the phases involved in building your project.
Office on the Web	Because Project is part of the Office family of products, this link is provided to the Office online Assistance Center.

Help Option	How to Use It
Detect and Repair	Automatically identifies errors and tries to correct them. Use this if you have serious problems using the software (for example, if the software constantly shuts down and gives you error messages).
Project Guide	The one option not accessed from the Help menu, Project Guide is new in 2003. Project Guide appears when you open a new project. It offers links to step-by-step information on how to build your project.

As you can see, it could take you a year just to learn all the help options in Project. Don't worry — they're there when you need them, and some, such as Project Guide, even pop up automatically to offer help.

Chapter 2

The Best-Laid Plans

In This Chapter

▶ Finding your way around Project

▶ Exploring Project views

▶ Customizing views

Homer (not Simpson — the other one) once said, "The evil plan is most harmful to the planner." In the interests of helping you get some good out of your Project plan, it's worth taking a moment to get comfortable with various aspects of it.

The file you create in Project is called a Project *plan,* or *schedule.* This plan is like a multidimensional chess game from *Star Trek,* with a plethora of data about various aspects of your project — as well as graphic representations of that information.

To see that information, Project provides more views than the Grand Canyon. These views help you observe the structure of your plan and see the progress in your project. Project also offers many ways to move around and display different information in your views. Navigating Project and displaying (and modifying) its views are the topics to explore in this chapter.

Navigating Around Project

Having a lot of views from which to observe your project information is great, but all those views won't do you any good if you don't know how to get from one to the other, or how to move around a view after you've found it.

Changing views

You can move from one view to another in Project using the view bar or the View menu. The view bar runs along the left side of every view. Simply click any view icon there to display that view.

If the view bar doesn't appear on your screen, choose Tools ➪ View Bar to display it.

In addition to the eight commonly used views displayed on the view bar, there are a few dozen other views that you'll need to use as you work through your project. To display views not shown on the view bar, follow these steps:

1. **Click the arrow at the bottom of the view bar to scroll down to the bottom.**

2. **Click the More Views icon.**

   The More Views dialog box appears, as shown in Figure 2-1.

Figure 2-1: Dozens of views are available for display in Project.

More Views
Views:
Bar Rollup
Calendar
Descriptive Network Diagram
Detail Gantt
Gantt Chart
Leveling Gantt
Milestone Date Rollup
Milestone Rollup
Multiple Baselines Gantt
Network Diagram
Relationship Diagram
Resource Allocation

New...
Edit...
Copy...
Organizer...

Apply   Cancel

3. **Use the scrollbar to locate the view you want.**

4. **Click Apply.**

You can also access the More Views dialog box by choosing View ➪ More Views. In addition, eight of the most commonly used views are available as selections on the View menu.

Scrolling around

The simplest views, such as the Calendar view, have a single pane, with horizontal and vertical scroll bars. Other views, such as the Resource Usage view (see Figure 2-2), have two panes. In that case, each pane has its own horizontal scroll bar but they share the vertical scroll bar, so the panes move up and down at once.

Figure 2-2:
Multiple
panes of
information
maximize
space in
many views.

In most views with two panes the pane to the left is called the *sheet,* which is a spreadsheet-like interface with columns of information. To the right of this view is the *chart.* The chart uses bars, symbols, and lines to represent each task in your project and the dependency relationships between them.

At the top of the chart area is the *timescale.* This tool is used as a scale against which you can interpret the timing of the *taskbars.* To see your plan in greater or lesser timing detail, you can modify the time units used in the timescale. For example, you can look at your tasks in detail over days or in a broader overview in months.

By using the horizontal scroll bars in each pane, you can view additional columns or additional periods of time in any pane with a timescale. Timescale panes cover the life of the project; in longer projects you may be able to scroll through years of time.

Use these different methods to work with scroll bars:

✔ **Click the scroll box and drag it until you reach the location in the pane that you want to look at.** When you click and drag the scroll box to move through a timescale display, the date display indicates where you are at any time in your scrolling calendar. Release the mouse button when the date display matches the date you want to view.

✔ **Click to the left or right of the horizontal scroll box to move one page at a time.** Note that a *page* in this instance is controlled to some extent by how you have resized a given pane. For example, with a timescale pane and a timescale set to weeks, you move a week at a time. In a sheet pane displaying three columns, you move to the next (or previous) column.

✔ **Click the right or left arrow at either end of a scroll bar to move in smaller increments.** With a sheet pane, you move about a half column per click. In a timescale view with weeks displayed, you move about a day at a time.

Go to!

To reach a particular area of your Project plan, you can also use the Go To command on the Edit menu. Using the Go To command, you can enter either of two items in the Go To dialog box when you want to find a task: You can select a date from a calendar, or you can enter a task ID.

You can also click the Go To Selected Task tool to scroll the timescale to show the taskbar for a selected task in the sheet pane.

The task ID is assigned automatically when you create tasks; this number provides a unique identifier for tasks in the plan.

A Project with a View

Views are one way that software designers organize information so that you can get at it in logical ways. Because of the complexity of information in a typical Project plan, many views are available to examine it. If you think of your average word-processed document as being about as complex as a cookie, your average Project plan is more like a five-tier wedding cake adorned with intricate flowers and garlands in delicate gobs of sugary icing.

In a typical Project plan, you have information about the following:

✔ **Resources.** The resource name, type of resource, rate per hour, overtime rate, assignments, department, cost per use, and more

✔ **Tasks.** The task name, duration, start date, finish date, assigned resources, costs, constraints, dependencies, and so on

✔ **Project timing and progress.** Several types of calendars, project start and finish dates, percent of tasks completed, resource hours spent, baseline information, critical path information, and more

✔ **Financial information.** Earned value, time and cost variance, projected costs for uncompleted work, and so on

You can see that finding out how to use the many Project views to enter, edit, look at, and analyze Project data is important. Don't worry that you'll be overwhelmed: After a while, using all those views is . . . well, a piece of cake.

Home base: Gantt Chart view

The Gantt Chart view is like a favorite room in your house, the place most people gravitate to. It's the place that appears first when you open a new project. This view, shown in Figure 2-3, is a combination of spreadsheet data and a graphical representation of tasks; it offers a wealth of information in one place.

Figure 2-3: The Gantt Chart view can display any combination of columns of data that you want.

The Gantt Chart view has two major sections, the sheet pane and the chart pane, and is actually an electronic version of the original Gantt Chart developed by engineer Henry L. Gantt in 1917 to deal with production-control projects in manufacturing. (See? Name a project-management tool and you too can become immortal.)

In the Gantt Chart view (and any view with a sheet pane), you can change what information is shown in the sheet by using tables. Tables are preset combinations of columns of data that you can easily display by choosing View ⇨ Table, and then selecting a table such as Entry or Cost from the menu.

You can also customize the column display for any table by displaying or hiding individual columns of data one by one. (See the section titled "Displaying different columns," later in this chapter, for information about this procedure.)

Go with the flow: Network Diagram view

Another view that you're likely to use often is the Network Diagram view, which is shown in Figure 2-4. The organization of information represents the workflow in your project, with a series of task boxes. The boxes include dependency lines running among them to reflect their timing relationships. You read this view from left to right, with the earlier tasks on the left flowing into later tasks and subtasks to the right.

Traditionally called a PERT chart, this method of diagramming workflow was developed by the Navy in the 1950s for use in building the Polaris submarine.

The Network Diagram view has no timescale because the view is used not to see specific timing but to see the general order of tasks in a plan. However, each task box does include specific timing information about each task, such as the start date, finish date, and duration. (You can customize the information in the task boxes, as described later in the "What Do You Want to See?" section.)

Call up Calendar view

Who can think of time without conjuring up a calendar? This familiar view of time is one of the many views offered in Project. The Calendar view, shown in Figure 2-5, shows tasks as boxes that fall across the blocks that represent days in a calendar.

You can modify the Calendar view to display from one to six weeks (or more using a Custom setting in the Zoom dialog box) on the screen at a time. The Calendar view also includes a timescale that you can modify to show a seven-day or five-day week and shading to indicate working and nonworking days based on a selected base or resource calendar.

Figure 2-4:
The
Network
Diagram
view puts
important
task
information
in task
boxes.

Figure 2-5:
The familiar
calendar
interface
shows you
how one
task can
straddle
several days
(or even
weeks).

Dozens of views are built into Project. You'll encounter many more as you work through specific elements of Project in this book.

What Do You Want to See?

Just when you thought you were starting to get a handle on the two dozen or so views available in Project, I'm going to dazzle you with even more possibilities: Every one of those views can be customized to show different information. Now the possible view variations become astronomical.

You can customize every view in Project to show different information; for example you can choose to show different columns of information in spreadsheets, different labels in Network Diagram boxes or taskbars, or different sets of data in graph views. You can modify the size of panes of information, and adjust the timescale.

Why all this flexibility with what you see on screen? At various times in a project, you'll need to focus on different things. Having a problem with costs? Take a look at the Resource Usage view and insert several columns of cost information, such as resource rates and total actual costs. Is your plan taking longer than the Hundred Years' War? You might want to display the Tracking Gantt view and look at a bunch of columns with timing and dependency data or examine the project's critical path in the chart pane. Need to display more of the sheet area so that you can read those columns without having to scroll? In this section, you find out how to do all the things you need to do to show a variety of information in each view.

Views with panes

In addition to the Gantt Chart view, there are several other views that include two panes, such as Task Usage, Tracking Gantt, and Resource Usage. You can modify the information you see in the sheet pane, and the scale for timing in the chart pane. You can also display information near taskbars in the chart pane.

It's a pane

In views that show more than one pane, you can reduce or enlarge each pane. This helps you see more information in one area, depending on what your focus is at the time.

The overall area taken up by the two panes is constant, so that when you enlarge one pane you reduce the size of the other.

Follow these steps to change the size of a pane in a view:

1. **Place your mouse cursor over the edge of a pane.**

2. **When you get a cursor that's a line with two arrows, one pointing left and one pointing right, click and drag to the left or right.**

   Dragging to the left enlarges the pane on the right; dragging to the right enlarges the pane on the left.

3. **Release the mouse button.**

   The panes are resized.

Note that if you display the Project Guide or another task pane such as New Project or Search Results, Project automatically resizes the sheet and chart panes to accommodate the additional pane.

Changing time

I wish I could tell you that Project actually lets you change time and give your project lots more of it, but it doesn't. What it does allow you to do is modify the timescale to display your plan in larger or smaller increments of time.

A timescale consists of a possible total of three tiers, as you can see in Figure 2-6. You can use these to display different increments of time. For example, the top tier could mark off months, the middle tier, weeks, and the bottom tier, days. This variety of detail lets you observe overall task length as well as points in time during the life of the task easily. You can use all three of these tiers, only the middle tier, or the middle and bottom tier.

Figure 2-6: The timescale is made up of three tiers so you can view time from several directions.

Zooming in and Out

One other way to modify your display for any Project view is to use the Zoom In and Zoom Out buttons on the Standard toolbar. This feature shows you a longer or shorter time period in your project without having to change the timescale settings. When you need to see several years in your project at once, for example, click Zoom In several times until you fit as many tasks as you like in the view. You can also choose View ⇨ Zoom and specify periods of time to display in the Zoom dialog box, or even choose to have the entire project appear on-screen.

You can modify the units of time and the alignment of each tier, and include tick lines to mark the beginning of each increment on the timescale. You also have the option of including or not including nonworking time on the timescale. For example, if you include an indication of nonworking time on a project where weekends are nonworking, Saturdays and Sundays will be indicated by a shaded area in the display.

You can also display text labels near taskbars and change what data is included. Labels can be placed above, below, inside, or to the left or right of the taskbars. Especially in projects where you are displaying many columns of data and a length schedule, a taskbar may be placed far to the right of the sheet pane data; including information such as task name or start date alongside the taskbar helps you read your plan more easily.

To modify the timescale, follow these steps:

1. **Right-click the timescale in any view that contains one and then click Timescale.**

   The Timescale dialog box shown in Figure 2-6 appears.

2. **Click a tier tab and select a style for Units, Label, and Align.**

3. **Set the Count.**

   For example, if your Units choice is weeks and you change Count to 2, the timescale appears in two-week increments.

4. **If you don't want to display a tier, click the Show option under the Timescale options section and select One Tiers or Two Tiers.**

5. **If you want Project to use fiscal year notation in the timescale, select the Use Fiscal Year check box.**

   For example, if your 2003 fiscal year begins July 1, 2002, 2003 is used on all months in the fiscal year. The fiscal year is set in the Options dialog box on the Calendar tab.

6. **To show marks at the beginning of each unit of time, select the Tick Lines check box.**

7. **Repeat Steps 2 through 6 for each tier you want to modify.**

8. **Click the Non-working Time tab.**

9. **In the Draw options, select the one you prefer.**

   Your choices are to have the shaded area for nonworking time appear behind taskbars, appear in front of them, or not appear at all.

10. **In the Color or Pattern list, select different options for the shading format.**

11. **Click the Calendar setting and select a different calendar to base the timescale on.**

    You can find out more about calendar choices in Chapter 3.

12. **Click OK to save your new settings.**

You can use the Size setting on the three tier tabs to shrink the display proportionately to get more information on your screen or the printed page.

Displaying different columns

Each spreadsheet view has certain default columns of data that are stored in tables. The Gantt Chart view with the Tracking table displayed, for example, has data related to the progress of tasks. The Resource sheet contains many columns of data about resources that can be useful for entering new resource information. In addition to displaying predefined tables of columns, you can modify any spreadsheet table to display any columns you like.

Follow this procedure to show columns of data:

1. **Right-click the column heading area and then click Insert Column.**

   The Column Definition dialog box appears, as shown in Figure 2-7.

Figure 2-7:
Here you can select new columns to insert.

Column Definition
Field name: ID
Title:
Align title: Center
Align data: Right
Width: 10   ☑ Header Text Wrapping
Best Fit   OK   Cancel

2. **In the Field Name list, select the field that contains the information you want to include.**

3. **If you want to enter a different title for the field, type it in the Title box.**

   The title appears in the column heading for this field in this view.

4. **Use the Align Title, Align Data, and Width options to modify the column format.**

5. **Click OK to insert the column.**

To hide a column, right-click its heading in the sheet pane and then click Hide Column.

You can also display preset tables of sheet data, such as Tracking for recording activity on tasks or Entry used for entering new task information. You do this by simply choosing View ⇨ Table, and then clicking the name of the table you want to display.

Modifying the contents of the network diagram box

When you first display the Network Diagram view, you see rectangular boxes, one for each task in your project. You can change the information contained in those boxes as well as the box formatting.

By default, a typical subtask contains the task name, task ID, start date, finish date, duration, and resource names. For a milestone, you get only the milestone date, milestone name, and task ID number.

Different categories of tasks (such as *critical* or *noncritical*) may contain different information, but you can change the information contained in any individual box or category of boxes.

What's in the box?

Sometimes you'll want to see information about task timing, other times you'll be focused on resources. To accommodate these various information needs, the Network Diagram view allows you to use various templates for what's contained in the diagram boxes.

To modify the information included in these boxes, do the following:

1. **Right-click anywhere in the Network Diagram view outside any box, and then click Box Styles.**

   The Box Styles dialog box appears, as shown in Figure 2-8.

Box Styles

Style settings for: Preview:

Critical
Noncritical
Critical Milestone
Noncritical Milestone
Critical Summary
Noncritical Summary
Critical Inserted Project
Noncritical Inserted Project
Critical Marked
Noncritical Marked
Critical External
Noncritical External
Project Summary

[Name]
Start: [Start]   ID: [ID]
Finish: [Finish]   Dur: [Duration]
Comp: [% Complete]

☐ Set highlight filter style   Show data from task ID: [   ] [↕]

Data template
[Summary   ▼]   [More Templates...]

Border
Shape: [▱   ▼]   Color: [■ Red   ▼]   Width: [———————— ▼]
☑ Show horizontal gridlines   ☐ Show vertical gridlines

Background
Color: [□ White   ▼]   Pattern: [■■■■■   ▼]

[Help]   [OK]   [Cancel]

Figure 2-8:
You can use
templates of
data for
Network
Diagram
view task
boxes.

2. **In the Style Settings For list, select a category of task.**

3. **To modify the data included in the task boxes, select a different template in the Data Template list.**

   You can choose additional templates (and edit any template to include whatever data you like) by clicking the More Templates button.

   A preview of the data included in the template appears in the Preview area.

4. **Click OK to save the new template.**

You can also apply different templates to each box separately by right-clicking a box (rather than clicking outside a box), clicking Format Box, choosing a different template from the Data Template drop-down list, and then clicking OK.

Making pretty boxes

Are you the creative type? Don't like the shape or color of the boxes in the Network Diagram boxes? Want to add shading to the background of the boxes? Project lets you do all that and more.

Follow these steps to modify the format of Network Diagram boxes:

1. Right-click anywhere in the Network Diagram view outside any box, and then click Box Styles.

The Box Styles dialog box appears, as shown in Figure 2-9.

Figure 2-9:
Modify the
format of all
boxes using
the settings
in this dialog
box.

2. Click the Shape drop-down list and select a different shape from the list that appears.

3. Click the Color drop down list and select a different color from the list of colors.

Note: This choice specifies the color of the line that forms the box, not a background color.

4. Click the Width drop-down list and select a line width from those displayed.

5. Click the Color drop-down list in the Background section and select a color for the background that fills the inside of each box.

6. **Click the Pattern drop-down list and select a pattern of lines that will fill the interior of each box.**

   Combinations of some patterns and colors in backgrounds can make the text in the box difficult to read, so look at the preview in this dialog box to be sure the combination works for you.

7. **Click OK to save the new settings.**

   You can also format individual boxes by right-clicking a box, selecting Format Box, and then making the settings outlined in the preceding steps.

Chapter 3

Mark It on Your Calendar

. . . .

. . . .

*M*ost people live their lives based on clocks and calendars. Think about it: You wake up and your first thoughts are what day is it, what time is it, what's for breakfast, and do you have to go to work that day.

You have a familiar definition for what your typical workday is, whether you're a 9-to-5 kind of person or your particular job calls for you to work from midnight to 8:00 a.m. You also vary from that routine now and then, putting in a 12-hour marathon in a crunch or slipping away after half a day to go fishing on a nice summer day.

Project calendars are sort of like your life in that they set some standards for a typical working time and then allow for variation. But unlike you, Project has several types of calendars to account for.

Base, Project, Resource, and Task Calendars — Oh My!

Now bear with me, because I won't kid you: This can be tricky. But understanding how calendars work in Project is essential to mastering the software.

Tasks are scheduled and resources are assigned based on the calendar settings you make. The costs accumulated by resource work hours will not be accurate if you haven't understood your calendar settings from the get-go.

How calendars work

When you create tasks and assign resources to work on them, Project has to base that work on some timing standard. So (for example) if you say a task is going to take one day, Project knows a day means eight hours (or 12 hours, or whatever) because that's the way you set up a standard workday in your project calendar. Likewise, suppose that you assign a resource to put in two weeks of work on a task in a company that has a standard five-day workweek. If that resource's own calendar is set for a standard four-day workweek, then the two weeks of work put in by that resource will total only eight days, deferring to the timing of the resource calendar.

The nature of a task can have an impact on resource time. A two-week effort-driven task won't be complete until the resources have put in two weeks (according to the Project or Task calendar) of effort. More about effort-driven tasks in Chapter 4.

Not everyone in a company works the same schedule, and not every task can be performed in the same eight-hour day. To deal with the variations in schedules that occur in most workforces, Project has three types of calendars: the Project calendar, Resource calendars, and Task calendars. The Project calendar sets general working times for the project. Task and Resource calendars allow you to specify working and nonworking hours and days; for example, you might block out a week of vacation as nonworking for a particular resource.

Project, Resource, and Task calendars can be set to use one of three base calendar templates built into Project. The three base calendar templates are

- ✔ **Standard.** The default. Sets a working day as 8 a.m. to 5 p.m. with an hour for lunch and a five-day, Monday-through-Friday workweek.

- ✔ **24 Hours.** Allows work to go on round the clock every day of the week.

- ✔ **Night Shift.** Sets the working time as 11 p.m. to 8 a.m. with an hour for dinner and a six-night, Monday-through-Saturday workweek. Working times for a Night Shift calendar are shown in Figure 3-1.

You can modify the standard calendar templates and base new templates on them. (See "Creating Calendar Templates," later in this chapter.)

Figure 3-1:
The legend
explains
how
different
hours are
shaded in
the calendar
display.

How one calendar relates to another

By default, all calendars in your project are controlled by the Project calendar setting. But here's the tricky part: When you change a Task or Resource calendar, you have to understand which setting takes precedence.

Here's how it works:

✔ With no other settings made, the base Project calendar you select when you first create the project controls the working time and days of all tasks and resources.

✔ If you make changes in the working hours for a resource, those settings take precedence over the Project calendar for that resource when you assign it to a task. Likewise, if you assign a different base calendar for a task, it takes precedence over the Project calendar for that task.

✔ If you've applied one calendar to a resource and a different calendar for a task that the resource is assigned to, Project uses only common hours to schedule the resource. So, if the Task calendar allows work from 8:00 a.m. to 5:00 p.m., and the Resource calendar allows work from 6:00 a.m. to 2:00 p.m., the resource will work from 8:00 a.m. to 2:00 p.m., the only hours the calendars have in common.

✔ You can set a task to ignore Resource calendar settings by opening the Task Information dialog box and clicking Scheduling Ignores Resource Calendars on the Advanced tab. (This setting is not available if the Task Calendar is set to None.) You might make this setting if you know that all resources will be required to be involved in a task (such as a quarterly company meeting), regardless of their usual work hours.

Calendar options and working times

Just when you thought you were out of the woods, I'm going to throw two more timing elements at you: calendar options and working times. Calendar options are used to change the standards for a working day, week, and year. So, if you set a Project calendar to Standard (by default 8 a.m. to 5 p.m., five days a week), the Calendar tab of the Options dialog box is where you could designate which five days are working days or modify the working hours to be 9:00 a.m. to 6:00 p.m., for example.

Working time is used to adjust the working time available on a particular date or days. For example, suppose that you make a change to the calendar options so that you have a 32-hour workweek but 8-hour days. You should also check your working time and be sure you've specified three days of the week that are nonworking to jive with the 32-hour week. If you want to set a certain date as nonworking for your project, such as your company offsite meeting day, you can do that with the working time settings.

Calendar options

When you make changes to a Resource or Task calendar, you're simply adjusting the times that a resource is available to work or the time during which a task will occur. You have not changed the standard workday for the project. A day will still be eight hours long if that's the Project calendar setting, even if you say that a task that takes place on that day will use the 24-hour base calendar.

If you want to change the standard workday to, say, ten hours instead of eight, you must do so in the Calendar tab of the Options dialog box.

Follow these steps to modify the calendar options:

1. **Choose Tools ➪ Options.**

   The Options dialog box appears.

2. **Click the Calendar tab, which is shown in Figure 3-2.**

Options

Save	Interface	Security	
Schedule	Calculation	Spelling	Collaborate
View	General	Edit	Calendar

Calendar options for 'Project1'

Week starts on: Sunday ▼

Fiscal year starts in: January ▼

☐ Use starting year for FY numbering

Default start time: 8:00 AM

Default end time: 5:00 PM

These times are assigned to tasks when you enter a start or finish date without specifying a time. If you change this setting, consider matching the project calendar using the Change Working Time command on the Tools menu.

Hours per day: 8.00

Hours per week: 40.00

Days per month: 20

Set as Default

Help   OK   Cancel

Figure 3-2:
Here's where you define your typical working day, week, month, and year.

3. **In Week Starts On, select a day from the list.**

4. **To modify the start of your fiscal year, select the month you want in the Fiscal Year Starts In box.**

5. **To change the working hours for a typical day, type new times in the Default Start Time and Default End Time boxes.**

   If you change this setting, it's a good idea to change the corresponding Working Times. See the section titled "Working times" to discover how it's done.

6. **Modify the Hours Per Day, Hours Per Week, and Days Per Month boxes as needed.**

7. **Click OK to save the settings.**

If your company uses these settings for most projects, consider clicking the Set as Default button in the Calendar tab of the Options dialog box to make your settings the default for any new project you create.

Working times

If you want to change the available working hours for a particular day (such as December 24th), you use the working time settings. For example, if you want the day before Christmas to be a half day, you can modify the working time settings for that day; then any resources assigned to a task on this date will put in only a half day of work. You also use these settings to specify global working and nonworking days to match the calendar options settings.

Here's how to change working times:

1. **Choose Tools ⇨ Change Working Time.**

   The Change Working Time dialog box appears, as shown in Figure 3-3.

Figure 3-3:
The working times you set for your project here should correspond to settings in the calendar options.

2. **In the Select Date(s) section, click the day you want to change.**

   For example, if you want to specify that Friday should be a nonworking day, click the column heading above Friday (labeled *F*) in the calendar to select all Fridays in the project.

3. **Change the From and To times to whatever schedule you like.**

   If you want to set nonconsecutive hours (for example, to build in a lunch break), you have to put two or more sets of numbers here (such as 8 to 12 and 1 to 5).

4. **If you want to block off a date or a day of the week as nonworking, click the Nonworking Time option.**

5. **Click OK to save your changes.**

TIP

The Nondefault Working Time setting that you find in the Change Working Time dialog box designates working time that is not part of the working time established by the base calendar.

Setting the Project Calendar

The first calendar setting you'll encounter is the Project calendar. You set the Project calendar in the Project Information dialog box (as in Figure 3-4), which you can display at any time by choosing Project ⇨ Project Information.

Figure 3-4:
The choice of calendars offered here includes one of three base calendar templates.

TIP

Project Guide offers a useful Calendar Wizard that can help you make calendar settings when you're new to Project. If it's not already visible, display Project Guide at any time as follows. Choose View ⇨ Toolbars ⇨ Project Guide. Then click the Resources button, and then click the Define Working Times for Resources item listed in the Project Guide task pane.

The Calendar setting offers the three base calendar templates: Standard, Night Shift, and 24 Hours. Remember, this is the typical working time for your company; if a few resources on your project will work the night shift but by and large your resources work a standard workday, choose the most commonly used calendar here. You can make changes to specific Resource and Task calendars later (though setting this up early in your planning process is a good habit to get into).

Modifying Task Calendars

Tasks can be set to use a different calendar template than the Project calendar. Doing so takes precedence over the Project calendar for that task. For example, suppose that you select a Standard calendar for a project and a 24 Hours calendar for a task. If you then specify that the task will have a duration of one day, it will be one 24-hour day.

To set a Task calendar, follow these steps:

1. **Double-click the task name.**

    The Task Information dialog box appears, as shown in Figure 3-5.

2. **Click the Advanced tab.**

3. **In the Calendar box, select a different base calendar.**

4. **Click OK to save your new calendar setting.**

Figure 3-5:
You can apply any calendar template to tasks in your project.

If a resource assigned to this task has a modified calendar, that resource will work only during the specific hours that the Task calendar and Resource calendar have in common.

Making Resource Calendar Settings

Even the most *resourceful* resources have only so many hours in a day to work. When you have to deal with variations in resource schedules, consider modifying the Resource calendars.

Each resource in your project — with the exception of material resources charged not by the time they put in but by the number of units used — can have its own calendar. You can change the base calendar for the resource and set specific dates as working or nonworking.

One word of caution about modifying Resource calendars: Unless a resource truly has a unique working schedule, don't change its calendar. For example, if a resource is working a night shift for a few days during the life of the project but usually works a day shift, don't change its base calendar to night shift. If one person works 10:00 a.m. to 7:00 p.m. because the company allows him to, it's probably not necessary to vary his schedule from the typical 8-to-5 work schedule set in the Project calendar, because he puts in eight hours a day like everyone else. Unless your project deals with the most detailed level of time, where hours and not days are the typical units of measure for tasks, making these types of changes is more work than it's worth.

To modify a resource's calendar settings, follow these steps:

1. **Display a view that includes a resource column, such as the Resource sheet.**

2. **Double-click a resource name.**

   The Resource Information dialog box appears.

3. **Click the Working Time tab, which is shown in Figure 3-6.**

4. **In the Base Calendar box, select a different base calendar: Standard, 24 Hours, or Night Shift.**

5. **In the Select Date(s) calendar, click a date and then click a Set Selected Date(s) To option.**

   You can select several dates or a day column instead of a single date by clicking and dragging.

6. **To change the hours that a resource works, enter new hours in the From and To boxes.**

7. **Click OK to save your settings.**

Resource Information

| General | Working Time | Costs | Notes | Custom Fields |

Resource Na_m_e: Developer   _B_ase calendar: Standard ▼

Set working time for selected date(s)

Legend: Sele_c_t Date(s):   Set selected date(s) to:

☐ Working

☐ Nonworking

◉ Use _d_efault
○ _N_onworking time
○ Nondefault _w_orking time

April 2003

S	M	T	W	Th	F	S
		1	2	3	4	5
6	7	8	9	**10**	11	12
13	14	15	16	17	18	19
20	21	22	23	24	25	26
27	28	29	30			

☐ Edited working hours

On this calendar:

T Edits to a day of the week

31 Edits to an individual day

_F_rom: _T_o:
8:00 AM   12:00 PM
1:00 PM   5:00 PM

He_l_p   Deta_i_ls...   OK   Cancel

TIP

Can resources work overtime even if their calendar says they're 9-to-5ers? Yes, but you have to tell Project to schedule overtime work. You can also set a different rate to be charged for overtime work for that resource. To find out more about overtime, see Chapter 8.

Creating Calendar Templates

If you've ever wanted to make your own time, here's your chance. Although the base calendar templates probably cover most working situations, you might want to create your own calendar template. For example, if your project involves a telemarketing initiative and most project resources work six hours from 4:00 p.m. to 10:00 p.m. (that's when they all call me!), it might be useful to create a new calendar template called Telemarketing.

If you want to save some time when creating a template (and time is what this is all about), start with an existing calendar template that is closest to your needs. Then modify it as you like, making changes to the working times and calendar options to make sure they're in agreement. (Use the Change Working Time dialog box and the Calendar tab of the Options dialog box.) After you create a new calendar template, it is available for you to apply in all three calendars: Project, Task, and Resource.

Remember, the Project calendar is the basis of your entire project and, as such, should represent the most common working schedule in your project. If only some resources in your project work odd hours, change the Resource calendars, not the Project calendar.

Follow these steps to create a new calendar template:

1. **Choose Tools ⇨ Change Working Time.**

   The Change Working Time dialog box appears.

2. **Click the New button.**

   The Create New Base Calendar dialog box appears, as shown in Figure 3-7.

3. **In the Name box, type a name for the new calendar.**

4. **Either select the Create New Base Calendar option or select the Make a Copy Of option and select an existing calendar from the list to base your calendar template on.**

5. **Click OK to return to the Change Working Time dialog box.**

   Now you'll make changes to the working time for the new calendar template.

6. **Click Options.**

   The Options dialog box appears with the Calendar tab displayed.

7. **Make changes to the start of the week or year, the start and end times for a workday, and the hour or day settings.**

8. **Click OK twice to save the new calendar settings.**

Figure 3-7:
Enter a name here, even if you're basing the calendar on an existing template.

Create New Base Calendar
Name: Copy of Standard
○ Create new base calendar
● Make a copy of Standard ▾ calendar
OK   Cancel

Sharing Copies of Calendars

You can make a calendar available for all projects in two ways. You can set a calendar as the default for all new projects by making that choice in the Change Working Time dialog box. Or you can make calendars from one project available for use in another project. The latter method is especially useful when you want to share calendars with other project managers in your company but don't want to change your own default calendar.

To copy a calendar from one project to another, follow this procedure:

1. **Open the project to which you want to copy a calendar.**

2. **Choose Tools ⇨ Organizer.**

   The Organizer dialog box appears.

3. **Click the Calendars tab, which is shown in Figure 3-8.**

4. **In the Calendars Available In box on the left side, select the Project file that contains the calendar you want to copy.**

Figure 3-8: You can copy your calendar to other projects.

5. **In the list on the left, click the calendar you want to copy, and then click the Copy button.**

   The calendar is copied to the current project.

6. **If you'd like to give the calendar a different name, click the Rename button, type a new name in the Rename dialog box, and then click OK.**

7. **Close the Organizer by clicking the close button (the X) in the upper-right corner.**

Here are a few pointers about copying calendars from project to project:

✔ **Make sure the name you give the calendar is descriptive.** That helps you remember its general parameters.

✔ **If your company has standard calendars, try having one resource create and disseminate them.** If ten versions of a management calendar are floating around and you grab the wrong one, it could cause problems.

✔ **Put the project manager's initials in each calendar template name you create. That way you know which one you created.**

Chapter 4

A Tisket, a Task Kit

A project manager is, by necessity, a taskmaster. That's because tasks form the to-do list of your project. They incorporate the what, when, who, and where information of your plan. Resources work on a project by getting assigned to tasks. The timing of tasks and the relationships between them form the timing for your project. By tracking the progress on tasks — mastering them — you can see your project advance over time.

Tasks can be created in a few different ways. You can create them by typing information in the sheet area of the Gantt Chart view (or any other view that displays information in columns) or by using a task information form. You can also import tasks from other programs such as Excel and Outlook.

You have to make some choices when you create tasks. For example, you consider and specify settings for a task that control its timing, its priority, and certain constraints regarding how it may or may not shift around during the life of your project.

In this chapter, you find out all about tasks and the various settings that give each task its own unique personality.

Your First Task

The first step in creating a task is to identify the individual action items in your project. Then you can create each of those steps as individual tasks in Project.

After you create some tasks, you'll begin to build some structure to your list, creating phases consisting of summary tasks with subtasks below them in an outline structure. For example, you might have a summary task named Permits with two subtasks, Submit Applications and Pay Fees.

You can find out how to organize tasks into outlines in Chapter 5. Here the focus is on making the settings required to simply create a task.

What tasks are made up of

Determining all the settings that characterize a task is a bit more complicated than writing an item on a to-do list. Think of each task in your project as a record — like a database record for a person that lists name, address, birthday, and shoe size. A task in Project contains data about that task: Not only a task name, but other vital data about how that task fits into your project.

To create a task, you enter not only a task name but also information such as a duration for the task, the task type, constraints for scheduling the task, and the task priority. Some things, such as task priority or task type, can often be left at default settings. Others, such as duration, require some input from you.

Pretty much everything in this list except the task name involves how the task timing is controlled. Several of these settings work in combination, with Project performing complex algorithms to set the timing of the task according to the value of each setting. Other elements, such as the task finish date, don't determine timing but rather cause Project to display a symbol in the Indicator column to alert you when a task has moved beyond its estimated deadline.

You can also specify a unique task calendar in the Task Information dialog box; calendars are covered in Chapter 3.

Let there be tasks

On the simplest level, you can create a task by entering a name for it. You can fill in the details of duration, task type, and so on at the same time or later.

You can enter task names in three ways: In a Gantt Chart view sheet pane, in a Task Information dialog box, or by importing them from Excel or Outlook.

Putting tasks in a column

For long projects, many people find that entering all task names in the sheet pane of the Gantt Chart view is the quickest and easiest way to go. You can simply enter one task name in the Task Name column, press the down arrow on your keyboard to move to the next blank row and enter another task, and so on.

Follow these simple steps to enter a task in the Gantt Chart view:

1. **In the Task Name column, click a blank cell.**

2. **Type a task name.**

   You can edit what you type by clicking in the entry box above the sheet and typing or using the Delete or Backspace key to clear characters (see Figure 4-1).

3. **Press the down arrow on your keyboard to move to the next cell in the column and type the next task name.**

4. **Repeat Step 3 until you've entered all task names.**

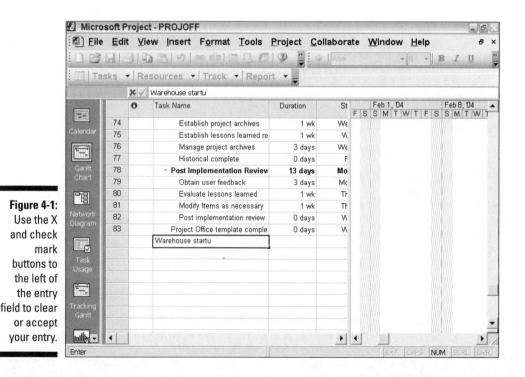

Figure 4-1: Use the X and check mark buttons to the left of the entry field to clear or accept your entry.

You can also display whatever columns you like in the Gantt Chart view to enter additional task information, such as duration, task type, start dates, and finish dates. To display additional columns, simply right-click any column heading, click Insert Column, and select the column to display from the Field Name list.

Naming your tasks in a dialog box

If you're a dialog box kind of person, consider using the Task Information dialog box to enter task information. The series of tabs in the Task Information dialog box contain all the information there is to know about a task.

Use these steps to create your task with the dialog box:

1. **In the Task Name column, double-click a blank cell.**

   The Task Information dialog box appears, as shown in Figure 4-2.

2. **In the Name field, type a task name.**

3. **Click OK to save the new task.**

   The task name now appears in the Gantt Chart view.

4. **Press the down arrow key to move to the next cell.**

5. **Repeat Steps 1 through 4 to add the next task.**

Figure 4-2:
The General and Advanced tabs of this dialog box contain various timing settings for the task.

As you name tasks, try to the keep task names in your project both descriptive and unique. However, if you can't make all the names unique (if, for example, you have three tasks called *Hire Staff*), you can use the automatically assigned task number or the WBS code to identify tasks; these numbers are always unique for each task.

Getting your tasks from Outlook

Once you get started, tasks are like rabbits breeding. What starts as a series of simple to-do tasks in Outlook often becomes a full-fledged project with hundreds of tasks. When that happens, you'll be glad to know that Microsoft has provided an easy-to-use import feature to take the tasks you created in Outlook and put them into Project.

Although Project has an import-mapping feature that allows you to map fields in a file created in another application to fields in Project to import data, it can be a tedious process. The Import Outlook Tasks feature is essentially an import map that's preset to work with Outlook task fields.

Follow these steps to import Outlook tasks into Project:

1. **Open the plan you want to insert tasks into, or open a new project (choose File ⇨ New).**

2. **Choose Tools ⇨ Import Outlook Tasks.**

   The Import Outlook Tasks dialog box appears, as shown in Figure 4-3.

Figure 4-3: Task name, notes, and duration entered in Outlook all come along for the ride.

3. **Click the options for the tasks you want to import, or click Select All to import all Outlook tasks.**

4. **Click OK.**

   The tasks are imported and appear at the end of your list of tasks.

By default, Outlook keeps tasks in a Tasks folder. Selecting the check box for the Folder: Tasks item is another way to select all tasks in Outlook.

When you import tasks from Outlook, the task name, duration, and any task notes are brought over. If a task in Outlook has no duration, Project creates the task with an estimated one-day time frame.

Importing an Excel task list

I am a firm believer that you should make things easy on yourself. If you like to noodle around with your task list for a project in Excel, you shouldn't have to retype everything into Project to build a Project plan. For that reason, Microsoft has provided an Excel Task List template. This template, located in the Microsoft Office template folder, can be opened from Excel.

The template provides four Excel worksheets, as shown in Figure 4-4, in which you can enter tasks, resources, and resource assignments, and then export that data from Excel to Project.

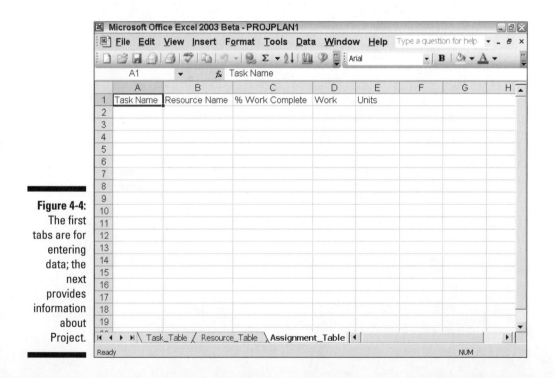

Figure 4-4: The first tabs are for entering data; the next provides information about Project.

Follow these steps to use this template:

1. **In Excel, open the template called Microsoft Project Plan Import Export Template.**

2. **Fill in information about Tasks, Resources, and Assignments on the appropriate tabs, and then save the file.**

3. **Open Project and choose File ➪ Open.**

   The Open dialog box appears.

4. **Locate the Excel Project Template file you just saved and then click Open.**

   The Import Wizard appears.

5. **Click Next to begin the wizard.**

6. **Choose the second option, Project Excel Template, for the format of the data you're importing. Then click Next.**

7. **On the next wizard screen, choose the method for importing the file.**

   You can import the file As a New Project, to Append the Data to the Active Project, or to Merge the Data into the Active Project. If you choose the third option, you have to create a *merge key* that delineates how the data should merge with existing tasks.

8. **Click Finish.**

   The project appears with whatever tasks, resources, and assignment information you entered in a project plan format.

Linking to tasks that live somewhere else

You can insert hyperlinks in a project outline; doing so allows you to quickly open another project by clicking the hyperlink.

The link text is placed in the Indicator column.

Inserting a hyperlink creates a task that you can use to represent the timing or costs of another project or subproject in your plan. However, you'll have to enter timing and cost information yourself — it isn't brought over from the hyperlinked project.

To insert a hyperlink to another Project file in your project, follow these steps:

1. **Click to select the blank task name cell where you'd like the hyperlinked task to appear.**

2. **Choose Insert ➪ Hyperlink.**

   The Insert Hyperlink dialog box appears, as shown in Figure 4-5.

Figure 4-5:
You can link
to a
document,
an e-mail
address, or
a Web page.

3. **In the Text to Display box, type a name for the hyperlinked file.**

   Make sure this text explains to readers of your plan what information is being summarized.

4. **In the Link To area, click the Existing File or Web Page option.**

5. **In the Look In list, locate and click the file to which you want to insert a hyperlink.**

6. **Click OK.**

   The link text is inserted and a hyperlink symbol appears in the indicator field. You can simply click that link symbol to open the other file.

Inserting one project into another

You can also insert an entire subproject into a Project file. This is a useful method when various project team members manage different phases of a larger project. The capability to assemble subprojects in one place allows you to create a master schedule from which you can view all the pieces of larger, more complex projects in one place.

Follow these steps to insert another Project file into your plan:

1. **In the Gantt Chart view, click the task in your task list above which you want the other project to be inserted.**

2. **Choose Insert ➪ Project.**

   The Insert Project dialog box appears, as shown in Figure 4-6.

3. **In the Look In list, locate the file that you want to insert and click it to select it.**

4. **If you want to link to the other file so any updates to it are reflected in the copy of the project you're inserting, select the Link to Project option.**

5. **Click Insert to insert the file.**

   The inserted project appears above the task you had selected when you began the insert process.

Figure 4-6:
You can insert a link to a project so that any changes appear in both.

Note that the inserted project's highest-level task appears at the level of the task you had selected when you inserted the project, with all other tasks falling below it in outline order. If you need to, use the Indent and Outdent tools on the Formatting toolbar (arrows pointing to the left and right, respectively) to place the inserted tasks at the appropriate level in your project.

You're in It for the Duration

In projects, as in life, timing is everything. Timing in your projects starts with the durations you assign to tasks. Although Project helps you see the impact that timing of your tasks has on the overall length of your plan, it can't tell you how much time each task will take: That's up to you.

Estimating the duration of tasks isn't always easy; it has to be based on your experience with similar tasks and your knowledge of the specifics pertaining to your project.

If you often do projects with similar tasks, consider saving a copy of your schedule as a template that you can use in the future, thereby saving yourself the effort of re-estimating durations every time you start a similar project. Find out about saving templates in Chapter 17.

There's more than one kind of task

Before you begin to enter task durations, you need to be aware of the three task types. These types have an effect on how Project schedules the work of a task.

Essentially, your choice of type determines which element of the task will not vary when you make changes to the task:

- **Fixed Duration task.** A task that takes a set amount of time to complete, no matter how many resources you add to the mix. For example, a test on a substance that requires that you leave the test running for 24 hours has a fixed duration even if you add twenty scientists to oversee the test.

- **Fixed Units task.** The default task type. With this task type, when you assign resources to a task with a certain number of units (hours of work expressed as a percentage of their working day), their assignments won't change even if you change the duration of the task, even though the work amount for the task does change.

- **Fixed Work task.** The number of resource hours assigned to the task determines its length. If you set the duration of a Fixed Work task at, say, 40 hours, and assign two resources to work 20 hours each (simultaneously) at units of 100 percent, the task will be completed in 20 hours. If you take away one of those resources, the single resource must put in 40 hours at units of 100 percent to complete the task. Understanding how the choice of task type causes your task timing or resource assignments to fluctuate is an important part of creating an efficient project.

Follow these steps to set the task type:

1. **Double-click a task.**

   The Task Information dialog box appears.

2. **Click the Advanced tab, if necessary, to display it (see Figure 4-7).**

3. **In the Task Type list, click one of the three choices.**

4. **Click OK.**

You can also display the Type column in a Gantt Chart sheet and make this setting there.

Task Information ⊠

| General | Predecessors | Resources | Advanced | Notes | Custom Fields |

Name: [   ]   Duration: [   ] ÷ ☑ Estimated

Constrain task

Deadline: [   ] ▼

Constraint type: [   ] ▼   Constraint date: [   ] ▼

Task type: [   ] ▼   ☑ Effort driven

Calendar: | Fixed Duration | ☑ Scheduling ignores resource calendars
          | Fixed Units |
WBS code: | Fixed Work |

Earned value [   ] ▼

☑ Mark task as milestone

[Help]   [OK]   [Cancel]

Figure 4-7:
The Task
Type list has
three
choices.

Tasks that take time

Most tasks in a project have a duration, whether it's ten minutes or a year or something in between. Deciding how finely to break down your tasks can affect how efficiently you track progress on those tasks: Tasks that wander on for a year are usually too broad, and tasks that take ten minutes are too narrow. But whatever your best guess at task duration, Project can accommodate you.

If your project is to run a one-day event, getting to the level of ten-minute tasks might make sense. In most projects, however, such finely detailed timing doesn't make sense because it defeats the point of all the tracking and reporting features of Project (unless you have people tracking their progress minute by minute — but then, what else would they have time to do?). On the flip side, creating a 12-month-long task suggests that you might be defining your project too broadly to keep accurate track of all that can happen in a year.

As with all task information, you can enter a duration in the Task Information dialog box or in a Gantt Chart sheet. Follow these steps to enter a duration by using the dialog box:

1. **Double-click a task to display the Task Information dialog box.**

2. **If necessary, click the General tab to display it.**

3. **In the Duration box, use the spinner arrows to increase or decrease the duration.**

4. **If the current duration units aren't appropriate (for example, days when you want hours), type a new duration in the Duration box.**

   You can use the following abbreviations for various units of time: *m* for minutes, *h* for hours, *d* for days, *w* for weeks, and *mo* for months.

   Note that changing the start and finish dates of a task does not change the duration.

5. **Click OK to accept the duration setting.**

If you are not sure about the timing of a particular task and want to alert people to your lack of certainty or have a way to find such tasks and enter more solid timing when you have better information, select the Estimated check box (in the General tab) when you enter the duration.

Milestones

I mentioned in the preceding section that almost all tasks have durations; the exception is a *milestone* — a task with no duration. (Now, that's the type I *like* to be assigned to.) In fact, milestones are less like tasks than they are like signposts that mark moments in time. Examples of milestones are the approval of a prototype (though the deliberations to make that decision may have taken months) or the completion of a phase of tests.

Some people include tasks such as *Design Complete* or *Testing Complete* at the end of each phase of their project. They can then create timing relationships to the moment of completion — for example, allowing production of a drug to proceed after the testing is over. Such milestones also alert you and your team members to a moment of progress in your project that can help to keep the team motivated.

Note that new tasks are created with an estimated duration of one day, unless you enter a duration. To create a milestone, you indicate that the task has a zero duration. The quickest way to do that is to simply type 0 in the Duration column of the Gantt Chart view or to click the Advanced tab of the Task Information dialog box and select the Mark Task As Milestone check box. When you do, the milestone is designated in the Gantt Chart with a black diamond shape rather than a task bar.

Like a bad penny: Recurring tasks

Some tasks occur again and again in projects. For example, attending a monthly project debriefing or generating a quarterly project report is considered a recurring task.

No one wants to create all the tasks for the monthly debriefing in a project that will take a year to complete. Instead, you can designate the recurrence, and Project creates the twelve tasks for you.

Here's how you create a recurring task:

1. **Choose Insert ⇨ Recurring Task.**

   The Recurring Task Information dialog box appears, as shown in Figure 4-8.

2. **In the Task Name box, type a name for the task.**

3. **In the Duration box, click the up or down arrows to set a duration, or type a duration, such as** 10d **for 10 days.**

4. **Select a recurrence pattern by selecting the Daily, Weekly, Monthly, or Yearly option.**

   What you select here provides different options for the rest of the recurrence pattern.

5. **Depending on the selections offered to you, make choices for the rest of the pattern.**

   For example, if you selected the Weekly option, you must choose a Week On setting, such as Every Other Week on Wednesday, or Every 5th Week on Friday. Or if you selected Monthly, you must set which day of every month the task will recur.

6. **In the Range of Recurrence area, type a Start date. Then click and fill in either the End After or End By option.**

   For example, you might start on January 1 and end after 12 occurrences to create a task that occurs every month for a year.

7. **Click OK to save the recurring task.**

Figure 4-8:
By completing this information, Project creates multiple occurrences of a task automatically.

If your choice causes a task to fall on a nonworking day (for example, if you choose to meet on the 8th day of every month and the 8th is a Sunday in one of those months), a dialog box appears asking you how to handle this. You can choose not to create the task, or you can let Project adjust the day to the next working day in that time period.

To assign resources to a recurring task, you can use the resource column in the Gantt Chart view. (The Recurring Task Information dialog box doesn't have a Resources tab.)

Getting Started

When most people start using Project, one of the first things they try to do is enter a start date for every task in the project. After all, you always include dates when you write up a to-do list. So why not, right? Well, for one thing, it's jumping the gun — and missing out on one of the great strengths of project-management software: The capability to schedule tasks for you according to sometimes-complex combinations of factors (such as dependencies between tasks and task constraints). By allowing Project to determine the start date of a task, you allow it to make adjustments automatically when changes occur.

If you enter a task duration and don't enter a start date for the task, by default that task starts as soon as possible after the project start date you set in the Project Information dialog box, based on any dependencies you have set up between tasks.

Typically, to establish a task's start date, you look for something in the project that would dictate its timing; for example, if you don't want construction to begin until you've obtained permits, link the permits task to the construction task in such a way that construction can't start before the permit task ends.

Certain tasks, however, must start on a specific date. Examples include a holiday, an annual meeting, or the start of the fishing season.

Project sets the finish date of a task based on when that task starts and the task duration. But if a task must finish on a certain date, you can set a finish date and let Project determine the start date.

Entering the Task Start date

Setting a start date or a finish date for a task applies a kind of constraint on it that may override dependency relationships or other timing factors. Task constraints, discussed in the "Constraints You Can Live With" section later in this chapter, are the preferred way to force a task to start or end on a certain day. But if you've determined that a particular task must begin or end on a set date, no matter what, you can enter a specific start or finish date. Setting the start or finish date is simple.

To enter a start or finish date for a task, simply follow these steps:

1. **Double-click a task.**

   The Task Information dialog box appears.

2. **Click the General tab if it's not already displayed.**

3. **Click the Start or Finish box.**

   A calendar appears.

4. **Click a date to select it, or use the forward or backward arrow to move to a different month and select a date.**

5. **Click OK.**

Note that setting a start date is not quite as strong a factor in how Project determines timing as applying the Must Start On constraint. You can find out more about how constraints work in the "Constraints You Can Live With" section.

Take a break: Splitting tasks

Did you ever start something — say your taxes — and find that you just had to drop everything before you were done and go do something else? (In the case of taxes, I usually need a break for a good cry.)

It's the same in projects. Sometimes you have tasks that start but then they have to be put on hold before they can start again later — for example, a work shutdown due to labor negotiations. In that case, you can use a Project feature to split a task so that a second or third portion starts at a later date, with no activity in between. You can place as many splits in a task as you like.

Use these steps to split a task:

1. **Click the Split Task button on the Standard toolbar.**

   A box appears, as shown in Figure 4-9.

2. **Click the task at the date where you want to split the task, and then drag until the box contains the date on which you want the task to begin again.**

3. **Release the mouse button.**

   The task is split.

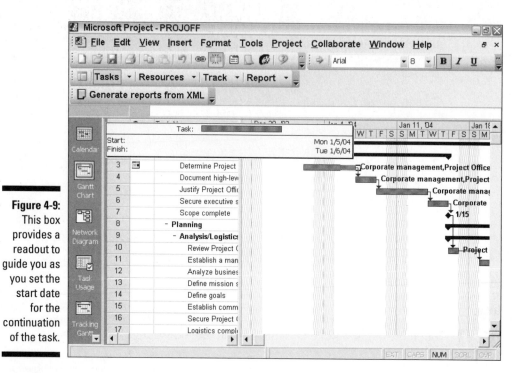

Figure 4-9:
This box
provides a
readout to
guide you as
you set the
start date
for the
continuation
of the task.

You can rejoin a split task by placing your mouse over the taskbar until the move cursor appears, and then clicking the split taskbar and dragging it back to join with the other portion of the taskbar.

Don't use the split-task approach to put an artificial hold on a task until some other task is complete. For example, suppose you start testing a product but then have to wait for final approval before finalizing the test results. In that case, you should create a Testing task, a Final Approval milestone, and a Finalize Test Results task — and then create dependency relationships among them. That way, if one task runs late, your final task will shift along with it, rather than being set in stone (as a split task can be).

It's Such an Effort: Effort-Driven Tasks

When you hear the word *effort* in Project you can think *work.* When you create a task, by default it is *effort-driven,* which means that if you adjust resource assignments, the duration might change but the number of hours of effort (work) you need to put in to complete the task stays the same. When you add or delete a resource assignment on an effort-driven task, work is spread around equally among resources.

So, here's how an effort-driven task works. Suppose that you have a two-day task to set up a computer network in a new office. With one resource assigned to it, working 8 hours a day, it will take 16 hours to complete (two 8-hour days). If you assign a second resource, the task will no longer take two days because the hours of effort required will be completed more quickly by the two people working simultaneously — in this case, in one 8-hour time period.

An example of a task that would *not* be effort-driven is attending a day-long seminar. No matter how many people attend or how many people are present, the seminar takes one day to complete.

Effort Driven is a simple check box choice on the Advanced tab of the Task Information dialog box (see Figure 4-7). Select this check box to activate or clear the Effort Driven box (it's selected by default). What happens when you clear this setting? Well, the same task that you set to run two days will *take* two days, no matter how much effort resources put in. In other words, adding resources will not cause the task to be completed sooner.

Constraints You Can Live With

A constraint is more than something you're forced to live with, such as dandruff or noisy neighbors. In Project, *constraints* are timing conditions that control a task. You tell Project what, if anything, to constrain for each task.

How constraints work

When you create a task, the As Soon As Possible constraint is selected by default. In other words, the task starts as soon as the project starts, assuming there are no dependency relationships with other tasks that would delay its start.

Task start and finish dates, working with dependencies, the task type, the Effort Driven setting, and constraints, set the timing of each task. However, in performing calculations to try to save you time in a project that's running late, constraints are the most sacred timing setting for Project. For example, if you set a constraint that a task Must Finish On a certain date, Project will shift around almost any other task in a schedule in recalculating timing before it suggests that that task might finish on another date. Therefore a word to the wise: Use constraints only when there is an absolute need to force a task's timing.

Table 4-1 lists all the constraints and an explanation of their effects on your task's timing.

Table 4-1	Task Constraints
Constraint	*Effect*
As Soon As Possible	The default setting; the task starts as early in the schedule as possible based on dependencies and the project start date.
As Late As Possible	The task occurs as late as possible in your schedule, based on dependencies and the project finish date.
Finish No Earlier Than	The end of the task will not occur any earlier than the date you specify.
Finish No Later Than	The end of the task will not occur any later than the date you specify.
Must Finish On	Sets an absolute date on which the task will finish.
Must Start On	Sets an absolute date on which the task must start.
Start No Earlier Than	The task will not start any earlier than the date you specify.
Start No Later Than	The task will not start any later than the date you specify.

Establishing constraints

You can set only one constraint for a task. Setting a constraint involves selecting the type of constraint you want in the Task Information dialog box. Some constraints work together with a date you choose. For example, if you want a task to Start No Later Than, you need to select a date by which a task must start. Other settings such as As Soon As Possible work off a different date — in this case, the start date you set for the whole project or any dependency relationships you've set up with other tasks (see Chapter 6 for more about dependency relationships).

To set a task constraint, follow these steps:

1. **Double-click a task.**

   The Task Information dialog box appears.

2. **Click the Advanced tab.**

3. **In the Constraint Type list, click a constraint to select it.**

4. **If the constraint requires a date, select one in the Constraint Date list.**

5. **Click OK to save the settings.**

Setting a deadline

I don't know about you, but sometimes I think deadlines were made to be overlooked. Project agrees, because strictly speaking, deadlines aren't constraints (although you'll find the setting for the deadline in the Constrain Task area of the Task Information dialog box's Advanced tab). Deadlines aren't the same as constraints because they don't force the timing of your tasks in any sense. If you set a deadline, it simply causes Project to display a symbol in the Indicator column if the deadline is past, alerting you so that you can panic (I mean *take action*) appropriately.

To set at deadline, follow these steps:

1. **Double-click a task.**

   The Task Information dialog box appears.

2. **Click the Advanced Tab.**

3. **In the Deadline list, click a date.**

   If necessary, use the forward or backward arrow to move to a different month.

4. **Click OK to save the deadline setting.**

You can also display a deadline column in your Gantt Chart sheet pane to show yourself and others what your targeted deadline date is.

Taking a Task Note

In spite of the wealth of information you can enter about a task and its timing, not everything can be said with settings. That's why every task includes an area to enter notes. You might use this feature, for example, to enter some background information about changes in timing or other changes that occur during the schedule, or to list vendor-contact information relevant to the task.

To enter task notes, follow these steps:

1. **Double-click a task.**

   The Task Information dialog box appears.

2. **Click the Notes tab (see Figure 4-10).**

3. **In the Notes area, type any information you like.**

Figure 4-10:
Enter
contact
information,
notes about
resources,
or other
useful
information
about the
task.

4. **Format the note.**

   Use the buttons at the top of the Notes area to change the font, to left-align, center, or right-align the text, or to format the text as a bulleted list.

5. **Click OK to save the settings.**

Saving Your Project

Now that you have some tasks in your project, don't lose 'em! Save your project on a regular basis.

You save a Project file using the same process you've used hundreds of times to save files in other software applications, with one exception: If you have not yet set a baseline when you save a Project file, then Project asks you — every time you save it — whether you want to save it with or without a baseline. You can find out more about baselines in Chapter 12, but to help you out with this decision, I'll give you a sneak preview.

A *baseline* is a saved version of your project plan against which you can track actual progress when the project gets going. It's like a photograph of your best-guess plan that's saved right along with the data you update as your project proceeds. You can save multiple baselines throughout the life of your project. If you haven't set a baseline and you save a Project file, a dialog box is displayed. If you don't want to save a baseline at that point, specify No; otherwise you can choose to save the baseline then and there.

To save a Project file, do this:

1. **Choose File ⇨ Save.**

   The Save As dialog box appears, as shown in Figure 4-11.
2. **In the Save In list, locate the folder in which you want to save the file.**
3. **In the File Name box, type a name.**
4. **Click Save.**

Figure 4-11: If you've used other software products, you've probably seen this dialog box many times before.

If you want to save changes to a previously saved Project file using a different file name, choose File ⇨ Save As and provide a new file name in the Save As dialog box.

Task Information in Action: Planning a Space Launch

To tie this all together, let's take a look at some of the task-setting information covered in this chapter in the context of a specific project. Say you are managing a space shuttle launch. You have these main tasks:

> ✔ Personnel training
>
> ✔ Launch public relations
>
> ✔ Equipment check
>
> ✔ Launch operation

Under the public-relations task, say you have three subtasks:

> ✔ Write press releases
>
> ✔ Hold press conference
>
> ✔ Set up interviews with astronauts

Your first step is to set durations for each task. These will be determined to a great extent by your experience with similar projects, but let's say you determine that writing press releases will take two days, a press conference will take two hours, and setting up interviews will take three days. You enter these durations in one of two locations: in the Durations column or in each individual task-information dialog box.

Next you have to determine the task types. Write Press Releases would be an effort-driven fixed-work task (if you get somebody to help you, it will take less time to complete the work). Hold Press Conference, on the other hand, has a fixed timing (two hours and then you cut the press off); in this case, it's a fixed-duration task. Finally, Setting Up Interviews with Astronauts could be a fixed-units task: It will take so many hours to make all the phone calls and arrangements, but when the arrangements are done you might still want the resources available for confirmations or to deal with changes. With a fixed-units task (which is Project's default), completing the number of units of work won't change the resource hours you've assigned.

Finally, what task constraints might you apply to these tasks? Although I'm not a fan of applying too many constraints to any project, here are some possibilities:

The Press Conference might take place **no later than** the task to launch the shuttle. Once the shuttle has left orbit, the press conference to brief the press on the mission has to already have been completed.

You could set the interviews with astronauts so that they **must start on** the day before the launch — when the media hold the most interest in the event and the astronauts are still available.

And if, in the end, the entire launch is scrubbed because of an annoying hurricane or faulty hatch door, won't you be glad that you used Project's dependency structure to cause all tasks to move out when you change the start date for the project, for the sixth time?

Chapter 5

Getting Your Outline in Line

In This Chapter

▶ Understanding the task/subtask structure

▶ Including a project summary task

▶ Promoting and demoting tasks

▶ Displaying and hiding outline levels

▶ Working with WBS codes

Certain things bring order to the universe: clocks, stop signs, and outlines, to name just a few. Whereas clocks bring order to time and stop signs bring order to rush hour, outlines bring order to information by imposing a hierarchy on it. An outline breaks down one idea, or topic, or category of information into smaller units with some logical sequence.

Project uses an outline structure to organize tasks in your project. The software also offers tools and functionality to help you build, reorganize, and view the outline structure. Learning how to create an outline is something you did back in Mrs. Plotkin's fourth-grade English class, but showing you how to use an outline to organize the many tasks in your project is my job. Welcome to Outlining 101.

Mama and Papa Tasks and Little Baby Subtasks

If you take a look at a project outline such as the one in Figure 5-1, you'll see that it organizes tasks into levels; each level represents a phase of your project. A task that has other tasks indented below it in this outline structure is what's often referred to as a *parent*, or *summary, task*. The tasks indented below it are referred to as *child tasks*, or *subtasks*. Summary tasks are indicated in bold in your Project outline. You can tell when a summary task has a family of subtasks clinging to its skirts: When subtasks are hidden, the summary task displays a little plus sign symbol next to it. When you click the plus sign, the task expands to show its whole clan of subtasks.

You can build several of these little families of tasks, representing project phases in your outline. Think of a project outline as being like those little wooden nesting dolls, with each successive doll representing a deeper level of detail. The highest-level task is the outer doll, the biggest of the bunch. The next doll in the group is a little smaller, just as the next level of tasks in an outline reflects a little narrower level of detail, and so on, right down to the littlest baby doll. The largest task in a project might be Build New Plant, and the smallest detailed task might be Empty Dumpster, with a whole lot of tasks in between.

Roll up, roll up!

All information about a family of tasks (that is, a *phase* of your project) is rolled up into its highest-level summary task. Therefore any task with subtasks has no timing or cost information of its own: It gets its total duration and cost from the sum of its parts.

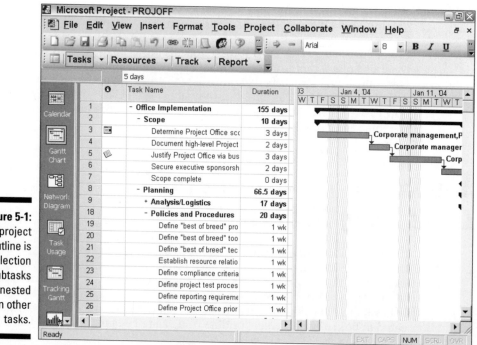

Figure 5-1:
A project outline is a collection of subtasks nested within other tasks.

You *can* assign resources and costs to a summary task — for example, assigning a project manager for that phase of tasks. But that task will also include the total of the costs of any tasks below it.

This roll-up functionality is cumulative: The lowest-level task rolls up to its parent, which may roll up into another summary task, which rolls up (for example) into a project-summary task. Any task with tasks below it gets its information from its subtasks, no matter how deeply nested it may be in the hierarchy.

The structure of phases in an outline is also useful when you need to reorganize an outline: When you move a summary task, all its subtasks come right along for the ride!

How many levels can you go?

There's really no limit to the number of levels of tasks you can create in an outline (except perhaps how much memory you have in your computer to accommodate a monster schedule!). But remember, at some point you have to deal with assigning timing and resources to each of these tasks — and then track their progress. Too much detail can make your project plan difficult to update.

Also, if you find you're building in three, four, or five levels of detail throughout your plan, consider that you might really be building *several* projects at once. Too many levels suggests that a few of these project phases might be more manageable if you broke them off and made them projects on their own — with their own project managers. Unless you want the maintenance of your Project plan to become a project itself, don't overdo the level of detail in your outline; two or three levels are usually sufficient.

The One-and-Only Project Summary Task

It's a good idea to create what I call a *project summary task;* this task represents the highest (least detailed) level of information, and is often simply the title of the project, such as New Product Rollout or Space Shuttle Launch. A project summary task is created when every task in the project falls under it in the outline, indented to become subordinate as in Figure 5-2. Just as there is only one captain on a ship, there can only be one task that summarizes all other tasks in each project.

Figure 5-2:
The highest-
level task in
the outline
with all
tasks
indented
below
it is the
summary
task.

When you think about it, an upper-level headline in an outline is the sum of its parts: It reflects the umbrella concept for all the items below it. The project summary task takes this a step further; this task rolls up all the actual data from other tasks into one line item. Thus the project summary task's duration reflects the duration of the entire project. From the monetary angle, the project summary task's total cost reflects the total of costs for the entire project. Figures like these can be handy to have at your fingertips, and that's one value of a summary task.

Now, not everyone uses project summary tasks. At the highest level of your outline, you can simply create tasks that represent major project phases — with subphases and subtasks below them — and not create one task that is higher in the order than all others. But my advice is to always have a project summary task, for two reasons:

✔ You get the ability to quickly view totals for the project at a glance in the columns of data in the Gantt Chart view and other views.

✔ You can place a link to your summary task in another project, so that all the data for one project is reflected in another. For example, if you create five schedules for new product launches in your company, you can easily create a master schedule for all company product launches by linking to the summary tasks in each of the projects. (Neat, huh?)

You can simply create a summary task yourself as you build your project, or you can use a Project feature to generate one automatically at any time — even after you've built all the phases of your project. To do this, follow these steps:

1. **Choose Tools ⇨ Options.**

   The Options dialog box appears.

2. **Click the View tab to display it.**

3. **Click the Project Summary Task option.**

4. **Click OK to insert the upper-level task.**

I'm Gonna Get Me Some Structure

Doubtless this tantalizing glimpse of how outlines work in Project has left you anxious to start building your own. But project outlines take a little upfront thought. You have to settle two important matters about your project before you start building a logical project outline:

✔ **The goal:** What do you want to achieve at the completion of your project? Is your goal to manage an entire space shuttle mission? Then you need as many tasks as it takes to get from here to splashdown. But if your goal is only to launch the space shuttle, your focus is narrower and the level of detail of certain tasks will probably be different.

✔ **The scope:** This matter is a little more specific: Do you want to build a new warehouse from scratch, outfit it with equipment and furniture, and deal with moving people into their offices by December 1 for a budget of $20 million? Or is the scope of your project to hook up the computer network by November 1 for a budget of $50,000? Understanding what your overall deliverables are helps you further define where to start and where to stop your project.

Look around your own office: you'll be surprised to find that many projects that go off track never had a clear goal to begin with. In fact, inputting project data into project management software is a waste of time if you don't know what your mission is. Go ahead: Ask three people working on the same project in your company to state the goal of the project. I'm betting the farm that you'll get three different answers. For an IT project, for example, the IT Director might tell you the goal is to reduce tech-support calls, the project manager might say the goal is to upgrade all server software to the latest version, and the technician might consider the goal to get all the software installed by next Thursday. (Sound familiar?)

To define a goal and scope for your project, answer these questions:

For a goal:

> ✔ What will be different when my project is complete?
> ✔ What will my project achieve? Will a building be built, a workforce trained, or a space shuttle launched?

For the scope:

> ✔ What will my project cost?
> ✔ How many people will be involved?
> ✔ On whom does my project have an impact: my workgroup, my division, my company, or my clients?
> ✔ What deadlines does my project have?

Everything but the kitchen sink: What to include

Once you have a clear picture of your project goal and the scope of the work to be done, you can begin to think about what your outline should contain. For example, here is the first of three approaches to an outline of tasks for planning a company party:

I. Send out invitations

II. Reserve Conference Room B

III. Order food

Perhaps a little more detail would be helpful:

I. Company Christmas Party

    A. Invitations

        1. Design invitations

        2. Mail invitations

    B. Location

        1. Reserve Conference Room B

        2. Order extra chairs

        3. Decorate space

    C. Food

        1. Hire caterer

        2. Clean up

Or, what about the really detailed approach:

I.   Company Events

    A.   Company Christmas Party

        1.   Planning

            a)   Set party date

            b)   Invitations

            c)   Design

            d)   Send out

            e)   Budget

            f)   Research costs

            g)   Create budget

            h)   Obtain budget approval

        2.   Location and Furniture

            a)   Location

                (1)   Reserve Conference Room B

                (2)   Arrange for carpet cleaning

                (3)   Pick decoration theme

                (4)   Decorate space

            b)   Furniture

                (1)   Order extra chairs

                (2)   Arrange for serving table

        3.   Food

            a)   Research caterers

            b)   Set food budget

            c)   Hire caterer

            d)   Provide kitchen access to caterers

            e)   Assign clean-up committee

            f)   Clean up

    B.   Halloween Party

        1.   And so on . . .

Which one of these outlines is best for this project? That depends on how complex these arrangements are — and on how narrowly you define the project. Are you planning the entire year of company events, or only one party? How many people will perform the tasks, over what period of time? Will one person research, budget, and hire the caterers in a single hour? If so, a single task, *Hire Caterer*, might be enough. Will one person do the research, another set the budget, and another do the hiring of the caterer — and might these tasks be separated by days (or even weeks)? If so, having several tasks might be the way to go.

If one task must happen before another can start, you may have to break the tasks down to reflect the causality between certain events. For example, if you can't begin a new manufacturing process before people have been trained, it's probably not prudent to lump training and the implementation of the new process into a single task.

The important thing to remember is that too little detail might let some tasks slip through the cracks, and too much detail might cause your project team to be inefficient, spending more time reporting their progress and breaking down their activities than they do working. Understand the scope of your project and the relationship of each task as you create your project outline.

Building the outline

People approach building a project outline in different ways. Some create all the tasks they can think of in whatever order, and then promote and demote tasks to different levels and move them around to be in the right order.

Others create upper-level tasks first, and then go back and fill in details below each. Still others work one phase at a time, creating one upper-level task and filling in every possible task underneath it. Then they go on to the next phase and create every task under that, and so on.

The approach you use depends to some extent on how you think. Some people think chronologically, and others group like information. You will eventually have to deal with all levels of structure in your final outline, but which you tackle first is up to you.

All the Right Moves

You discover how to create tasks in Chapter 4. In this section, you move those tasks around to create the outline structure. If you've used any word-processing outlining feature, this will be pretty easy stuff. If you haven't — it's still easy!

The outdent-and-indent shuffle

Outdenting and indenting are the functions you use to move tasks to higher or lower levels of detail in your outline. In some software programs, this is referred to as *demoting* and *promoting*.

> ✔ **Outdenting** a task moves it up a level in the outline (literally shifting it to the left in the outline). The concept behind outdenting is that a task is now at a higher level of detail (in other words, less detailed).

> ✔ **Indenting** a task moves it down a level in the outline (literally indenting the task to the right in the outline) and putting it at a deeper level of detail.

You use tools on the Formatting toolbar (shown in Figure 5-3) to indent and outdent tasks in a project outline. The Outdent tool looks like a left-facing arrow; the Indent tool looks like a right-facing arrow. You can outdent and indent tasks from any view, even the Network Diagram view. However, it's a lot trickier to see the effect in the Network Diagram view, and I recommend the Gantt Chart view for manipulating tasks in an outline structure.

Figure 5-3: Click these tools as many times as you like to move a task up or down the levels of a multiphase outline.

If you've used an outlining feature in other software, you may be tempted to press Tab to demote a task and Shift+Tab to promote a task in an outline. In a word, don't. It won't cause disaster, but it will only move your cursor from one column to the other in a columnar view. In the Network Diagram view, it will move the cursor from field to field in a single task box.

To promote or demote a task, follow these steps:

1. **Click a task in a columnar view to select it.**

   An example of a columnar view is the Gantt Chart view.

2. **Click the Outdent or Indent button according to what action you want to take.**

Moving tasks

It's practically a maxim of project management that things change: tasks you thought you could do early on can't happen yet because the people, materials, or money are in short supply. Or a task you thought you couldn't start until next July gets bumped up in priority when your customer changes his mind (again) about deliverables. Because of this changeability, when you enter tasks in a project outline, odds are you'll need to move those tasks around at some point. You can move subtasks to other phases of the outline by simply clicking and dragging them.

You should understand that moving a task can change its outline level. A task retains its level in the outline when you move it to follow a task at the same level. If you move a lower-level task to a section of tasks at a higher level — for example, move a third-level task to a section of second-level tasks — the task will take on the level of the task preceding it. This is also true when you take a higher-level task and move it to follow a lower-level task. However, the exception is when you move a lower-level task to follow a summary task. If you move, say, a second-level task to immediately follow a summary task, it will stay at the second level (not take on the summary-task level of the task that now precedes it).

Moving is a drag

If you ask me, click-and-drag is to computing what the remote control is to television. It's a quick, no-brainer method of moving stuff around in software that just makes life simpler. Here's an example: The quickest way to move a task in an outline is to use the click-and-drag method.

To move a task with this method, follow these steps:

1. **Display a columnar view, such as the Gantt Chart.**

2. **Select a task by clicking its task ID number.**

3. **Drag the task to where you want it to appear in the outline.**

   A gray line appears, indicating the new task position, as shown in Figure 5-4.

4. **When the gray line is located where you want to insert the task, release the mouse button.**

   The task appears in its new location. If you want the task to be at a different level of the outline, you can now indent or outdent it as needed.

If you want to move more than one task at a time, click and drag to select multiple task IDs, and then drag them to a new location. Note that you can also use the Shift+click and Ctrl+click selection methods to select multiple tasks in a Project outline. Using Shift+click, however, means you can only move contiguous selected tasks.

Cut!

Clicking and dragging is fine in most cases, but in very large projects — with, say, a few hundred or more tasks — it can be like dragging a peanut to Tibet: It's not the difficulty; it's the distance you have to travel.

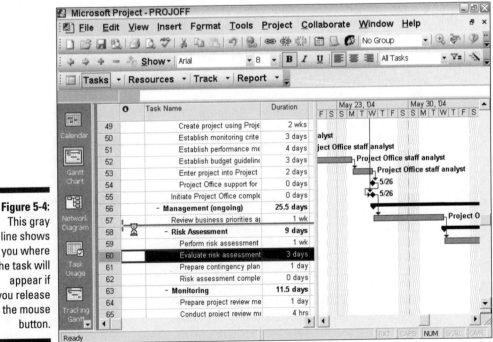

Figure 5-4:
This gray line shows you where the task will appear if you release the mouse button.

In a larger outline, simply use the cut-and-paste method as follows:

1. **Select a task by clicking its task ID number.**
2. **Click the Cut Task tool on the Standard toolbar.**

   The task is removed from its current location and placed on the Windows Clipboard.

3. **Scroll to display the location where you want the task to appear.**
4. **Click the task after which you want to insert the task.**
5. **Click the Paste tool.**

If you want to insert a copy of a task in a project outline, you can use the preceding steps, but click Copy Task instead of Cut Task.

If you are cutting and copying only a single cell and not a whole task, click in the cell and the toolbar buttons will be named Cut Cell and Copy Cell.

Now You See It, Now You Don't

Since caveman days (or whenever the first fourth-grade teacher taught the first set of kids how to outline their book reports), outlines have allowed you to focus on different levels of detail. Outlines do this on paper by essentially ordering information so you can more easily focus on the level of information you need and ignore the rest.

With the invention of computer outlining, the capability to focus on only certain portions of an outline comes into its own. That's because you can easily open and close an outline to show or hide different levels of information — or entire sections of your outline. The project outline in Figure 5-5, for example, is open to show details of just one phase of the project.

What does that capability mean to you? It means you can hide all but the upper level of tasks in a project to give your manager an overview of progress. It means you can close every phase of your project except the one currently in progress — and your team can focus on just those tasks — in a status meeting. It means you can close most of your outline so that jumping to a late phase of a very large schedule doesn't involve more scrolling than a Baroque fireplace.

A summary task with all tasks displayed has a minus sign to the left. A summary task with hidden subtasks has a plus sign to its left. To display or hide different levels of information in your outline, do the following.

When a summary task has a minus sign next to it, you can select the summary task and do one of three things:

✔ Click the minus sign to hide all subtasks.

✔ Click the Hide Subtasks button on the Formatting toolbar to hide all subtasks.

✔ Click the Show button on the Formatting toolbar and then click the level of detail you'd like to leave open in the entire outline. (For example, you can click Outline Level 1 for only the highest level in the outline — which shows the fewest details.)

If you don't want to see plus and minus outlining symbols, you can remove them from all views by deselecting the Show Outline Symbol option on the View tab of the Options dialog box.

When a summary task has a plus sign next to it, you can select the summary task and do one of three things:

✔ Click the plus sign to display one level of subtasks.

✔ Click the Show Subtasks button on the Formatting toolbar to display one level of subtasks.

✔ Click the Show button on the Formatting toolbar (as in Figure 5-6) and click the level of the outline you want to reveal for the entire outline.

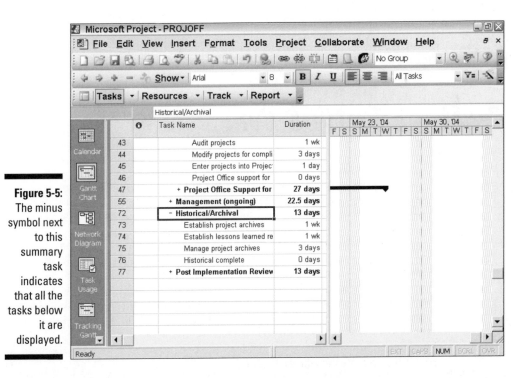

Figure 5-5: The minus symbol next to this summary task indicates that all the tasks below it are displayed.

```
Microsoft Project - PROJOFF
File  Edit  View  Insert  Format  Tools  Project  Collaborate  Window  Help
```

			0				Duration	May 23, '04	May 30, '04
				Show ▾	Arial	▾ 8 ▾			
		Tasks ▾	Re		All Subtasks	ort ▾			
					Outline Level 1			F S S M T W T F S S M T W T F S	
Calendar		27			Outline Level 2	s c	0 days		
		28			Outline Level 3	Co	28 days		
		29			Outline Level 4	sp	3 days		
Gantt		30			Outline Level 5	ers	5 days		
Chart		31			Outline Level 6	ng	2 days		
		32			Outline Level 7	g i	1 wk		
		33			Outline Level 8	ies	3 days		
Network		34			Outline Level 9	es	2 wks		
Diagram		35			Project Standards and cor	0 days		
		36			Empower Project Office	1 day		
		37			Announce Project Office	4 hrs		
Task		38			Planning complete	0 days		
Usage		39			− **Initiate Project Office**	**27 days**		
		40			Staff Project Office personne	1 wk		
		41			− **Project Office Support for**	**11 days**		
Tracking		42			Determine existing projec	2 days		
Gantt		43			Audit projects	1 wk		

Ready   EXT CAPS NUM SCRL OVR

Figure 5-6:
Choose
whatever
level of
detail you'd
like to see
from this
drop-down
list.

To quickly reveal all subtasks in a project, click the Show button and then click All Subtasks.

Cracking the WBS Code

Some codes are used for disguising things (think Mata Hari). In Project, however, codes are used to make the elements of a project easier to identify. These codes, which are called *work breakdown structure,* or *WBS,* codes, can be generated automatically to give a unique identity to each task in your project by its order in the project outline.

For example, the fourth task in the third phase of a project would have a code similar to this: 1.3.4. This code helps you identify all tasks that belong to Phase One, no matter at what level of the outline they may lie, as shown in Figure 5-7. Quite simply, assigning a WBS code to an outline helps you to identify the location of individual tasks in the outline so that people can find and reference them easily. This is similar to the way page numbers in a book's table of contents help you go right to a specific page.

Figure 5-7:
With larger
projects,
this code
can get
quite
lengthy!

	WBS	🛈	Task Name	Duration
27	1.2.2.9		Policies and procedures c	0 day
28	**1.2.3**		− **Project Standards and Co**	**28 day**
29	1.2.3.1		Define security/roles/resp	3 day
30	1.2.3.2		Define system parameters	5 day
31	1.2.3.3		Create project numbering	2 day
32	1.2.3.4		Define financial reporting i	1 v
33	1.2.3.5		Identify project categories	3 day
34	1.2.3.6		Create project templates	2 wl
35	1.2.3.7		Project standards and cor	0 day
36	1.2.4		Empower Project Office	1 d
37	1.2.5		Announce Project Office	4 h
38	1.2.6		Planning complete	0 day
39	**1.3**		− **Initiate Project Office**	**27 day**
40	1.3.1		Staff Project Office personne	1 v
41	**1.3.2**		− **Project Office Support for**	**11 day**
42	1.3.2.1		Determine existing projec	2 day
43	1.3.2.2		Audit projects	1 v

The United States government often requires the use of such a code, so companies doing business with them will find this automatic application of a WBS code useful.

A standard WBS code uses numbers for each level of the code. You can also create custom codes that provide a few options for how the code is defined.

New to Project 2003 is a Visio WBS Chart Wizard. If you have Microsoft Visio installed on your computer, you can use this wizard to generate a Visio WBS chart for selected tasks — or all the tasks in your project. You can use the settings in the wizard to generate a chart for a specified level in the project outline, such as only level-1 tasks, or level-1 and level-2 tasks, and so on.

Display a WBS code

Here's the good news: You don't really have to create a WBS code per se because the very structure of your outline creates the code. All you have to do is display it. To do that, follow these steps:

1. **Click the Gantt Chart icon in the View bar.**

   The Gantt Chart view appears.

2. **Right-click anywhere in the column headings and then click Insert Column.**

   The Column Definition dialog box appears, as shown in Figure 5-8.

3. **Click the arrow on the Field Name box and then select WBS.**

   Use the scroll bar if necessary to locate that field name.

4. **Click OK.**

   The WBS column is displayed. If you add a task, or move, promote, or demote a task in your project outline, the WBS code is updated automatically.

Customize it

By default, the WBS code would look like this for the fourth task under the second phase of the first phase in the project:

> 1.2.4

Figure 5-8: You can use this dialog box to set options such as column width and alignment, as well.

Now, often such off-the-rack WBS code works just fine for projects. But for those times when you want to make changes, Project allows you to modify the code to use a prefix — say the name of your project, a client ID, or your department number — and to vary the use of numerals or letters to indicate the various levels of your code structure. An example of a customized code is shown in Figure 5-9.

The elements used to make up the code are called *code masks.* You can specify the following choices for WBS code masks:

- ✔ **Numbers (ordered)** uses a numerical code.

- ✔ **Uppercase Letters (ordered)** uses letter codes (such as A, B, C to correspond to the first, second, and third phases of a project) with uppercase formatting.

- ✔ **Lowercase Letters (ordered)** also uses letters, but with lowercase formatting.

- ✔ **Characters (unordered)** is used for combinations of letters and numbers. This choice generates an asterisk; you can replace the asterisk with whatever characters you like in a columnar view.

Figure 5-9: Customized WBS codes can help you identify your tasks by categories such as division, client, or company.

To customize a WBS code, follow these steps:

1. **Choose Project ⇨ WBS ⇨ Define Code.**

   The WBS Code Definition dialog box appears, as shown in Figure 5-10.

2. **In the Project Code Prefix box, type a prefix.**

3. **Click at the top of the Sequence column, and then select a mask for the first level.**

4. **Click the Length column, and then select a length for the mask sequence that corresponds to the number of tasks you expect to have at that level.**

   Each number represents a single character. If you choose 4, for example, your first task at this level is numbered 0001. If you aren't sure, leave the default choice of Any to allow for any length.

5. **Click under the Separator column, and then click a choice of separator.**

   The choices are a period, a hyphen, a plus sign, or a forward slash.

6. **To define WBS code elements for additional levels of your outline, repeat Steps 3 through 5.**

7. **When you're finished, click OK to save the new code.**

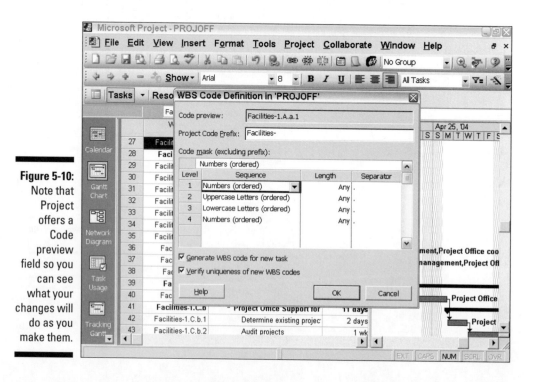

Figure 5-10:
Note that
Project
offers a
Code
preview
field so you
can see
what your
changes will
do as you
make them.

The essential point of a WBS code is to provide a unique identifier for each task in your project. The WBS Code Definition dialog box does offer an option to Verify Uniqueness of New WBS Codes that is active by default. If you turn this option off, you won't be alerted if, for example, you insert a subproject that contains duplicate WBS numbers.

If you don't want Project to automatically add a custom WBS code when you insert new tasks, clear the Generate WBS Code for New Task option in the WBS Code Definition dialog box (Project ➪ WBS ➪ Define Code). If at a later point you want to renumber all tasks to accommodate new tasks, subprojects you've inserted, and changes, choose Project ➪ WBS ➪ Renumber. This can be useful if you want to try what-if scenarios but don't want all of your tasks to change.

Chapter 6

Timing Is Everything

. . . .

. . . .

*I*magine this: If you create a hundred tasks, leave their default constraints so they start As Soon As Possible, and have no dependencies, all those tasks will start on the project start date and occur simultaneously. The project of a hundred tasks will take exactly as long as the longest task.

But wander back over here to reality for a moment. When was the last time every task in your project could be performed at the same time? When did you last have enough resources to even begin to make that feasible? When did you ever have a set of tasks where not a single task had to be completed before another could start? Imagine if you poured a building's foundation before you got the building permit. Or what if you tried to train your employees to use a new piece of equipment before the equipment even arrived?

Tasks in a project don't all start at the same time. To reflect that reality in a Project plan, you have to build in a timing logic. That logic consists of dependency links between tasks. *Dependencies* are timing relationships between tasks — for example, if one task depends on the completion of another. They're caused either by the nature of the tasks (you can't build the house frame until the concrete foundation is dry; otherwise the building will sink) or lack of available resources (you can't have your operations manager attend two plant inspections simultaneously).

Becoming Codependent

In Chapter 4, I mention that you shouldn't set task start dates very often. That's because projects are fluid — they change and grow faster than bad guys come at you in the average computer game. If you build in a timing logic, rather than assign specific dates to tasks, Project can reflect changes by adjusting your project based on that logic.

So, if the task of getting materials in-house is delayed by a week, the dependent task of starting the manufacturing process automatically moves out a week. You can note the change when tracking activity in your plan, and Project will make adjustments accordingly. The alternative is to go in and change the start date of just about every task in your schedule *every time a task is running late* — you don't even want to think about doing that!

When tasks depend on each other

As with human relationships, every dependency relationship involves roles: Every task is either a *predecessor* or a *successor*. Any two tasks can be a predecessor-and-successor pair, even if the timing of the two tasks overlaps or they're set to happen concurrently.

Figure 6-1 shows how the taskbars in the Gantt Chart view graphically depict the predecessors and successors in dependency relationships between tasks. Notice how taskbars represent the relationship when a task starts after (or during the life of) another task. Notice also the lines drawn between tasks. These lines indicate dependency links.

 Here's some important advice about dependencies, so listen up: You can have more than one dependency link to a task, but don't overdo it. Many people who are new to Project make the mistake of building every logical timing relationship that could exist. If things change and they have to delete or change dependencies (for example, shorten a schedule), the web of dependencies starts to get convoluted — and can easily create a nightmare.

For example, both obtaining a permit and pouring a foundation for a building have to be completed before you can start framing the building. However, if you set up a dependency between the permit and pouring the foundation, then setting a dependency from foundation to framing is sufficient to establish the correct timing. Because you can't start pouring the foundation till you have a permit, and you can't frame till you pour the foundation, there's no way framing could start before you have a permit. (Who knew common sense could be so refreshing?)

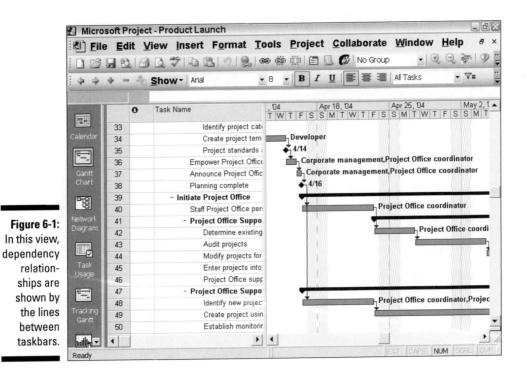

Figure 6-1:
In this view,
dependency
relation-
ships are
shown by
the lines
between
taskbars.

Dependency types

You can establish four types of dependency links: finish-to-start, start-to-finish, start-to-start, and finish-to-finish. Using these types efficiently can mean the difference between a project that finishes on time and one that is still going on long after you retire.

In Chapter 4, I cover task constraints and priorities. These settings work in concert with dependencies to determine the ultimate timing of tasks in your project.

Here's how the four dependency types work:

- **Finish-to-start.** A finish-to-start dependency is the most common type of dependency link. In this relationship, the predecessor task must be completed before the successor task can start. When you create a dependency, the default setting is finish-to-start.

  An example of a finish-to-start dependency is when the *Print Invitations* task must be completed before you can begin the *Send Out Invitations* task. Figure 6-2 shows two tasks with the finish-to-start relationship indicated by a successor taskbar that starts where the predecessor taskbar leaves off.

Figure 6-2:
The taskbar for the *Print Invitations* task ends where the milestone symbol for *Send Out Invitations* begins.

✔ **Start-to-finish.** In a start-to-finish dependency, you can finish the succes-sor task only after the predecessor task has started. If the predecessor is delayed, the successor task can't finish.

Suppose that you're planning the building of a new cruise ship. You might start selling tickets for the ship's maiden voyage while the ship is being built, but you don't want to stop selling tickets until the ship is ready to leave. So, the predecessor is *Ship Ready for First Voyage* (a mile-stone) and the successor task is *Sell Tickets for Maiden Voyage.* If the ship is not ready, you can keep selling tickets. When the ship is ready to go, the ticket windows close, and that task can finish. Bon voyage!

✔ **Start-to-start.** Start-to-start does what it says: Two tasks must start simultaneously. For example, you might want to ensure that a new block-buster movie you're producing is released to theaters the same day that the new action figures are available in fast-food chains.

Figure 6-3 shows such a start-to-start relationship between two tasks.

✔ **Finish-to-finish.** Finish-to-finish has nothing to do with warm relations between citizens of Finland. Finish-to-finish — you guessed it — means two tasks must finish at the same time.

Suppose you're preparing the annual report for your adventure-travel company. You have to obtain photographs of travel destinations and have the brochure copy typeset. You have to have both items in hand before you can forward the report to the printer. If you set a finish-to-finish dependency between these two, you allow both tasks the most time to be completed. (Why have the photos sitting around for four weeks when the copy isn't ready?)

Allowing for Murphy's Law: Lag and lead time

Now that you understand the four types of dependency links, it's time to show you how dependencies can get a little more complex. You can use lag time or lead time to get your timing relationships even more finely tuned.

Lag time occurs when you add time to the start or finish of a predecessor task; lag time causes a gap in timing. *Lead time* is when you subtract time from the start or finish of the predecessor; lead time causes an overlap between two tasks.

Figure 6-3:
Because you're sending the posters and invitations to the printer at the same time, these tasks have a start-to-start relationship.

Here are some examples:

✔ Suppose you want to launch a new toy product into the market, and set up a start-to-start dependency relationship between the *Begin Print Media Advertising* predecessor task and the *Begin TV and Radio Advertising* successor task in your project. With a simple start-to-start relationship, both tasks start at the same time. But what if you want the TV and radio ads to come out a week after the print ads begin? In that case, you'd want to build in a week of lag time to the start-to-start relationship where *Begin Print Media Advertising* is the predecessor and *Begin TV and Radio Advertising* is the successor. TV and Radio ads will now start one week after print ads begin to appear.

✔ In a project to train a new set of volunteer docents to give tours of an historic mansion, suppose you create a finish-to-start relationship between the *Locating Recruits* and *Training Recruits* tasks. However, to save time in your project, you decide to incorporate two days of lead time — that is, allow the training of the earliest hires to start before all the recruits are hired. In that case, you essentially deduct time from the finish-to-start relationship that allows you to start training two days before the finish of the Locating Recruits predecessor.

Making the Connection

Making dependency relationships is simple. You simply create a dependency, make settings to select the dependency type, and build in any lag or lead time. What's important is that you understand how each type of dependency affects your plan when your project goes live and you start to record actual activity that resources perform on tasks.

Adding the missing link

When you create a dependency, by default it's a finish-to-start relationship — one task must finish before another can start. If that's just the kind of dependency you want, that's all there is to it. If not, then after you create this link, you can edit it to change the dependency type or to build in lag or lead time.

To establish a simple finish-to-start link with your mouse, follow these steps:

1. **Display the Gantt Chart view, making sure that the two tasks you want to link are visible.**

2. **Click the predecessor taskbar and drag your mouse pointer to the successor taskbar.**

   As you drag, a box appears, as shown in Figure 6-4, and your cursor changes to the shape of a sideways 8.

3. **When the readout indicates the task number that you want to link to, release your mouse button.**

You can also establish the finish-to-start relationship by clicking the predecessor and dragging to link it to the successor task, then click the Link Tasks button on the Standard toolbar.

To establish a link in a Task Information dialog box or modify an existing relationship, make note of the task ID number of the predecessor task, then follow these steps:

1. **Double-click the successor task.**

   The Task Information dialog box appears.

2. **Click the Predecessors tab, which is shown in Figure 6-5.**

3. **Click the ID box and type a task ID number of the Predecessor task.**

4. **Press Tab.**

   The task name and the default finish-to-start dependency type with 0 lag time are entered automatically.

Task Information

| General | Predecessors | Resources | Advanced | Notes | Custom Fields |

Name: Send Out Invitations   Duration: 0d   ☐ Estimated

Predecessors:

ID	Task Name	Type	Lag

Help   OK   Cancel

Figure 6-5:
You can build as many dependency relationships here as you like.

5. **Click the Type box to display the dependency types, and then click the appropriate one for your dependency.**

6. **If you want to add lag or lead time, click the Lag box and use the spinner arrows.**

   Click up to a positive number for lag time or down to a negative number for lead time.

7. **Repeat Steps 3 through 6 to establish additional dependency relationships.**

8. **When you're finished, click OK to save the dependencies.**

The Gantt chart displays your dependencies with lines and arrows, as shown in the project displayed in Figure 6-6.

Most dependency links are between tasks that are reasonably close to each other in the Project outline. However, if you have to link tasks that won't fit on a single screen of information, the click-and-drag method can be tricky. In that case, use the successor Task Information dialog box to create the relationship by entering the predecessor task ID number.

Extending your reach with external dependencies

No person is an island — and no project exists in a vacuum. Many times, another project you're managing or another project going on somewhere else in your organization will affect your project. Perhaps resources or facilities are shared or perhaps the timing of tasks in other projects affects the timing of tasks in yours. For example, if your project is to plan the opening of a new store, you may have to create a dependency from your *Begin Move-In* task to the *Final Building Inspection Complete* task in someone else's construction project.

To deal with this balancing act, you can create a hyperlinked task in your project that represents the timing of the other project (or of a particular task in it). Enter a start date and duration for the task. You can then create dependencies between that task and other tasks in your project, reflecting the external timing. Use the hyperlink to jump quickly to the other project any time you want to update your timing information. (See Chapter 4 for information about hyperlinking tasks and entering the start date and duration.)

You can also insert an entire project and include a link to it so updates to the other file are reflected in your plan automatically. See Chapter 4 to read more about hyperlinked tasks and inserted projects.

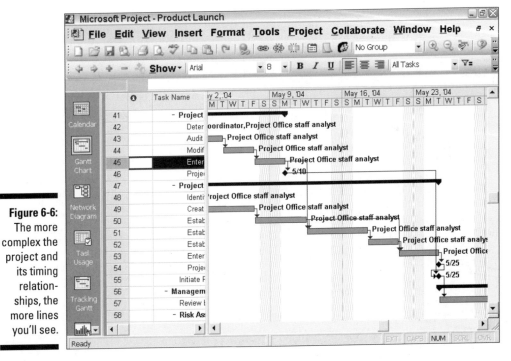

Figure 6-6:
The more complex the project and its timing relationships, the more lines you'll see.

Things change: Deleting dependencies

Just when you think you can depend on some folks, sometimes you find you can't depend on them at all. That kind of change can occur with Project dependencies as well. When you need to get rid of a dependency, you can undo what you did either in the Gantt Chart or in the Task Information dialog box.

In the Gantt Chart, follow these steps:

1. **Select the two tasks whose dependency you want to delete.**

   For two adjacent tasks, you can click and drag to select their ID numbers. For nonadjacent tasks, click one task, press and hold the Ctrl key, and then click a nonadjacent task.

2. **Click the Unlink Tasks button on the Standard toolbar.**

Be careful when you use this method: If you click only one task and then click the Unlink Tasks button, you get a somewhat drastic result: *All* dependency relationships for that task are removed.

To remove dependency relationships in the Task Information dialog box, here's the drill:

1. **Double-click a successor task name.**

   The Task Information dialog box appears.

2. **Click the Predecessors tab to display it.**

3. **Click the Type box for the dependency that you want to delete.**

   A list of dependency types appears, as shown in Figure 6-7.

Figure 6-7:
This tab can
be used to
both create
and delete
dependency
links.

Task Information

| General | Predecessors | Resources | Advanced | Notes | Custom Fields |

Name: Project Office support for new projects   Duration: 0d   ☐ Estimated

Predecessors:

Finish-to-Start (FS)

ID	Task Name	Type	Lag
53	Enter project into Project Office management	Finish-to-Start (FS)	0d
42	Determine existing projects for Project Office	Finish-to-Start (FS) ▼	0d
		Finish-to-Start (FS)	
		Start-to-Start (SS)	
		Finish-to-Finish (FF)	
		Start-to-Finish (SF)	
		(None)	

Help   OK   Cancel

4. **Click None.**

5. **Click OK to save the change.**

The dependency line on the Gantt Chart is gone, and the next time you open that Task Information dialog box, the dependency will be gone.

Just Look At What You Did!

Project provides several ways to view dependencies in your project. The method you choose will probably relate to how you visualize data, so there's no absolute right or wrong here!

Case study: Launching a new product

To put all this timing information in practice, imagine a project to launch a new product into the market. Here are six tasks that might exist in such a project:

Design Product Packaging

Meet with Focus Group

Send Press Release

Submit Web Site Content to Management

Approve Web Site Content

Add Product Page to Web Site

What logical timing relationships exist among these tasks? Some of these relationships will depend on whether resources would be available to work on these tasks if they happened simultaneously. But here are the likely dependencies:

Predecessor, Design Product Packaging, Successor, Meet with Focus Group. You couldn't have a focus group give feedback on the packaging if it hasn't been designed. This could be a start-to-start relationship, with some lag time between the start of design and holding the focus group. You're not going to finalize the package design *before* you have focus group feedback, but you can't hold the focus group until at least initial designs are available, so you might have the focus group task start, say, three weeks after design has started.

Predecessor, Submit Web Site Content to Management, Successor, Approve Web Site Content. You might want to make this a finish-to-start relationship with a week or so of lag time between the submitting of the content and the approval task to give management a week to review the content. (You could also create a week-long task named Review Web Site Content and put it between these two tasks — either approach is valid.)

Predecessor, Approve Web Site Content, Successor, Add Product Page to Web Site. The logic here is obvious: You have to have approved content before you can place it on a Web page. This is also a finish-to start relationship.

Predecessor, Send Press Release, Successor, Add Product Page to Web Site. You might want to create a finish-to-finish relationship here, such that the press release goes out at the same time that the Web site is ready to be viewed. If the Web site isn't ready, the press release won't be sent out.

You've already seen the dependency link lines that appear in the Gantt Chart (refer to Figure 6-6). Another great way to see the flow of dependencies is in the Network Diagram. This workflow view uses similar lines and arrows to reveal dependency relationships, but it allows you to get a different perspective on them.

Figure 6-8 shows the Network Diagram view of an engineering project. Notice that each task has a node containing its vital statistics. Between nodes are lines revealing dependency relationships among tasks. Although you can't see it in black and white, by default any task dependency links on the critical path are in red and noncritical tasks are in blue. (*Critical-path tasks* are tasks that have no slack: They can't be delayed without delaying the entire project.)

A neat trick in the Network Diagram view is to edit the layout to show link labels. (Right-click outside any task nodes, click Layout, and then select the Show Link Labels check box.) A code (such as FS for finish-to-start) is displayed to explain the type of dependency that each dependency line represents.

Figure 6-8:
Following
the flow of
dependency
lines is a bit
easier in the
Network
Diagram
view.

You can also display columns that itemize successors or predecessors for each task by task ID number in any view with a sheet area, such as the Gantt Chart view. Figure 6-9 shows the Gantt Chart view for the same engineering project with successor and predecessor columns displayed. These columns also include a notation of the type of dependency (other than the default finish-to-start) and any lead or lag time using percentages or amounts of time. For example, 71SS+50% is a start-to-start link to task 71, with lag time set so that the successor begins halfway through the predecessor task. Similarly, 71SS+2 days is a start-to-start link to task 71, with lag time set so that the successor begins two days after the predecessor task starts.

Note that you can also edit the contents of Network Diagram nodes to include predecessor and successor data.

Figure 6-9:
Of course,
you have to
know which
task number
is which
before you
can use the
information
in these
columns!

		Predecessors	Successors	Task Name
	5	4	6	Justify Project Office via
	6	5	7	Secure executive spons
	7	6	10	Scope complete
	8			– Planning
	9			– Analysis/Logistics
	10	7	11	Review Project Office
	11	10	12	Establish a managem
	12	11	13	Analyze business ob
	13	12	14	Define mission stater
	14	13	15	Define goals
	15	14	16	Establish communica
	16	15	20,21,22,23	Secure Project Office
	17	16		Logistics complete
	18			– Policies and Procedu
	19	16	24	Define "best of breed"
	20	16	24	Define "best of breed"
	21	16	24	Define "best of breed"
	22	16	24	Establish resource re

Part II
People Who Need People

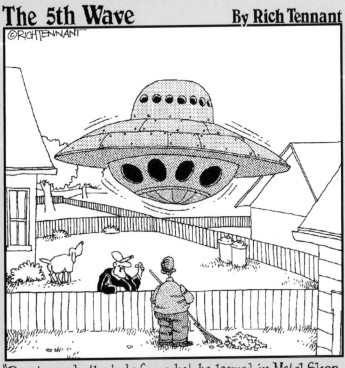

The 5th Wave   By Rich Tennant

©RICHTENNANT

"Ronnie made the body from what he learned in Metal Shop,
Sissy and Darlene's Home Ec. class helped them in fixing up
the inside, and then all that anti-gravity stuff we picked
up off the Web."

In this part . . .

*H*ere's where you get to know Project resources —
human and otherwise — and how to orchestrate
resources and material costs most effectively to dispatch
your project's tasks. This part also shows how to save
some administrative hassle by incorporating smaller projects into larger master projects — and getting various
projects to share resources and play nice.

Chapter 7

Using Your Natural Resources

*P*rojects are like giant water coolers — they're gathering places for people. Projects also utilize equipment and materials. Those people, equipment, and materials are your project *resources*.

Unlike water coolers (you can take an analogy only so far), resources are also the means by which Project tallies up costs in your plan. Assign a resource to work for ten hours on a task, give that resource an hourly rate of $20, and you've just added a $200 cost to your project. Create a resource called cement, give it a unit cost of $200, and assign ten units (for example, ten tons of cement), and you've added a whopping $2,000 to the bottom line.

Using resources wisely in Project doesn't involve only assigning them a cost. It's a delicate art of combining the right resource, with the right skills, and assigning that resource to put in the right amount of time (or units) on tasks. And you have to do this all without overbooking anyone at any point in your schedule.

Because they affect timing and costs, resources are a big deal in Project. Resources are so important that many tools are available to help you create them, make settings for how and when they'll work, assign them to tasks, manage costs, and manipulate their workload. The first step in working with resources is to create them and enter certain information about them. That's what this chapter is all about.

Resources: People, Places, and Things

Many people hear the word *resources* and think of people. Well, people are a frequently used Project resource, but they're not the whole story. Resources can also be equipment that you rent or buy, and materials such as paper clips or scrap iron. You can even create resources that represent facilities you have to rent by the hour, such as a laboratory or a meeting space. You could (for example) create a resource named Plant Visit and assign it a unit cost of $400 — the average cost for a trip to your plant, including airfare, hotel, and rental car.

Here are some typical and not-so-typical project resources:

- Engineers
- Trade show booth
- Office supplies
- Hotel ballroom
- Administrative assistants
- Rocket fuel
- Speaker fees
- Furniture
- Computer software
- Printing services
- Prototype design

You get the picture. Resources can be practically anything or anyone that you use to complete your Project.

Becoming Resource-full

After you create and organize the tasks in your project, the next typical step is to create resources. You can also borrow resources that have been created by others and assign them to your project. But before you start creating resources willy-nilly, it's important that you understand how they affect your project.

Understanding resources

The key to understanding resources is to realize that resources in Project equal costs. If you want to account for costs in your project — such as a person putting in hours working on a task or computers you have to buy or rent — you must create resources and assign them to one or more tasks. When you do, you can see the resulting costs in the Cost column of the Gantt Chart spreadsheet, as shown in Figure 7-1.

		Microsoft Project - PROJOFF3						

Menu bar: File   Edit   View   Insert   Format   Tools   Project   Collaborate   Window   Help

Show ▾   Arial   ▾ 8 ▾   **B** *I* U   All Tasks

Tasks ▾ | Resources ▾ | Track ▾ | Report ▾

Project Office Template

	Task Name	Fixed Cost	Fixed Cost Accrual	Total Cost	3, 03 T W T F S S	Jan 4, 04 M T W T F
2	− **Scope**	**$0.00**	**Prorated**	**$8,500.00**		
3	Determine Project Of	$0.00	Prorated	$2,400.00		Corporate
4	Document high-level	$0.00	Prorated	$1,600.00		Co
5	Justify Project Office	$0.00	Prorated	$2,400.00		
6	Secure executive spc	$500.00	Prorated	$2,100.00		
7	Scope complete	$0.00	Prorated	$0.00		
8	− **Planning**	**$0.00**	**Prorated**	**$70,390.00**		
9	− **Analysis/Logistics**	**$0.00**	**Prorated**	**$11,510.00**		
10	Review Project Off	$2,500.00	Prorated	$2,940.00		
11	Establish a manag	$0.00	Prorated	$2,400.00		
12	Analyze business	$0.00	Prorated	$880.00		
13	Define mission sta	$0.00	Prorated	$880.00		
14	Define goals	$450.00	Prorated	$1,770.00		
15	Establish commur	$0.00	Prorated	$440.00		
16	Secure Project Off	$0.00	Prorated	$2,200.00		
17	Logistics complete	$0.00	Prorated	$0.00		
18	− **Policies and Proce**	**$0.00**	**Prorated**	**$38,400.00**		

Ready   EXT   CAPS   NUM   SCRL   OVR

Figure 7-1: Tasks with assigned resources show the associated total costs in the Cost column.

Calendar   Gantt Chart   Network Diagram   Task Usage   Tracking Gantt

One other way to add costs to a project is to use a fixed cost. Fixed costs are not assigned through resources because they don't accumulate costs by hours of work or units used. Instead, a fixed cost is a set cost applied directly to individual tasks. (For more on fixed costs, see Chapter 8.)

If a cost is not task-specific — such as a flat $10,000 consulting fee to a firm that's advising you on an overall project — you can create and assign a resource or fixed cost to the summary task for the entire project.

After you create the resources that Project uses to tally your project costs, you'll need to manage the workflow for any resource that has limited time availability for your project. You create resources that are available so many hours a day and so many days a week. When you assign those resources to your project, you can use various views, reports, and tools to see whether any resource is overbooked at any point during your project. You can also see whether people are sitting around twiddling their thumbs when they might be available to help out on another task. You can even account for resources that work on multiple projects across your organization and make sure they're being utilized efficiently. Views such as the Resource Usage view (shown in Figure 7-2) help you visualize resource working time in your project.

Figure 7-2:
You can see
total hours
on the
project by
resource
and an
itemization
of the hours
assigned
task-by-task
for that
resource.

Finally, it's important to understand that the number of resources you assign to work on a task will usually have an effect on the duration of that task. In others words, if you have a certain amount of work to perform but few people to do it, a typical task will take longer to finish than if you had scads of folks.

TIP

The task type determines whether or not a task's duration will change based on the number of resources assigned to it. Take a look at Chapter 4 for more about task types.

Resource types: Work and material

Although people and things come in all shapes and sizes, to Project there are only two types of resources: work resources and material resources.

✔ **Work resources** are typically (but not always) people. Their costs are associated with the amount of work time they put in, usually at an hourly rate. Work resources are assigned to tasks based on a Working Time calendar (shown in Figure 7-3), where you specify their working and nonworking hours.

✔ **Material resources** can have an hourly rate or a unit cost, and they have an unlimited working time. This type of resource has no calendar, and you make no settings for working and nonworking time.

A typical work resource is a person working eight hours a day at a standard rate of $20 an hour and an overtime rate of $30 an hour. Another example of a work resource is a meeting facility available only eight hours a day at an hourly rate. Even though it's not a person, the meeting facility would probably be created as a working resource because it has limited "working" hours.

The three kinds of calendars are Project, Task, and Resource. Calendars, their settings, and how those settings interact are discussed at some length in Chapter 3.

A typical material resource is any material — such as steel, rubber, paper or books, chairs, and shoes — assigned to a task with an associated unit cost. A resource called *Books* with a unit price of $12.95, assigned to a task called *Computer Training* at ten units, will accrue a cost of $129.50 to the task. Another example of a material cost is anyone performing a service for a fee where working time is not an issue. A speaker who presents at a conference for a fee of $1,000 but whose working calendar and time are not your concerns might be created as a material resource with a unit cost of $1,000.

Figure 7-3:
You can select one of three base calendars and then modify specific working hours.

Fear of commitment?

If you've ever asked somebody to work on your project and gotten a half-hearted, "Well, maybe, if I have time, if my manager says it's okay, if it falls on a Leap Year . . ." in response, you may well ask: So is that resource available or not? It's not always easy to tell. How can Project help? One feature new to Project 2003 is the capability to designate a resource as either *proposed* or *committed*. You can use the Booking Type field in the Resource Information dialog box to make this setting.

What does this setting do? Well, if you're not quite sure about a resource's commitment to your project, you call that resource *proposed*. Then you can display the booking type column in a resource view (such as the Resource Sheet), and keep track of resources you may have to firm up as you get closer to finalizing your project plan.

How resources affect task timing

For a fixed-unit or fixed-work task type, the addition or removal of resources assigned to the task will have an impact on the time it takes to complete the task. In essence, the old saying that "two heads are better than one" might be modified to "two heads are faster than one."

Here's an example: Suppose that one person is assigned to the *Dig Ditch* task, which should take four hours of effort. Two people assigned to the *Dig Ditch* task will finish the job in two hours because two hours are being worked by each resource simultaneously — which achieves four hours of effort in half the time.

One BIG word of warning here: Assigning additional people to tasks doesn't always cut work time down proportionately, though that's the way Project calculates it. When you have more people, you have meetings, memos, duplicated effort, conflicts, and so on. If you add more resources to a task, you might consider upping the amount of effort required to complete that task to account for inevitable workgroup inefficiencies.

Estimating resource requirements

You usually know how many material resources it takes to complete a task: In most cases, you can calculate the number of pounds, tons, yards, and so on with a standard formula. But how do you know how much effort it will take on the part of work resources to complete the tasks in your project?

As with many aspects of information you put into a Project plan, this judgment rests to a great degree on your own experience with similar tasks and resources. But remember these guidelines:

- ✔ **Skill counts.** A less skilled or experienced resource is likely to take more time to finish something.

- ✔ **History repeats itself.** Look at previous projects and tasks. If you've tracked people's time, you can probably see how much effort was required to complete various types of tasks.

- ✔ **Ask and you shall receive.** Ask the resources themselves how long they think it will take. Then add 10 percent to that time to cover yourself!

The Birth of a Resource

When a person is born, someone fills out a birth certificate with his or her name, parents' name, date of birth, and so on. Creating a resource in Project involves filling out a form, too. On the Resource Information form, you enter information such as the resource name, rate per hour or cost per use, and availability. You can also enter optional information such as the workgroup the resource belongs to or the resource's e-mail address.

You can create a resource as a single person or thing, as a generic resource (that is, a skill set with no person attached such as Assistant or Engineer), and even as a group of several resources that work together.

One at a time

On the simplest level, you create a resource — whether it's a person, a piece of equipment, or a material — as a single entity. In this case, you're thinking of a particular person, or meeting room, or piece of equipment. You create the resource by entering information in the Resource Information dialog box.

Another method for entering resource information is to display the Resource Sheet view and enter information in the columns included there. This is often a faster way to create several resources at once.

When you create a resource, you must at a minimum type the Resource Name, but you can also include as much information as you want. Some people prefer to create all the resources first and deal with contact and cost information at a later stage.

To create a resource, follow these steps:

1. **Click the Resource Sheet view in the View bar.**

2. **Double-click a blank Resource Name cell.**

   The Resource Information dialog box appears, as shown in Figure 7-4.

3. **In the Resource Name box, type a name.**

4. **In the Type box, click Work or Material.**

   The settings available to you differ slightly depending on what you choose.

5. **In the Initials box, type an abbreviation or initials for the resource.**

   If you don't enter anything here, the first letter of the resource name is inserted when you save the resource.

6. **Continue to enter any information you want to include for the resource.**

   That information might include an e-mail address, the group (a department, division, or workgroup, for example), Material Label (for example, pounds for food coloring or tons for steel), Booking Type, or Code (such as a cost-center code). Note that a material resource won't have the E-mail box available, and a work resource won't have the Material Label box available.

   If you enter information in the Group box, you can then use filters, sort features, and the Group feature to look at sets of resources. See Chapter 11 for more about filtering and working with groups.

7. **Click OK to save the new resource.**

If you use Project Server (a feature of Project Professional used for online collaboration) you can choose the Microsoft Project Server option in the Workgroup box. You can also use the Windows Account option in the Resource Information dialog box to specify how you'll communicate with the team.

Getting generic

In the planning stages of a project, you'll often find that all your resources aren't assembled. Sometimes even well into the project, you don't know what resource you'll be using; you know only that you need a resource with a certain skill set to complete upcoming tasks. In that case, you might be better off creating some resources as generic resources.

Figure 7-4:
These five
tabs can
hold a
wealth of
information
about any
resource.

If you want to create a generic resource, you should give it a name that describes its skill, such as Engineer, or Designer, or even Meeting Space (as opposed to a specific resource named Conference Room B). Then, in the Resource Information dialog box, be sure to select the Generic check box.

You can display a Yes/No column titled *Generic* to identify these resources, and you can create a resource filter to filter for a Yes or No entry in the Generic column to filter resources by this characteristic.

No formula takes the Generic setting into account in recalculating your schedule based on resource availability. However, many people find this setting useful in long-range planning and in situations where they aren't responsible for specific resource assignments (for example, assigning a temporary worker to a task when the specific worker will be chosen by the temp agency).

Resources that hang out together

Although you'll probably have little use for chain gangs in your project, they exemplify the principle of a resource that represents multiple resources. Rather than assigning people one by one to some tasks, you'll want to assign a group of people who typically work together. Being able to make one assignment of such a *consolidated resource* rather than several separate resources and assignments can be a timesaver in larger projects.

Here's an example of a consolidated resource: Suppose that you are managing a project to get a new Web site up and running. You have four Web designers of equal skill at your disposal, so you create a resource named Web Designers. You can assign Web Designers to a task at 400 percent, and have all four designers working at once. Or you can assign the Web Designer resource to work on a task at 100 percent, thereby assigning two resources to it.

There is no special setting to designate a multiple resource: however, you might want to include some indication of the number of resources in the resource name. For example, you could name your designer resource *Four Web Designers* (if you know the Web design group consists of four people) or *Web Design Group.* What really defines this type of resource is the maximum assignment units; 400 percent would indicate four resources in the group.

Sharing Resources

Many organizations have lots of projects going on at the same time. Some, such as a project to organize an office move, will be the only project of its type happening in a company. Others, such as a building design project in an architectural firm, will happen simultaneously with several other similar projects and draw on many of the same resources, such as architects and draftspeople.

When an organization has projects of a similar nature going on at the same time, it's often useful to create centralized resources. This can save you time because you don't have to create resources when they already exist. It can also help to track resources across projects.

Another timesaving Project feature allows you to pull existing resources from a company address book or your own address book in Outlook.

In the swim: Drawing on resource pools

If you use Project throughout your company, it can be beneficial to create a centralized repository of common resources and allow project managers to assign those resources to their various projects. This collection of enterprise resources is called a *resource pool.* By using a resource pool, you can get a more realistic idea of how busy resources are across all projects at any point in time.

Both individual resources and consolidated resources can be created in a blank project as a resource pool, and saved to an accessible location on your company server. Then, any project manager can call on those resources for his or her own projects; those projects are then referred to as *sharer files* because they share resources with the resource pool. For example, if you have a pool of maintenance people that everyone in your manufacturing company assigns to projects, create a project called *Resource Pools* and then create all your enterprise resources in this project. Or you could create a resource called *CEO* and let all the people managing projects that require the CEO's involvement assign him or her from that central location. Then use the resource-sharing tools in Project to assign these resources to your plan.

When anyone makes resource assignments in a sharer file, that information is also saved in the resource pool file. Then, anyone can use that file to look at resource allocations across all projects in the organization.

To access a resource that's available to your entire organization, follow this procedure:

1. **Choose Tools ⇨ Resource Sharing ⇨ Share Resources.**

   The Share Resources dialog box appears, as shown in Figure 7-5.

Figure 7-5: When many people pull on the same resources in a company, sharing resources becomes a good idea.

2. **Specify the resources for the project.**

   If you want to specify that a project will use only its own resources (the default), select the Use Own Resources option. If you want to share resources, select the Use Resources option and then select a project in the From list.

3. **Specify what Project should do when a conflicting resource setting, such as the resource base calendar, exists.**

   If your project's setting will take precedence, select the Sharer Takes Precedence option. If you want the pool setting to rule, select Pool Takes Precedence.

4. **Click OK to complete the process.**

   All resources in the specified resource pool are added to your own project's resource list, ready to be assigned to tasks.

After you've added a shared resource to your project, you can update shared resource information. You would want to do this in case the person who maintains those shared resources has made a change, such as upping the resource's rate per hour. To do this, choose Tools ⇨ Resource Sharing ⇨ Refresh Resource Pool.

If you combine separate projects into one master project at any point, Project allows you to have duplicated resources. If you link the combined projects and then delete a duplicate resource in the master project, it's deleted in the subproject as well.

Importing resources from Outlook

If you're like me, you've spent months or years building up your list of e-mail contacts in Outlook. You might as well have a way to leverage all that work: Project supplies this in its capability to pull resources from Outlook.

You must have Outlook specified as your default e-mail program in order for this to work. Do that by opening Outlook, and when you're asked if you want it to be your default program, say yes.

When you insert one or more Outlook resources in your project, they're added to your project list, taking the resource name and e-mail address as they exist in the Outlook address book. The default first-letter initial and work type is also preassigned. You can then add any details you like to the resource.

Drowning in the resource pool

Drawing resources from resource pools saves you time because you don't have to recreate those resources again and again. However, should you track your resource's time in the resource pool file to see whether the resource is overbooked? Most projects in the real world use resources who are not solely dedicated to a single project. New users of Project often get confused because almost every person working on their projects puts in time on other work, from general communication with co-workers and clients to efforts put in on other projects. Should they build resource pools to account for time shared among several projects at one time?

Generally speaking, it would be chaos to try to track every minute of all your resources' days to see whether they're working 100 percent or 50 percent on your tasks or are being shared among multiple projects. Ask yourself this question: When this resource works on a task in your project, "Will he or she put his entire focus on that task at that time?" If so, you may not need to fool around with tracking shared resources across many projects. Especially on shorter tasks, not trying to micromanage the efforts of your resources outside of your own project usually works just fine. If, on the other hand, you have resources who work only half time or split their time between two projects routinely, consider using shared resource tools to keep track of those resources across projects.

To insert resources from your Outlook address book, display the Resource view, and then follow these steps:

1. **Choose Insert ⇨ New Resource From ⇨ Address Book.**

   The Choose Profile dialog box appears.

2. **Select Outlook.**

   The Select Resources dialog box appears.

   If you use Outlook as your e-mail client, this is how Microsoft makes it easy to use contacts you've stored in Outlook as resources in your project.

3. **Specify a name.**

   You can type a name in the Type Name or Select from List box, or you can click a contact name in the Name list.

4. **Click Add to place the selected name in the Resources list.**

5. **Repeat Steps 2 and 3 to add all the resource names that you want to import to your project.**

6. **When you're finished, click OK.**

The names now appear in your project resource list, ready for you to add additional information.

If you use Project Server, you can access a feature called Build Team from Enterprise through the Tools menu of Project. This allows you to choose resources from among various projects and your enterprise resource pools to build a project team. See Chapter 20 for more about this feature.

Say, When Do These Guys Work?

Chapter 3 is all about calendars, including Project, Task, and Resource calendars. Now that you're working with resources, it's worth a closer look at how Resource calendars work.

First, there's a base calendar that can be Standard, Night Shift, or 24 Hours. (You can also create custom calendars.) Standard is a typical 9-to-5 day and five-day week. Night Shift is an eight-hour day scheduled between 11 p.m. and 8:00 a.m. with an hour off for a meal from Monday through Friday.

The 24 Hours base calendar shows just what it says: 24 hours, seven days a week.

After you specify a base Resource calendar, you can specify working hours, such as 9:00 a.m. to 12:00 p.m. and 1:00 p.m. to 5:00 p.m. for a standard eight-hour day or 8:00 a.m. to 12:00 p.m. and 1:00 p.m. to 4:00 p.m. for a variation on that eight-hour day. Finally, you can select specific days when a resource is not available (for example, when someone will be on vacation, at an off-site seminar, or busy with another commitment) and mark them as nonworking.

Avoid micromanaging nonworking time for your resources — it could leave you no time to manage anything. For example, if someone is taking half a day to go to a doctor's appointment, it's probably not necessary to block a day off. But if a resource is taking a two-week vacation or a three-month sabbatical, it's probably useful to modify the resource's working time calendar.

To make all these settings, you can use the Working Time tab of the Resource Information dialog box, which is shown in Figure 7-6.

To make changes to a resource's calendar, follow these steps:

1. **Display the Resource sheet.**

2. **Double-click a resource name.**

   The Resource Information dialog box appears.

3. **Click the Working Time tab to display it.**

Figure 7-6:
The legend
on the left
explains
how
nonworking
and working
days
appear.

4. **In the Base Calendar box, select a base calendar.**

5. **If the default base calendar hours don't match your organization's, click the From and To boxes and type new times.**

   Note that to build in a break or lunch hour, you must enter two sets of numbers.

6. **If you want to mark any days as nonworking, click them in the Select Date(s) calendar, and then select the Nonworking Time option.**

   To display other months or years, drag the scroll bar box.

7. **Click OK when you're finished.**

To find out more about calendars or to create a custom Resource calendar, see Chapter 3.

Now I've Got 'Em, How Do I Manage 'Em?

Before I leave the topic of resources, I'd be remiss if I didn't tell you a bit about the vital project-management skill of *resource management*. Here, in a nutshell, is your nickel tour of the art of managing the people who will make your project happen.

Acquiring the right resources

Just as an award-winning performance in a movie begins with casting the right actor, resource management starts with finding the right resources for your tasks. What makes a resource is a combination of factors. The right resource for a task is somebody who has:

- The right skills for the task at hand (or is trainable, if training is part of your budget).
- Enough time available to complete the task according to your schedule.
- The ability to commit to the project (this sometimes involves getting another manager's buy in).
- A cost that fits in your budget.

Though the above list covers the basic requirements, consider other details, such as whether the resource is set up to work with the project team, and whether the technology to communicate and share documents is available. Also, give some thought to how well each resource you choose will work as part of the team, and whether the resource can be considered dependable.

In Project, you have several ways to flag and find resources, categorizing them by skill or other criteria:

- Use the Resource Notes area to record information about a resource's skills and abilities. Then use the Find feature to search notes fields for words such as "highly skilled," "dependable," and "trainable."
- Use the Code field in the Resource Information form to rank resources by skill, cost, or ability to work well with others.
- Create Custom Fields for resources to note specific skills and search for resources by those skills.

Sometimes it's worthwhile to consider a less experienced, cheaper resource to save money. But be sure to factor in the time and money needed for any training required.

Balancing workload

Another important part of resource management is managing the assignment of resources so that nobody is as overbooked as a CPA at tax time. Although occasional overtime is expected of most workers, constant overtime causes burnout and poor work quality. Keep in mind that a less skilled worker will take longer to do a task than a skilled worker. Take that into account when scheduling the time that resource might need to complete his or her work.

You get the scoop about making resource assignments in Chapter 9, and more about resolving resource overallocation in Chapter 10.

You can do three main things to stay aware of resource workload when working with Project:

Keep an eye on your Project plan. Various tools such as a resource usage view (shown in Figure 7-7) allow you to spot overbooking on tasks.

When tracking activity on tasks, you will receive an accounting from resources about the actual time they're spending on tasks. Notice the people who have to constantly put in overtime to keep their heads above water.

Ask people. That's right. This isn't a feature of Project, but it's an old fashioned communications device that works amazingly well. Check in with resources often and ask whether things are going okay — including whether your human resources are being run ragged. Then help those who are overworked by modifying your schedule or adding other resources to help.

Figure 7-7:
The
Resource
Usage view
shows
resource
assign-
ments and
helps you
see problem
times in
your project.

	❶	Resource Name	Work	Details	T	F	S	S	M	
		Localize identifie	40 hrs	Work						
		Refine compone	16 hrs	Work		8h			8h	
		Review identifiec	8 hrs	Work						
		Localize identifie	40 hrs	Work						
		Refine compone	16 hrs	Work						
		Review identifiec	8 hrs	Work						
		Localize identifie	40 hrs	Work						
		Refine compone	16 hrs	Work		8h			8h	
		Review identifiec	8 hrs	Work						
		Localize identifie	40 hrs	Work						
		Refine compone	16 hrs	Work						
		Review identifiec	8 hrs	Work						
		Localize identifie	40 hrs	Work						
		Refine compone	16 hrs	Work		8h			8h	
7	◇	⊟ **Technical reviewer**	272 hrs	Work	40h					
		Test component	16 hrs	Work	8h					
		QA review cycle	8 hrs	Work						
		Test component	16 hrs	Work	8h					
		QA review cycle	8 hrs	Work						
		Test component	16 hrs	Work						

Managing conflict gracefully

Although the fine art of managing people and the conflicts they seem to get into is beyond the scope of a book on Microsoft Project, this topic is worth a word to the wise. *Conflict resolution* is a necessary skill for project managers — and it involves creating an environment of cooperation and respect, building consensus (agreement) among team members, and encouraging honest communication.

As a project manager, you can set up well-designed communications tools (such as frequent status meetings or reports) so people stay in touch throughout your project. You can also make a point of staying alert to conflict — and nipping it in the bud. (A conflict ignored will only fester and become something worse.) Try to keep the focus of discussions on the project goal, not on personalities.

Chapter 16 tells you all about designing and generating reports in Project.

Chapter 8

What's All This Gonna Cost?

There's no such thing as a free lunch — and if you use Project to track costs, there's no such thing as a free resource. That's because Project uses resources working on tasks as a way of calculating most of the costs on your project.

When you create a resource, you specify a work resource rate (by default, this rate is tallied up per hour) or a material resource per use cost. You can also create *fixed costs* — that is, a set cost for a task that isn't calculated using a per-use or hourly rate, such as a trade-show fee.

Some other factors come into play as well, such as how many hours a day a resource is available to work and any overtime rates. At the end of the day, all these settings come together to put you over — or under — budget.

In this chapter, you explore the relationship between resources and costs — and find out how to set resource standard and overtime rates, create fixed costs, and set the availability of resources on individual tasks in your project.

Mary, Mary, How Do Your Costs Accrue?

Project helps to account for costs on your various tasks with a combination of costs per hour, costs per unit, and fixed costs. Before you begin to flesh out cost information about your resources, you have to understand how these calculations work.

You'll have two main pictures of the budget in your project: one at the moment you freeze your original plan (called a *baseline plan*) and the ongoing picture of actual costs that comes from the actual activity and material usage you record as your project moves along. You record a certain amount of work effort on tasks, and tasks with resources assigned to them then run up costs based on the effort expended or units of materials used.

It all adds up

The best way to understand how costs add up in your project is to look at an example. John Smith (that's not his real name) is managing a project involving the building of a new gourmet ice cream packaging plant. John has created a task called *Install Ice Cream Mixers.* Here are the costs John anticipates for that task:

- ✔ About ten person-hours of effort to do the installation
- ✔ A fixed cost of $500 paid to the mixer manufacturer to oversee the installation and train workers on the machine
- ✔ Twenty pounds of ice-cream ingredients to test the mixers

The ten hours of effort will be expended by work resources. The total cost for the ten hours is a calculation: 10 times the resource rate. If the resource rate is $20, this cost totals $200. If two resources work on the task, one at a rate of $20 and one at a rate of $30, then (by default) Project splits the ten hours of effort between them, and the resulting cost is $250.

The fixed cost of $500 for a fee to the manufacturer is not assigned through a resource. Instead, you enter it in a Fixed Cost field for the task. This cost won't change based on the number of resources nor the time involved.

Finally, the cost for 20 pounds of ice cream (any flavor you like) is calculated as 20 times the unit cost of the ice cream ingredients. If the unit cost is $2, this cost would be $40.

 And that's how costs are assigned and add up on your projects.

You can create and assign resources that have no associated costs — for example, if you want your boss to be available to review status reports, but your company doesn't require that your boss be charged to your project, you can simply use those resource assignments to remind you about the need for your boss's availability on that day or at that time.

When will this hit the bottom line?

In business, you rarely get to choose when you'll pay your own bills. In Project, however, you can choose when your costs will hit your budget.

Both resources and fixed costs can be set to accrue at the start or end of the task they're associated with or to be prorated throughout the life of the task. So, if a three-month-long task begins April 1, a $90 fixed cost could be added to your actual costs to date on day 1, on day 90, or at a dollar a day until the end of the task.

This isn't exactly a purely realistic reflection of how you have to pay for costs, because let's face it: Most bills come due 30 days after they hit your desk. It's more a factor of when you want that cost to show up for the purposes of tracking costs and reporting expenses on your project.

It's Pay Day!

Most projects involve a combination of cost types: fixed, work, and material. You'll have to do your homework before you can enter the information at the task or resource level. You have to find out the fixed costs as well as the hourly or unit rates for all your resources.

During the planning stages, it may not be possible to anticipate exactly what a particular cost will be or know every resource's rates. If you have to, build the resource or fixed cost with your best estimate. Then at least some cost will be reflected in your plan, and you can go back to enter more accurate information as soon as you know it.

Use the Estimated check box in any task to which you assign estimated fixed or resource costs. That way you can easily go back to those tasks and update the estimates as your plan progresses.

There's no avoiding fixed costs

Maybe it's that huge fee for the consulting company your boss insisted you use, even though you knew their report wouldn't tell you a thing you didn't already know. Or perhaps it's the $2,000 for a laptop computer you talked your boss into getting you so you could manage your project when you're on the road. Whatever it is, it's a cost that won't change no matter how many hours the task goes on or how many people work on the task. It has no unit cost or rate per hour. It's what's called a *fixed cost.*

You can enter fixed costs for tasks by using the Fixed Cost column in the Gantt Chart sheet. The easiest way to display this is to use the Cost table.

Tables are preset column combinations that make entering certain information in a sheet pane easier.

Follow these steps to enter a fixed cost for a task:

1. **Display the project in the Gantt Chart view.**

2. **Choose View ➪ Table ➪ Cost.**

   The table of columns appears, as shown in Figure 8-1.

3. **Click the Fixed Cost column for the task to which you want to assign the cost, and then enter the amount.**

That's all there is to it, but because you can enter only one fixed-cost amount for a task, you should also enter a task note where you can itemize fixed costs if you have more than one. Note also that the default fixed-cost accrual method is prorated; if you prefer to have your fixed costs hit your budget at the start or end of a task, use the Fixed Cost Accrual column in this table to select another option.

Figure 8-1:
You can
insert the
Fixed Cost
column in
any sheet,
but the Cost
table is
ready for
you to use.

	Task Name	Fixed Cost	Fixed Cost Accrual	Total Cost
2	– **Scope**	$0.00	Prorated	$1,000.00
3	Determine Project Of	$0.00	Prorated	$0.00
4	Document high-level	$1,000.00	Start	$1,000.00
5	Justify Project Office	$0.00	Prorated	$0.00
6	Secure executive spc	$0.00	Prorated	$0.00
7	Scope complete	$0.00	Prorated	$0.00
8	– **Planning**	$0.00	Prorated	$3,250.00
9	– **Analysis/Logistics**	$0.00	Prorated	$3,250.00
10	Review Project Off	$0.00	Prorated	$0.00
11	Establish a manag	$0.00	Prorated	$0.00
12	Analyze business	$2,500.00	Prorated	$2,500.00
13	Define mission sta	$0.00	Prorated	$0.00
14	Define goals	$0.00	Prorated	$0.00
15	Establish commur	$0.00	Prorated	$0.00
16	Secure Project Off	$750.00	Prorated	$750.00
17	Logistics complete	$0.00	Prorated	$0.00
18	– **Policies and Proce**	$0.00	Prorated	$0.00

When resources get paid per hour

Whether it's minimum wage or the astronomical fees your lawyer charges you every time you sneeze, most people get paid something per hour. To represent most people involved in your project, you create work resources and charge them to your project at an hourly rate.

After a resource has an hourly rate, when you then enter the estimate of how many hours that person will work on each task that he's assigned to, Project totals his estimated costs in your plan. When you track actual effort expended on tasks, a calculation of actual effort times the hourly rate returns actual costs.

By comparing estimated costs and actual costs, you get an ongoing picture of whether or not your project is on track.

To set resource rates per hour, follow these steps:

1. **Display the Resource Sheet view.**

2. **Click the Std. Rate column for the resource to which you want to assign a cost.**

3. **Type a dollar amount.**

    If you're entering a rate for a unit other than hours, type a slash (/) and then the unit (for example, **minute** or **month**).

4. **Press Enter and the entry is saved.**

Note that you can also make cost-rate entries in the Resource Information dialog box. The Costs tab of this dialog box, which is shown in Figure 8-2, offers a Standard Rate, an Overtime Rate, and a Per Use Cost.

In addition, five tabs labeled A through E allow you to enter different rates for the resource. By using the Effective Date column, a resource could work for several months at one rate and then start working at a different rate on a preset date. This helps you account for periodic raises or seasonal shifts in rates (for example, paying a premium for construction resources in months with better weather when they are more in demand).

If you use ten gallons at $2 a gallon . . .

This one may feel like a problem from your high-school algebra class. (*So many gallons of water in a bathtub with a leak. . . .*) Well, unless your project is to raise the *Titanic,* no leaks are involved, but there is a pretty straightforward calculation Project makes to arrive at *cost per use.*

Figure 8-2:
You can set
several sets
of rates for
a resource.

Technically speaking, you can have a cost per use for either a work or material resource. You could, for example, have a consultant who costs $500 per use (that is, each time you use him to consult on a task, you get hit with a $500 fee). More commonly, you use a cost per use for a material resource such as rubber or milk, assign a cost for a single unit (per yard, or ton, or gallon, for example), and assign so many units to each task. The cost is tallied by the number of units times the cost per use.

To assign a cost per use, follow these steps:

1. **Display the Resource Sheet view.**

2. **Click the Cost/Use column for the resource you want to set, and then type an amount for the per-use cost.**

3. **Click the Material Label column for that resource, and then type a unit name (such as gallon).**

4. **Press Enter to accept your entry.**

Note that you can use the Resource Information dialog box also to enter up to five per-use costs with effective dates to account for fluctuations in unit cost over the life of your project.

Making allowances for overtime

Overtime is a fact of life: It's great for people who earn it — and hard on the project manager with a budget. If you have resources that shift into earning overdrive after so many working hours, you can enter an overtime rate for them. Overtime kicks in when their calendar indicates that their regular day is over. For example, a resource with a standard eight-hour-day calendar who puts in ten hours on a one-day task will be charged by Project with eight hours at the standard rate and two hours at the overtime rate.

To enter an overtime rate for a resource, follow this procedure:

1. **Display the Resource Sheet view.**
2. **Click the Ovt. Rate column for the resource.**
3. **Type an amount.**
4. **Press Enter.**

    The entry is saved.

It's an Availability Thing

Lots of Project features deal with resources — in particular, helping you spot resource overallocation. *Overallocation* is a calculation involving the resource's calendar and availability.

So, consider Monica Melendez, an engineer who works a standard, eight-hour day based on her calendar. Monica is assigned to the *Write Final Report* task at 50 percent of her availability and to the *Create Design Specs* task — which occurs at the same time as the report task — at 100 percent of her availability. Monica is now working at 150 percent of her availability, or 12 hours per day. Poor Monica is overbooked.

By default, a resource is assigned to a task at 100 percent availability, but you can modify that if you know someone will be busy with several tasks and is likely to put in only part of the resource's time over the course of a task.

Setting availability

Availability is easier to estimate for some than for others. A manager isn't likely to give an entire day over to any single task because he has to deal with all the people who report to him, or she has to sign authorizations, go to meetings concerning various projects, work on budgets, and so on. With a production worker, it might be simpler to pin down availability to a single task: If one manufacturing job is going through the line for three days and one person is working on the line all that time, it's closer to the mark to say that he or she is working on that task full time.

One big mistake that new users of Project make is to micro-think availability. Of course, no one actually *spends* eight hours every day on a single task in one project. People spend part of their days reading e-mail about company holidays, chatting with co-workers, and answering phone calls about non-project-related stuff (you know — J Lo's love life, UFOs landing at the UN, the usual). A resource might spend seven hours on a task one day but only three the next. Don't get hung up on a day-by-day resource schedule in estimating availability. If *over the life of a task* the person is pretty much devoted to it, 100 percent availability is a good setting. If that person will put in only, say, five days of work on a ten-day task, whether they work four hours a day for ten days or five full days at any point, that's 50 percent availability.

The Availability setting is there to help you spot overbooking of a resource that might work on multiple tasks at the same time in a project schedule.

To set resource availability, follow these steps:

1. **Display the Resource Sheet view.**

2. **Double-click a resource.**

   The General tab of the Resource Information dialog box appears, as shown in Figure 8-3.

3. **In the Units column (in the Resource Availability area), click the arrows to raise or lower the availability in 50 percent increments or type a number.**

   For example, type 33 for a resource available a third of the time, or 400% for a pool of four resources all available full time. The most common entry here (and the default entry) is 100% for a single resource working full time on the task.

4. **Click OK to save the setting.**

When a resource comes and goes

In addition to being available only a certain percentage of the time on any task or project, a resource may be available for only a certain period of time during the life of the task or project. Another scenario might be a resource that is available half time for the first few days of the project and then full time for the rest of the project. In that case, you enter a date range in the Available From and Available To columns of the Resource Availability area in the Resource Information dialog box (see Figure 8-3) to specify varying availability.

Show ▾ | Arial | 8 | **B** *I* U | All Tasks

$97,994.00

	Task Name	Fixed Cost	Fixed Cost Accrual	Total Cost
1	− **Project Office Template**	$0.00	Prorated	$97,994.00
2	− **Scope**	$0.00	Prorated	$15,400.00
3	Determine Project Of	$0.00	Prorated	$4,320.00
4	Document high-level	$1,000.00	Start	$3,880.00
5	Justify Project Office	$0.00	Prorated	$4,320.00
6	Secure executive spo	$0.00	Prorated	$2,880.00
7	Scope complete	$0.00	Prorated	$0.00
8	− **Planning**	$0.00	Prorated	$58,210.00
9	− **Analysis/Logistics**	$0.00	Prorated	$10,930.00
10	Review Project Off	$0.00	Prorated	$240.00
11	Establish a manag	$0.00	Prorated	$4,320.00
12	Analyze business	$2,500.00	Prorated	$2,980.00
13	Define mission sta	$0.00	Prorated	$480.00
14	Define goals	$0.00	Prorated	$720.00
15	Establish commur	$0.00	Prorated	$240.00
16	Secure Project Off	$750.00	Prorated	$1,950.00
17	Logistics complete	$0.00	Prorated	$0.00
18	− **Policies and Proce**	$0.00	Prorated	$25,600.00

Ready

Figure 8-3:
You can
enter any
number you
like in the
Units box.

Adding It Up: How Your Settings Affect Your Budget

In Chapter 9, you explore assigning resources to tasks. But to help round out this discussion of costs, you should know that in addition to a resource cost per hour or use and a resource base calendar and availability, you will assign resources to tasks at certain percentages. All these factors work together in calculating the cost of the resource when assigned to tasks.

Don't worry about the calculations — Project does those for you. That's the beauty of this: After you make settings for your resources, Project does the work of tallying and showing total costs to you in views such as the Cost table of the Gantt Chart view shown in Figure 8-4.

For example, suppose you want to assign a mechanic to a task. Here are the specifics:

Base calendar: Night Shift (eight hours, six days a week, between 11:00 p.m. and 8:00 a.m.)

Cost per hour: $20

Overtime cost: $30

Availability: 100 percent

Assigned to a two-day task: 50 percent

What is the cost of this resource? Here's how it works: two days at half-time availability based on an eight-hour calendar is a total of eight hours (four hours each day). The resource incurs no overtime, so the cost is 8 times $20, or $160.

Change one setting for the same resource, and see what you get:

Assigned to a two-day task: 150 percent

Now the resource is working 12 hours a day (150 percent of 8 hours) over two days. With 16 total hours at the standard rate ($20) and 8 hours of overtime ($30), this person will cost $560.

Figure 8-4:
Total costs at the summary-task level give you a quick idea of your total budget and costs in this table.

	Task Name	Fixed Cost	Fixed Cost Accrual	Total Cost
1	− **Project Office Template**	$0.00	Prorated	$97,994.00
2	− **Scope**	$0.00	Prorated	$15,400.00
3	Determine Project Of	$0.00	Prorated	$4,320.00
4	Document high-level	$1,000.00	Start	$3,880.00
5	Justify Project Office	$0.00	Prorated	$4,320.00
6	Secure executive spc	$0.00	Prorated	$2,880.00
7	Scope complete	$0.00	Prorated	$0.00
8	− **Planning**	$0.00	Prorated	$58,210.00
9	− **Analysis/Logistics**	$0.00	Prorated	$10,930.00
10	Review Project Off	$0.00	Prorated	$240.00
11	Establish a manag	$0.00	Prorated	$4,320.00
12	Analyze business	$2,500.00	Prorated	$2,980.00
13	Define mission sta	$0.00	Prorated	$480.00
14	Define goals	$0.00	Prorated	$720.00
15	Establish commur	$0.00	Prorated	$240.00
16	Secure Project Off	$750.00	Prorated	$1,950.00
17	Logistics complete	$0.00	Prorated	$0.00
18	− **Policies and Proce**	$0.00	Prorated	$25,600.00

Customizing Cost Fields

When you display the Cost table with fields such as the Standard Resource Rate, you can click in any cost column and enter a rate for each resource. A neat shortcut is to customize those fields with a value list.

A *value list* allows you to create a drop-down list of values in a field to select from. So if your company has a few standard hourly rates or per-use costs for materials, customizing these fields can make your information entry faster, and help avoid the data-entry mistakes that can occur when you enter all rates manually.

To customize a field, follow these steps:

1. **Display a table with the column you want to customize.**

2. **Right click the column heading and select Customize Fields from the shortcut menu that appears.**

   The Customize Fields dialog box shown in Figure 8-5 appears.

Figure 8-5:
You can use the Rename button in this dialog box to rename a cost field if you like.

3. Click the Value List button.

The Value List dialog box appears, as shown in Figure 8-6.

Value List for "Cost1"	☒

Enter values to display in dropdown list

| Cut Row | Copy Row | Paste Row | Insert Row | Delete Row |

Row	Value	Description
1		
2		
3		
4		
5		
6		

Move ▲ ▼

☐ Use a value from the list as the default entry for the field

Set Default (Click button after selecting a value above)

Data entry options

○ Restrict field to items in the value list
● Allow additional items to be entered into the field
　☑ Append new entries to the value list
　　☐ Prompt before adding new entries

Display order for dropdown list

● By row number　　○ Sort ascending　　○ Sort descending

| Import Value List... | OK | Cancel |

Figure 8-6:
Create
preset
values for
the field by
building a
value list.

4. Enter a value (if you're filling in a cost field, this would be a dollar amount) in the Value column.

5. Enter a description (for example, plant worker or engineer for the category of resource charged at this rate) in the Description column.

6. Repeat Steps 4 and 5 to enter additional values for this field.

7. If you want to restrict the field to accept only the values in this list, select the Restrict Field to Items in the Value List check box.

8. If you want to allow other values not on the list to be entered in this field, select the Allow Additional Items to be Entered into the Field check box.

9. Select an order for the list.

By Row Number lists the items as you've listed them in this dialog box; Ascending lists them in ascending value order, lowest value first; Descending lists them in descending value order with the highest value first.

10. Click OK, then OK again to save the list and close all dialog boxes.

A good view to use if you want to see all of a resource's work assignment information is the Resource Allocation view. You can display it by clicking the Resource Allocation View button on the Resource Management toolbar, or select it from the More Views dialog box. (Read more about the Resource Management toolbar function in Chapter 9.)

Chapter 9

Your Assignment, Should You Choose to Accept It

*Y*ou might have entered a cost per hour (or per use) for every resource in your project, but they won't cost you a thing — or, for that matter, get anything done — until you assign them to tasks.

When you do begin making assignments, several interesting things happen. Not only will your budget start to swell, but also some of your tasks may actually change duration. You may also start to see evidence of people who are overbooked on several tasks that happen around the same time. Understanding how those results occur is key to making intelligent assignments.

But your work won't be over even when everything about your assignments looks hunky-dory. That's when you have to communicate the assignments to everyone and make sure they agree to take them on. If they don't, it's back to the assignment drawing board.

In fact, assigning resources is something of an ongoing process throughout your project. As usual, Project provides the tools to help you manage this entire process relatively painlessly.

You'd Be Surprised What Assignments Can Do to Your Timing

The three task types (described in Chapter 4) are fixed units, fixed work, and fixed duration. Each defines the relationship that balances a task's duration, the work required to complete the task, and resource availability.

Your selection of task type — in combination with a setting that determines whether a task is effort-driven — has an impact on the timing of your tasks relative to your resource assignments.

Pinning down your type

Essentially, task types specify what will remain constant in a task when you add or remove work resources to it after making the initial resource assignment. Although this whole work and duration and resource assignment percentage calculation can be complicated, it's important that you understand it if you want Project to accurately determine task durations in your plan according to resource assignments.

The default task type is fixed units. With a fixed-units task, the task duration you enter and the resource effort (work) assigned to that task jointly determine the timing of the task. With this task type, the assignment units you specify for your resources won't change even if the number of hours required to complete the task shrinks or grows.

With a fixed-units task, if you increase the duration of Task A from two to three days, your resources will continue to work on it at the assigned units for the specified duration; Project increases the Work amount accordingly. When you add or take away resources, Project changes the task duration accordingly, based on the assignment units you specify.

The fixed-work task type, on the other hand, takes a specified number of work units to be completed. A one-day task requires eight hours to be completed (assuming a Standard calendar). This type of task changes its duration in response to the number of resource units you assign.

With a fixed-work task, resource assignments may change in response to a work change. For example, suppose Task A takes four days to complete when one person is assigned; with a fixed-work task, the same task takes only two days when two people are assigned. Project will not modify the hours of work required to complete the task, but will modify resource assignment units to complete that work within the specified timeframe. So if you up the duration of Task A, resource assignment units shrink in response. If you reduce the time to complete Task A, resource assignments increase to complete the unchanged amount of work hours in less time.

A fixed-duration task does not vary its length, no matter what resource assignments you make.

With a fixed-duration task, Task A will take four days. If you assign additional resources or remove resources, the task will still take four days, but the resource-assignment units will change.

Figure 9-1 shows the same task with the three different types. Each task was created with a four-day duration and one resource at 100 percent. Then an additional resource was added at 100 percent. Note the resulting change — or lack of change — with each type. The fixed-duration task didn't change duration but *did* reduce resource assignments. The fixed-units task kept resource assignments constant at 100 percent — but reduced the task's duration. Fixed work was accomplished faster, and the work (32 hours) stayed constant.

Figure 9-1:
Select the task type that reflects what is variable on your task.

When effort is in the driver's seat

Project's complex calculation of work, task duration, and assignment units involves not only task types but also the effort-driven setting. (In Figure 9-1, the effort-driven setting is active for all tasks.)

With the *effort-driven* setting active, if you add resources to a task, Project distributes the specified work equally among them and may change the task duration according to the total resource effort, depending on the task type.

With all three task types, Project assumes (by default) that each task is effort-driven. You can turn on the effort-driven setting — or turn it off if you choose the fixed-duration or fixed-units task type. With the fixed-work task type selected, the effort-driven setting is turned on automatically and can't be turned off.

Follow these steps to change the settings for an effort-driven task:

1. **Double-click a task.**

   The Task Information dialog box appears.

2. **Click the Advanced tab, which is shown in Figure 9-2.**

Figure 9-2: The effort-driven setting is selected and unavailable to you if you select a fixed-work task.

3. **To turn off the effort-driven setting, select the Effort-Driven check box to remove the check mark.**

   The effort-driven setting is on by default.

4. **Click OK to save the new setting.**

Suppose task calendars prevail?

One other setting on the Advanced tab of the Task Information dialog box, Scheduling Ignores Resource Calendars, has an effect on how resources are scheduled when you make task assignments. You can instruct Project to let the Task calendar override any Resource calendar setting for resources assigned to it. Then, if a task is set to use the Standard calendar and a resource assigned to it uses a Night Shift calendar, that resource will work standard hours on that task.

There are situations where certain calendar settings won't be available. Chapter 7 provides details about how all kinds of resource calendar settings work if you need a refresher course about this.

Use this setting, for example, if someone who normally works the night shift will be called on to attend a two-day seminar that takes place during standard working hours.

Finding the Right Resource

Sometimes there's no one in the world who can perform a certain task like Albert, and you'll get Albert to do that job if it kills you. Other times, just about anyone could handle the work.

If any Tom, Dick, or Mary with a certain skill level (or a certain rate per hour) will do, you can use Project features to find the right resource and make sure he or she has enough time to take on just one more task.

Needed: One good resource willing to work

You've probably used the Find feature in other software to find a word or phrase or number. That's child's play: Project's Find feature can find you a backhoe, a corporate jet, or an entire person! You can use Project's Find feature to look for resources with certain rates or in a certain workgroup. You can search for resources by their initials, their maximum assignment units, their standard or overtime rate, and so on.

For example, you might need to find a resource whose standard rate is less than $50. Or you might want to find someone who can put in extra work on a task, so you search for any resource whose maximum units are greater than 100 percent. (In other words, the resource can put in a longer than usual day before he or she is considered overallocated.) Perhaps you need to find a material resource that is a chemical measured in gallons, but you can't remember the exact chemical name. In that case, you can search for resources whose material label includes the word *gallons*.

First display any resource view, then follow these steps to find resources in Project:

1. **Choose Edit ➪ Find.**

   The Find dialog box appears, as shown in Figure 9-3.

Figure 9-3:
Searching
is a
combination
of looking
for some
element in a
particular
field that
meets a
certain
criterion.

Find

Fi_n_d what: 1000

Look in field: Remaining Cost   T_e_st: is greater than

_S_earch: Down   ☐ Match Case

_F_ind Next   _R_eplace...   Close

2. **In the Find What box, type the text you want to find.**

   For example, type **50** if you want to search for a resource with a standard rate of $50 or less, or **laboratory** if you want to find a resource whose material label contains that word.

3. **In the Look In Field list, click the name of the field you want to search in.**

   For example, to search for resources that have a maximum unit assignment percentage of more than 100 percent, click the Max Units field here.

4. **In the Test box, select a criterion.**

   For maximum units of more than 100 percent, for example, this choice would be Is Greater Than.

5. **If you prefer to search backwards from your current location (that is, the currently selected cell in the task list) instead of forward, click Up in the Search box.**

6. **If you want to match the case of the text, select the Match Case check box.**

7. **To begin the search, click Find Next.**

8. **Continue to click Find Next until you find the instance you're looking for.**

You can use the Find feature also to find and replace an entry. For example, if your Design Services department changes its name to Multimedia Production, you can search the Group field for the words *Design Services,* click the Replace button, and type the words *Multimedia Production,* as shown in Figure 9-4. Then click the Replace button to replace each instance one by one, or click the Replace All button to replace every instance of that entry in that field, wherever it occurs in your project.

Figure 9-4:
The Replace feature offers a fast way to change every instance of some text in your project field by field.

Custom fields: It's a skill

When assigning resources, you'll often need to take a person's skills into account. If a person with less skill or experience could work on a particular task (and save you money because he or she has a lower rate per hour), wouldn't it be nice to be able to find such resources easily?

Well, Project doesn't include a Skill field, but it does allow you to add fields of your own. You can use these fields for anything, but one great way to use them is to code your resources by skill level. You can use a rating system such as A, B, and C, or use terms such as *Exp* for an experienced worker and *Beg* for a beginning-level worker.

Here's how to add a custom field:

1. **Display the Resource Sheet (or whatever sheet you want to view the custom field in).**

2. **Right-click a column heading and select Insert Column.**

   The column is inserted to the left of the column you clicked.

3. **In the Field name box, select one of the custom fields, designated as Text 1 through Text 30.**

4. **In the Title box, type a name for the field.**

5. **Click OK to insert the column.**

You can enter whatever you like in this column for each resource in your project. Then you can search for specific entries in that field using the Find feature, or turn on a filter to display only resources with a certain skill level in that field. (Read more about filters in Chapter 10.)

Some organizations designate custom fields for certain company information such as an accounting code or vendor rating. If you have a Project administrator who is in charge of these enterprise-wide standards, check with him or her before you choose a custom field to designate skill level.

A Useful Assignation

If you understand how task types and effort-driven scheduling can affect your tasks' timing, you've fought 95 percent of the battle in assigning resources. The rest is just the software equivalent of paperwork. First, you have to create resources before you can assign them. (If you haven't, wander to Chapters 7 and 8 for a refresher course.) After you create resources, you can use a couple of methods to assign them to tasks, and specify the resource assignment units. These assignment units differ slightly between work resources and material resources, however, so read on.

Determining work and material-resource assignment units

Work resources, which are typically people, are assigned to a task using a percentage, for example 100 percent, 50 percent, or 150 percent. When you assign a resource at a percentage, the assignment is based on the Resource calendar. A resource with a Standard calendar will put in eight hours a day if you assign it at 100 percent assignment units. Theoretically, a resource with a 24-hour calendar will work a grueling 24 hours a day at 100 percent (and probably fall right over) or 12 hours at 50 percent.

A material resource is assigned in units, such as gallons, consulting sessions, yards, or tons. When you assign a material resource to a task, you designate how many units of that resource will go to that task.

Note that material resource units are part of the entire work-unit-duration calculation that can cause work resource assignments to change task durations.

Making your assignments

You have four methods of making resource assignments in Project. You can select resources from the Resources tab of the Task Information dialog box, enter resource information in the Resource column in the Entry table (displayed in Gantt Chart view), split the window and use the Resources and Predecessors form in a pane, or use the Assign Resources dialog box.

Which method you use depends to some extent on your own preferences, but generally speaking, here are some parameters for using each method:

✔ When you use the Resource column, you're assigning at a default 100 percent assignment; if you want to assign a different percentage, don't use this method.

✔ Use the Assign Resources dialog box if you may want to replace one resource with another (there's a handy Replace feature in this dialog box) or if you want to filter the list of available resources by a criterion (for example, resources with a cost of less than a specified amount). This is very useful for making multiple resource assignments.

✔ Work in the Task Information dialog box if it's helpful to have task details (such as task type or the constraints contained on other tabs of this dialog box) handy when you make the assignment.

Picking resources from the Resource column

You can use this method to add resources in a resource column, whether from the Gantt Chart view or the Tracking Gantt view.

The Task Usage view, though it lists tasks in its sheet pane and can even display a Resource column, cannot be used to add resource assignments.

Follow these steps to assign resources at a default percentage:

1. **Display the Gantt Chart view by clicking it in the View Bar.**

2. **Choose View ➪ Table ➪ Entry.**

3. **Click in the Resource column for the task on which you want to make a resource assignment.**

   An arrow appears at the end of the cell.

4. **Click the arrow to display a list of resources.**

5. **Click the resource you want to assign.**

   The resource name appears in the Resource column, assigned at 100 percent.

You can always change the assignment units later by opening the Task Information dialog box and changing the assignment units on the Resources tab.

Using the Assign Resources dialog box

To assign a work or material resource to a task, you can select a task and then use the Assign Resources dialog box to make assignments. To do so, follow these steps:

1. **Click a task to select it.**

2. **Click the Assign Resources button on the Standard toolbar.**

   The Assign Resources dialog box appears, as shown in Figure 9-5.

Figure 9-5: Every resource you've created is shown in this list.

Assign Resources

Task: Secure Permits

Resource list options

Filter by:

☐ All Resources   More Filters...

☐ Available to work   0h

Add Resources ▼

Resources from Project1

John Smith

	Resource Name	R/D	Units
✓	Albert Smythe		100%
	John Smith		
	Mary Jones		

Assign

Remove

Replace...

Graphs...

Close

Help

Hold down Ctrl and click to select multiple resources

3. **Click a resource to select it, and then click the Assign button.**

   A check mark appears next to the assigned resource in the Resource Name column.

4. **Click the Units column for the resource you just assigned.**

   If it's a work resource, the default assignment of 100% appears. If it's a material resource, the default is one unit.

5. **Specify a percentage of assignment units for the resource.**

   Click the spinner arrows in the box to increase or decrease the setting. For a work resource, change the percentage units in 50 percent increments by clicking the arrows, or type a percentage. For a material resource, use the spinner arrows in the Units column to increase or decrease the unit assignment, or type in a number of units.

6. **Repeat Steps 3 to 5 to add all resources.**

7. **If you want to replace one resource with another, click an assigned resource (indicated with a check mark), click Replace, select another name on the list, set its units, and click OK.**

8. **Click the Close button to save all the assignments.**

You can also get to the Assign Resources dialog box from the Resource Management toolbar. This toolbar also offers handy tools for adding resources to your project from sources such as your Outlook Address Book, and managing overallocated resources.

Adding assignments in the Task Information dialog box

Finally, you can assign resources on the Resources tab of any Task Information dialog box by following these steps:

1. **Double-click a task name in the Gantt Chart view.**

   The Task Information dialog box appears.

2. **Click the Resources tab to display it.**

3. **Click in a blank Resource Name box, and then click the arrow that appears at the right side of the box.**

   A drop-down list of resources appears.

4. **Click the resource you want to assign.**

5. **Click the Units column and use the spinner arrows to set an assignment percentage.**

6. **Repeat Steps 3 through 5 to assign additional resources.**

7. **Click OK.**

If assigning a material resource, the Units default is a single unit (if your units are pounds, the default assignment is 1 lb). Use the spinner arrows in the Unit field to assign additional material units.

Getting the contour that's right for you

When you make a work resource assignment, Project spreads the work out evenly over the life of the task. However, you can modify the level of work that goes on during the life of the task, called a work *contour,* so that more work takes place near the beginning, middle, or end of the task.

For example, if you know that the people on a task to install a new computer network will have to spend some time up front studying the manuals and reviewing the schematics for the wiring before they can begin to make measurable progress on the installation, you might use a late-peaking contour. Or if you know that people are likely to put in a lot of work up front on a survey — and then sit back and wait for the results to come in — then you might choose an early-peaking contour.

Using a different contour on a particular resource's task assignment could free up that resource to work on a second task that occurs during the life of the first task. This can help you resolve a resource conflict.

The contour you select will have slightly different effects depending on the task type. Trust me: Most project managers don't even want to try to understand this complex equation. Simply try a different contour and see whether it solves your problem and doesn't make too dramatic a change to your task duration or other resource assignments.

To set a task's contour, follow these steps:

1. **Display the Task Usage view.**

   This view shows resource assignments by task.

2. **Double-click a resource.**

   The Assignment Information dialog box appears, as shown in Figure 9-6.

3. **In the Work Contour box, select one of the preset patterns.**

4. **Click OK to save the setting.**

   A symbol for the contour pattern is displayed in the Indicator column for the resource.

   If none of these patterns fits your situation, you can manually modify a resource's work by changing the number of hours the resource puts in day by day on a task in the Task Usage view.

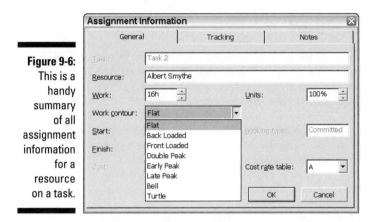

Figure 9-6:
This is a
handy
summary
of all
assignment
information
for a
resource
on a task.

Before you save, make sure your modifications add up to the number of hours you want, or you could inadvertently change the resource's assignment.

The Resource Allocation view is useful for reviewing resource assignments at this stage. This view gives a side-by-side comparison between a single resource's workload and all the tasks going on during a particular time period in your project.

Communicating an Assignment to Your Team

When you've worked out all your resource assignments on paper, it's time to see whether your ideas will work for your resource's schedules.

Of course, you should check to see who is available for your project. But in the time it takes to work out your plan and make assignments, things can change. So, before you commit yourself to a final plan, make sure your resources are committed to you.

If you use the Project Server product with Project, you can use collaborative tools to publish assignments to the server, where people can review them and accept or decline. For more on Project Server, see Part V.

You can send your entire project plan to resources as an e-mail attachment or just send selected tasks. You can also generate a resource assignment report and send that to people so that they can review their assignments in detail.

It's in the e-mail

E-mail can be a project manager's best friend. You can use it to communicate throughout the life of your project and to send your project plan for review at various stages. One of those stages is the point at which you want your resources to commit to their task assignments.

You can send your project as an e-mail attachment or as a schedule note, which is an e-mail with only updated tasks attached. You also have the choice of sending an entire plan (or just selected tasks from it).

To send a project as an e-mail attachment, follow these steps:

1. **Choose File ➪ Send To ➪ Mail Recipient (as Attachment).**

   An e-mail form is displayed.

2. **Fill in a subject and your e-mail message.**

3. **Click Send to send the message.**

If you want to send a schedule note, follow these steps:

1. **Choose File ➪ Send To ➪ Mail Recipient (as Schedule Note).**

   The dialog box in Figure 9-7 appears.

Figure 9-7:
Use this
dialog box
to specify
who will
receive
your note.

2. **Choose any intended recipients of the message from among Project Manager, Resources, and Contacts.**

3. **Select either Entire Project or Selected Tasks to specify what to include in the schedule note.**

4. **In the Attach area, choose what to attach to the e-mail message.**

   If you select the File option, the entire file will be attached. If you instead select the Picture of Selected Tasks option, Project will attach a bitmap picture of the selected tasks in the view you had active when you started the Send procedure.

   Note: If you were in a Resource view when you began this process, this option will read *Picture of Selected Resources* and the resources you had selected will be sent.

5. **Click OK.**

   An e-mail form is displayed.

6. **Fill in a subject and your e-mail message.**

7. **Click Send to send the message.**

To help you track e-mails to resources on your project, set your e-mail program to provide return receipts when messages are received or read.

Report your findings

Remember the days when you read a report on paper, instead of on your computer screen? Those days aren't gone — in lots of situations, a printed report is your best bet for clear communication about your project.

You can use several assignment reports to inform your human resources of their assignments on projects. To help you out, the four assignment report types provide the following information:

- ✔ **Who Does What report:** Provides a list of tasks organized by resource with total work hours, number of days delay from the original schedule, and start and finish dates. It also reflects a total number of work hours for a resource on all tasks in the project.

- ✔ **Who Does What When report:** Shows a calendar listing that organizes tasks by time period with resource-assignment totals.

- ✔ **To-Do List report:** Generated for a single resource (not all resources, as with the other report types) week by week in a project. It lists the task names, durations, start and finish dates, as well as predecessor tasks by task number.

- ✔ **Overallocated Resources report:** Shows resource assignments for human resources who are overbooked on tasks during the project — including total hours, unit assignments, total hours of work on each task, and any delay from the original schedule.

Follow these steps to generate an assignment report:

1. **Choose View ⇨ Reports.**

2. **Click Assignments, and then click Select.**

   The Assignment Reports dialog box appears, as shown in Figure 9-8.

3. **Click one of the four reports.**

4. **Click Select.**

   A preview of the report appears. Figure 9-9 shows a sample Who Does What report.

5. **If you need to modify the Page Setup, click Page Setup.**

   For example, you might want to modify the margins or set the document to print landscape or portrait.

6. **To print the report, click Print.**

If you want to print to a fax machine or a file, change your printer choice in the Print dialog box.

Figure 9-8:
Assignment
reports
deal with
resource
assign-
ments to
individual
tasks.

Figure 9-9:
A wealth of assignment information can be contained in these reports.

Part III
Well, It Looks Good on Paper

The 5th Wave   By Rich Tennant

"Why, of course. I'd be very interested in seeing this new milestone in the project."

In this part . . .

When you've charted a course for your project, it's time for the critical eye: Does your project plan pass muster in terms of budget and timing? If not, you can use the built-in Project tools to tinker with resource assignments, adjust task timing, trim costs, and meet deadlines. Result: a better final plan. You also get a look at modifying how items in your project are formatted. (After all, a polished presentation, whether on-screen or in print, is invaluable.)

Chapter 10

Fine-Tuning Your Plan

As they say, the best-laid schemes of mice and project managers go oft awry (or is that "gang aft agley?"), and your plans are no different. When you've taken your best shot at laying out your project plan, created every task, and assigned every resource, and you think you're ready to start your project — think again.

A close look at almost any plan will reveal some issues that you should resolve before you begin working on your first task. These might include a schedule that ends a month after your deadline, human resources who are assigned to work 36-hour days, or a budget that exceeds the national debt. (Details, details. . . .)

But even if you don't see any glaring problems in the areas of time, workload, or money, you should do a few things to make sure that your project is as realistic as possible before you commit to it. So take a moment to give your project the once-over.

Everything Filters to the Bottom Line

A first step in making sure that your plan is solid is simply looking at it from a few different perspectives. It's like turning around in front of the mirror to see your outfit from every angle before you go out on a date. Filters and groups are two Project features that help you get that kind of perspective.

Two major problem areas that filters and groups can help you examine at this stage are *overallocated resources* — that is, resources working more than the number of hours you specified — and tasks that are on the critical path. The *critical path* consists of the series of tasks in your project that must happen on time for the project to meet its final deadline. Any task that has *slack* — that is, any length of time that it could be delayed without delaying the entire project's timing — is not on the critical path. If your project has little in the way of slack, any delays that occur are likely to derail your project.

Predesigned filters

Filters are to Project what a magnifying glass was to Sherlock Holmes. They give you a closer look at various aspects of your plan and help you spot clues about problems (such as overallocated resources). You can set a filter to highlight tasks or resources that meet certain criteria or to remove any tasks or resources from view that don't meet such criteria.

Project provides predesigned filters that you can simply turn on for tasks or resources, using criteria such as

- ✔ Tasks with a cost greater than a specified amount
- ✔ Tasks on the critical path
- ✔ Tasks that occur within a certain date range
- ✔ Milestone tasks
- ✔ Tasks that use resources in a resource group
- ✔ Tasks with overallocated resources

Several filters, such as Slipping Assignments and Work Overbudget, help you spot problems after you've finalized your plan and are tracking actual progress. (See Chapter 13 for more about tracking.)

You can access filters in a couple of ways. When you use the Filter button, you choose from a list of predesigned filters. The filters act to remove any tasks from view that don't meet specified criteria.

To turn on such filters from the Formatting toolbar, follow these steps:

1. **Display a resource view (such as Resource Sheet view) to filter for resources or a task view (such as Gantt Chart view) to filter for tasks.**

2. **Click the Filter list on the Formatting toolbar, and then click a criterion.**

The Filter list is a drop-down list; when no filter is applied, All Tasks or All Resources appear in the list. If you choose a filter that requires input, you'll see a dialog box such as the one in Figure 10-1. Otherwise, the filter is applied immediately and removes from view any resources or tasks that don't match your criteria.

3. If a dialog box is displayed, fill in the information and then click OK.

The filter is applied.

Figure 10-1:
Some filters
require
additional
input.

Cost Greater Than	⊠
Show tasks/assignments whose cost is greater than:	OK
5,000	Cancel

To redisplay all tasks or resources, click Filter on the Formatting toolbar and then click either All Resources or All Tasks (depending on whether a Resource or Task filter is currently applied).

You can also use the AutoFilter button on the Formatting toolbar to turn on an AutoFilter feature. When you click the AutoFilter button, arrows appear at the head of columns in the currently displayed sheet. Click the arrow for the Task Name column (for example) and the name of every task in your project is listed. Click a task name, and all tasks but that task and any parent tasks for it are removed from view. You can also choose a Custom setting from each of these menus (as in Figure 10-2) to customize AutoFilter with certain criteria.

Follow these steps to activate and use AutoFilter:

1. Display the view that contains the fields (columns) you want to filter.

2. Click the AutoFilter button.

Arrows appear at the top of each column.

3. Click the arrow on the column that you want to filter.

4. Click the criterion you want for your filter.

For example, if you are filtering for task duration, in the Duration column you can choose >1 day, >1 week, or a specific number of days (such as 5 days or 100 days). All tasks or resources that don't meet your criteria disappear.

If you want to apply a highlight to each item that meets your filter criteria rather than remove nonmatching items from view, choose Project ⇨ Filtered For ⇨ More Filters. Click the filter you want, and then click Highlight.

Figure 10-2:
AutoFilter
choices are
specific to
each field of
information
in your
sheet.

Do-it-yourself filters

You don't have to use predesigned filters: You can get creative and design your own filters. To define a new filter, you specify a field name, a test, and a value.

For example, the following filters for any task on the critical path:

Critical (field name) **Equals** (test) **Yes** (value)

You can also include additional qualifiers to the filter. The following filters for tasks that are both on the critical path and have a baseline cost of more than $5,000:

Critical (field name) **Equals** (test) **Yes** (value)

and

Baseline Cost (field name) **Is Greater Than** (test) **5000** (value)

Here's how to build your own filter definition:

1. **Choose Project ➪ Filtered For ➪ More Filters.**

   The More Filters dialog box appears, as shown in Figure 10-3.

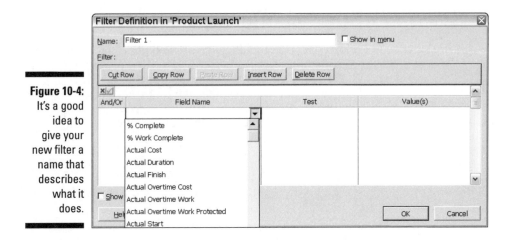

Figure 10-3:
This dialog
box lists all
available
filters —
both
predesigned
and custom.

2. **Click either the Task or Resource option to specify which list of filters you want the new filter to be included in.**

3. **Click New.**

   The Filter Definition dialog box appears.

4. **In the Name box, type a name for the filter.**

5. **Click the first line of the Field Name column, and then click the arrow that appears to display the list of choices, as shown in Figure 10-4.**

Figure 10-4:
It's a good
idea to
give your
new filter a
name that
describes
what it
does.

6. **Click a field name to select it.**

7. **Repeat Steps 5 and 6 for the Test and Value(s) columns.**

   The Test is a condition that must be met, such as does not equal or greater than; the Value would be either a value you enter, such as a specific date or cost, or predetermined values such as baseline cost.

8. **If you want to enter a qualifier, such as a dollar amount, click the entry box above the column headings and then type the amount at the end of the filter definition.**

   For example, if you choose Cost for the field name and Equals for the test, you might enter the number $5000 at the end of the definition in the entry box.

9. **If you want to add another condition, choose And or Or from the And/Or column, and then make choices for the Field Name, Test, and Value(s) boxes.**

   Note that you can cut and paste rows of settings you've made to rearrange them in the list, or use the Copy Row or Delete Row button to perform those actions for filters with several lines of criteria.

10. **If you want the new filter to be shown in the list when you click the Filter box on the Formatting toolbar, select the Show in Menu check box.**

11. **Click OK to save the new filter, and then click Apply to apply the filter to your plan.**

You can click the Organizer button in the More Filters dialog box to copy filters you've created in one Project file to another file.

Looking at things in groups

Remember those groups you used to hang out with in high school? (I'm sure *you* were part of the *cool* group!) Groups helped you see the underlying order of your adolescent hierarchy. Project lets you group things, too. The Group feature essentially allows you to organize information by certain criteria. For example, you can use the Group feature if you want to see resources organized by work group, or you might organize tasks by their duration, shortest to longest.

Like filters, groups come predefined or you can create custom groups.

Follow these steps to apply a predefined group structure to your project:

1. **Display either a resource view (such as Resource Sheet view) to group resources, or a task view (such as Gantt Chart view) to group tasks.**

2. **On the Standard toolbar, click the Group By list, and then click a criterion.**

   The information is organized according to your selection. Figure 10-5 shows an example.

Figure 10-5:
Organizing
tasks by
duration
provides
this view of
your project.

To redisplay all tasks or resources in their original order, click the arrow in the Group box on the toolbar to display the list, and then click No Group. (When no group is applied, the Group box displays No Group.)

Devising your own groups

Custom groups include three elements: a field name, a field type, and an order. For example, you might create a group that shows the field name (such as Baseline Work) and a field type (such as Tasks, Resources, or Assignments) in order (Descending or Ascending). A group that shows Baseline Work for Tasks in Descending order, for example, would list tasks in order from the most work hours required to the least. Other settings you can make for groups control the format of the group's appearance such as the font used, or a font color applied.

Follow these steps to create a custom group:

1. **Choose Project ⇨ Group By ⇨ More Groups.**

   The More Groups dialog box appears, as shown in Figure 10-6.

Figure 10-6:
This dialog
box is
organized
by task- or
resource-
oriented
groups.

2. **Click either Task or Resource to specify in which list of groups you want the new group to be included.**

3. **Click New.**

The Group Definition dialog box appears, as shown in Figure 10-7.

Figure 10-7:
Use your
own groups
to organize
data.

4. **In the Name box, type a name for the group.**

5. **Click the first line of the Field Name column, click the arrow that appears to display the list of choices, and then click a field name to select it.**

6. **Repeat Step 5 for the Field Type and Order columns.**

   Note that if you want the Field Type option of grouping by assignment rather than by resource or task, you must first select the Group Assignments, Not Tasks check box to make that field available to you. Otherwise the Field Type of Task or Resource appears by default.

7. **If you want to add another sorting criteria, click a row titled Then By, and make choices for the Field Name, Field Type, and Order columns.**

8. **If you want the new group to be shown in the list when you click the Group box on the Formatting toolbar, select the Show in Menu check box.**

9. **Depending on the field name you've chosen, you can make settings for the font, cell background, and pattern to format your group.**

   For example, the font and color of each duration group heading in Figure 10-5 was determined by making choices from these three lists.

10. **If you want to define intervals for the groups to be organized in, click the Define Group Intervals button.**

    This displays the Define Group Intervals dialog box; use the settings here to set a starting time and an interval. For example, if the Group By criterion is Standard Rate, and you select a Group Interval of 10.00, groupings would be in $10 intervals (those making 0-$10 an hour in one grouping, those making $11-$20 in another, and so on).

11. **Click OK to save the new group, and then click Apply to apply the group to your plan.**

If you want to make changes to an existing predefined group, apply the group and then choose Project ➪ Group By ➪ Customize Group By. This takes you to the Customize Group By dialog box for that group. This dialog box — identical to the Group Definition dialog box — allows you to edit all those settings for an existing group.

It's About Time

We've all had this experience: Your boss asks you to commit to getting a project finished by a certain date. Your palms sweat, you get a sick feeling in the pit of your stomach, you add a week onto the deadline the boss suggests to cover yourself, and then you promise to deliver the impossible. You hope you can do it. You want to do it. But *can* you do it?

Project allows you to feel much more confident about committing to a time-frame because you can see how long all your tasks will take to complete. Before you go to your boss and make any promises, make sure you're comfortable with two things: the total time it takes to complete the project and the critical path (the longest series of tasks that must be completed on time in order for you to meet the overall project deadline).

The timing data for your project summary task tells you how long the entire project will take. Just display the Gantt Chart view and look at the Duration, Start, and Finish columns. If your finish date doesn't work, you'll have to go back and modify some tasks.

You should also make sure that there's room for error. You can use filters and groups to identify the critical path in, for example, the Gantt Chart view or the Network Diagram view. If you judge that too many tasks are on the critical path, it's wise to add some slack to the plan to allow for inevitable delays.

Giving yourself some slack

How many tasks should be on the critical path in your project and how many should have some slack — that is, some time that they could be delayed without delaying the entire project? I wish I could give you a formula, but sadly, it's not a science. Ideally, every task in your project *should* have slack because things can come up that you never expected (shortages of vital materials, asteroid strikes . . . management turnover that places you in an entirely different department). If you add slack to each and every task, however, your project is probably going to go on into the next millennium. Figure 10-8 shows a more typical scenario, with a mix of noncritical and critical tasks.

Some tasks have slack naturally because they occur during the life of a longer task with which they share a dependency. The shorter task could actually be delayed until the end of the longer task without delaying the project.

Think about this example: You can start installing the plumbing and electrical elements of a new office building as soon as the framing inspection is complete. The plumbing takes two weeks and the electrical work takes one week. The next task, mechanical inspection, can't happen until both the plumbing and electrical tasks are finished. The shorter of the two, electrical, has a week of slack because nothing else can happen until the dependent task, plumbing, is finished (as in Figure 10-9). However, if electrical runs one week late, the situation becomes critical.

These natural cases of slack occur in any project. But in many cases, you have to build in slack. Slack can be added in a few ways.

Figure 10-8:
Follow the
critical path
in the
Network
Diagram
view.

Figure 10-9:
Taskbars
will help you
visualize
slack
available to
tasks that
are not on
the critical
path of your
project.

First, you can simply inflate task durations: Add two days to the duration of all the tasks in your project, or go in and examine each task to figure out the risk of delay and pad each duration accordingly. This method is a little problematic, however, because when changes occur, you may have to go into many tasks and adjust durations to deal with a schedule that's ahead or behind. You also have to keep track of exactly how much slack you built into each task.

The second method of building in slack is the one I like best. You build one task or several tasks that occur throughout your project — say, one at the end of each phase of the project, as shown in Figure 10-10.

Now, there's one must-do here, even if it seems obvious: Don't call this task *Slack*. Nobody in a position of responsibility would be caught dead approving *slack* time for anybody. The resounding "No!" response would make your (ahem) slack wither away, and you'd be left with the expectation of hitting an impossible deadline. Give slack tasks appropriately respectable names that reflect useful (but yeah, somewhat generic) activities — say, *Engineering Analysis,* or *Debriefing,* or *CYA Meeting.* Then give the task a duration that provides breathing space for the other tasks in that phase. For example, at the end of a two-month phase of designing a new product package, you might add a task called *Design Debriefing* and make it one week long (and if a sudden mandate for design tweaks comes out of nowhere, you're covered). Then create a dependency between that task and the last "real" task in the phase. We're not talking dishonesty here — just reality. In the real world, slack is indispensable.

Figure 10-10: Each phase of this project ends with an Analysis task that actually represents slack.

As things slide in your project (and they will, trust me), you'll spot that slack is being eaten up because the slack task is suddenly ending later than the date you'd wanted the phase to end. You can change the duration of the slack task, reflecting the fact that your slack is being used up. The duration of that task will give you a good indication of how much more time you have before the entire phase will go critical.

Doing it in less time

If you do your homework and add slack to tasks, you're making your plan realistic, but the price you pay is that you're adding time to your project. What happens when your project finish date just won't cut it with the powers-that-be? That's when you have to try a few tactics to chop your timing down to size.

Check your dependencies

The timing of your plan is determined, to a great extent, by the timing relationships you build among tasks — that is, by dependencies. So ask yourself, *Did I build all my dependencies in the best way I could?* Perhaps you didn't start one task until another was completely finished, but you could actually start the second task two days before the end of its predecessor. Building in that kind of overlap will save you time.

Here's an example: You created a finish-to-start relationship for the *Do Research* and *Write Speech* tasks, such that you could not start writing the speech until your research was finished. But is that true? Couldn't you do a first draft of the speech starting three-fourths of the way through the research? Especially when you have two different resources working on those tasks, getting the second task going before the first is complete can save you time.

Over the life of a project with hundreds of tasks, adding that kind of overlap to even a few dozen tasks could save you a month of time or more!

You can take a refresher course in creating and changing dependencies in Chapter 6.

We could use some help here!

Another reason for timing is the availability of resources. Sometimes you set a dependency relationship where one task can't start before another is over simply because the resources aren't available until the predecessor task is over. Here are a few things to look for with resource-dependent timing:

✔ Maybe you delayed the start of a task because a resource wasn't available. But could some other resource do the work? If so, switch resources and let the task start sooner.

✔ Project calculates the duration of some tasks (fixed work and fixed units with effort-driven scheduling) according to the number of resources available to do the work. If you add resources to those tasks, Project shortens their duration.

✔ If you assign a more skilled resource to some tasks, you might be able to shorten the task durations because the skilled person will finish the work more quickly.

✔ Could you hire an outside vendor to handle the work? If you have money but no time, that's sometimes a viable option.

Chapter 9 covers the mechanics of making and changing resource assignments.

Cut to the chase: Deleting some tasks and slashing slack

When all else fails, it's time to cut some very specific corners. Can you skip some tasks, such as that final quality check, the one that occurs after the *other* three you already built in? Or should you pull back on some of the slack you've allowed yourself?

Never, I repeat, NEVER get rid of all the slack in your schedule. Otherwise it will come back and haunt you like the Ghost of Christmas Past. Just tell your boss I said so.

Could you get some other project to handle some of your tasks for you with different sets of resources? If your buddy has a project that involves writing specs for a new product, could you convince him to also write the user's manual, which was your responsibility in designing product packaging? It's worth a shot.

Getting It for Less

When you've assigned all your resources to tasks and set all your fixed costs, it's time for sticker shock. Project will tally all those costs and show you the project's budget. But what if those numbers just won't work? Here are some tips for cutting down that bottom line:

✔ **Use cheaper resources.** Do you have a high-priced engineer on a task that could be performed by a junior engineer? Did you assign a high-priced manager to supervise a task that could be handled by a lower-priced line supervisor?

✔ **Lower fixed costs.** If you allowed for the travel costs of four plant visits, could you manage with only three? Could you book flights ahead of time and get cheaper airfares? Could you find a cheaper vendor for that piece of equipment you allocated $4,000 to buy? Or could you make do with the old equipment for just one more project?

✔ **Cut down on the overtime.** Are resources that earn overtime overallocated? Try cutting down their hours or using resources on straight salary for those 14-hour days.

✔ **Do it in less time.** Resource costs are a factor of task durations, hourly wages, or number of units. If you change tasks so that fewer work hours are required to complete them, they'll cost less. However, don't be unrealistic about the time it will *really* take to get the work done. (Rome isn't the only thing that wasn't built in a day.)

Your Resource Recourse

Before you finalize your plan, you should consider one final area: resource workload. As you went about assigning resources to tasks in your project, you probably created some situations where resources are working round the clock for days on end. It may look okay on paper, but in reality it's just not going to work.

Your first step is to see how to spot those overallocations. Then you have to give those poor folks some help!

Checking resource availability

To resolve issues with resource assignments, you have to first figure out where the problems lie. You can do that by taking a look at a few views that focus on resource assignments.

The Resource Usage view (shown in Figure 10-11) and the Resource Graph view (in Figure 10-12) are useful in helping you spot overbooked resources.

First, keep in mind that resources are flagged as overallocated in these Resource views based on their assignment percentage and calendars. A resource based on a standard eight-hour-day calendar, assigned at 100 percent to a task, will work eight hours a day on it. If you assign that same resource at 50 percent to another task that happens at the same time, the resource will put in 12-hour days (8 plus 4) and be marked as overallocated.

Figure 10-11:
The Resource Usage view spells out workflow resource by resource.

Figure 10-12:
The Resource Graph view gives you a visual clue to overworked resources.

In the Resource Graph view, work is summarized in the Peak Units row, and all work in the part of the bar graphic that's above the 100 percent mark is highlighted. In the Resource Usage view, any overallocated resource has a yellow diamond with an exclamation point in the Indicator column. The total hours that the resource is working each day on his or her combined tasks is summarized on the line that lists the resource's name.

Deleting or modifying a resource assignment

So, you discover that poor Henrietta is working 42 hours on Tuesday and 83 hours on Friday. What to do?

You have a few options:

✓ **Remove Henrietta from a few tasks to free up some time.**

✓ **Change Henrietta's resource calendar to allow for a longer workday — for example, 12 hours.** Keep in mind that this means a 100 percent assignment will have Henrietta working 12 hours on any one task in a day. If you stretch a resource's workday, you should probably reduce the resource's assignments. For example, if someone frequently puts in 16 hours on two tasks in one day (based on an 8-hour calendar) and two 100 percent assignments, try changing to a 12-hour calendar and 50 percent assignments (6 hours on each of the two tasks, totaling 12 hours a day). However, if the person typically works an 8-hour day and 12- or 16-hour days *are the exception,* you shouldn't change the resource's base calendar because that will have an impact on *all* assignments for that resource.

Keep in mind that the two previous options may lengthen the tasks that the resource is assigned to, regardless of whether you remove the resource or reduce the resource's assignment.

✓ **Change Henrietta's availability by upping her assignment units to more than 100 percent in the Resource Information dialog box.** For example, if you enter 150% as her available units, you're saying it's okay for her to work 12 hours a day, and Project will then consider her fair game and not overallocated until she exceeds that 12 hours.

✓ **Ignore the problem.** I don't mean this facetiously: Sometimes someone working 14 hours *for a day or two* during the life of a project is acceptable, and there's no need to change the resource's usual working allocation to make that overwork indicator go away. (However, consider telling Henrietta it's okay to order pizza on the company on those long workdays — and make sure you don't let them become the norm.)

Getting some help

When one person is overworked, it's time to look for help. You can free up resources in several ways.

One way is to assign someone to help out on a task, and reduce the over-booked resource assignment now that he or she is not needed for as many hours. Reduce the resource's work assignment on one or more tasks — say, reducing 100 percent assignments to 50 percent. You do this in the Task Information dialog box on the Resources tab, or by selecting the task and clicking the Assign Resources tool to open the Assign Resources dialog box shown in Figure 10-13.

Figure 10-13: You can change assignment units for a resource on a particular task.

Assign Resources

Task: Project Office Template

- Resource list options

Filter by:

☐ All Resources   More Filters...

☐ Available to work   0h

Add Resources ▼

Resources from Product Launch

Project Office staff analyst		
Resource Name	R/D	Units
✔ Analyst		100%
✔ Corporate managemer		100%
✔ Developer		150%
✔ Project Office coordina		50%
✔ Project Office staff ana		100%

Assign
Remove
Replace...
Graphs...
Close
Help

Hold down Ctrl and click to select multiple resources

Note that you can quickly check a work graph for any resource by clicking the Graphs button in the Assign Resources dialog box.

You'll also find that by adding resources to some tasks, you'll shorten the task duration. That means you might free up your resource in time to eliminate a conflict with a later task in the project.

Try changing the work contour for the resource. By default, Project has a resource work on a task at the same level for the life of the task. You can modify the work contour, for example, so that a resource puts in the most effort at the start of a task, which frees up the resource's workload later when a conflict with another assignment might occur.

To level or not to level?

As both a process and a program feature, resource leveling has pros and cons. It can make changes that you might not want it to make — for example, taking a resource off a task where you absolutely need that person's unique skills. It frequently delays your project's finish date, which might not be acceptable to you (or your boss).

The safest setting for Resource Leveling — that is, the one that makes the least drastic changes to your timing — is to level only within slack. This setting may delay some tasks, but it won't delay your project completion date.

If you just can't live with everything Resource Leveling did, the capability to turn Resource Leveling on and off is your best ally. You can turn the feature on and look at the things it did to resolve resource problems, and then turn it off and manually institute the portions of the solution that work for you.

Getting your resources level

Resource leveling sounds something like the St. Valentine's Day massacre, but it's not. It's a calculation that Project goes through to try to resolve resource overallocation in your project. The feature works in two ways: by delaying a task until the overbooked resource frees up, or by splitting tasks. Splitting a task involves (essentially) stopping it at some point, thereby freeing up the resource, and then resuming it at a later time when the resource is available.

You can make such changes yourself or let Project do the calculation. Project will first *delay* tasks that involve overallocated resources to use up any available slack. When no more slack is available on these tasks, Project makes changes based on any priorities you've entered for tasks, dependency relationships that are affected, and task constraints (such as a Finish No Later Than constraint).

But don't worry: You can turn on leveling to see what changes Project would make, and then clear the leveling to reverse those actions if you don't like them.

To level the resources in your project, follow these steps:

1. **Choose Tools ➪ Level Resources.**

   The Resource Leveling dialog box appears, as shown in Figure 10-14.

2. **Make a choice between allowing Project to do Automatic or Manual leveling.**

   Automatic tells Project to level every time you change your plan. The Manual option requires that you go to the Resource Leveling dialog box and click Level Now.

Figure 10-14:
You can
control
some
aspects
of the
resource-
leveling
calculation.

3. **If you choose to level automatically, be sure to check the setting in the Clear Leveling Values Before Leveling option depending on whether you want previous leveling actions reversed before you level the next time.**

4. **Select Level Entire Project, or select Level and fill in a date range by making choices in the From and To boxes.**

5. **In the Leveling Order box, click the arrow and make a selection.**

   Standard considers slack, dependencies, priorities, and constraints. ID Only delays or splits the task with the highest ID number — in other words, the last task in the project. The Priority, Standard choice uses task priority as the first criteria in making choices to delay or split tasks (rather than using up slack).

6. **Select any of the three check boxes at the bottom to control how Project will level.**

   You can level within available slack, meaning that no critical tasks are delayed and your current finish date for the project is retained. You can level by adjusting resource assignments, allowing Project to remove or change assignments. You can level by splitting tasks only for unstarted work in the project, which can put some tasks on hold for a period of time until resources are freed up for work. Finally, you can level relative to booking type. Booking type (proposed or committed) relates to how firm you are in using that particular resource. Allowing resource leveling to consider a resource's booking type means that committed resource assignments are considered more sacred when Project goes about making changes than proposed assignments.

7. **Click Level Now to have Project perform the leveling operation.**

To reverse leveling, go to the Resource Leveling dialog box (Tools ➪ Level Resources) and click Clear Leveling.

Getting in the Mix

One final word about all the solutions suggested in this chapter to deal with time, cost, and overallocation problems. To be most successful, you'll probably have to use a combination of all these methods. Solving these problems is often a trial-and-error process, and although you might initially look for one quick fix (who doesn't?), in reality the best solution might come through making a dozen small changes. Take the time to find the best combination for your project.

Chapter 11

Making Yourself Look Good

Some old chestnut would have you believe clothes make the man. Well, in the same spirit, there are times when the presentation makes the project. Having a project that looks good serves two purposes. It impresses people with your professionalism (sometimes to the point where they'll overlook a little cost overrun), and it allows people looking at your project to easily make out what the different boxes, bars, and lines indicate.

Project uses default formatting that's pretty good in most cases. But you may have certain company standards for reporting that require (for example) baseline data to be yellow and actual data to be blue, or more frequent gridlines to help your nearsighted CEO read Project reports more easily.

Whatever you need, Project provides tremendous flexibility in formatting various elements in your plan.

Putting Your Best Foot Forward

Microsoft has decided to capitulate to the artist in all of us by allowing us to modify shapes, colors, patterns, and other graphic elements in our Project plans. This gives you great flexibility in determining the way your plan looks.

When you print Project views, you can print a legend on every page. The legend helps those reading the plan understand the meaning of the various colors and shapes you've set for elements.

One important thing to realize is that all the views and formatting choices that Project offers you aren't confined to the screen. You can print your project or reports. What is displayed on your screen when you print a view is what will print. So knowing how to make all kinds of changes to what's on your screen allows you to present information to team members, managers, vendors, and clients in hard copy.

It's useful to be able to print in color, so you can get the full visual impact and nuance of the various colors used for graphic elements (such as taskbars and indicators). If you print in black and white, you may find that certain colors that look good on-screen aren't as distinct when you print. Being able to modify formatting allows your project to look good in both color *and* black and white, both on-screen and in print.

Formatting Taskbars

Taskbars are the horizontal boxes that represent the timing of a task in the chart pane of the Gantt Chart view. You can format each bar individually or change global formatting settings for different types of taskbars.

You can change several things about taskbars:

- ✔ **The shape that appears at the start and end of the bar; you can change the shape's type and color.** Each end can be formatted differently.

- ✔ **The shape, pattern, and color of the middle of the bar.**

- ✔ **The text that you can set to appear in five locations around the bar: left, right, above, below, or inside the bar.** You can include text in any or all of these locations, but keep in mind that too many text items can quickly become impossible to read. As a rule, use just enough text to help readers of your plan identify information, especially on printouts of large schedules where a task may appear far to the right of the Task Name column that identifies it by name in the sheet area.

When you track progress on a task, a progress bar is superimposed on the taskbar. You can format the shape, pattern, and color of the progress bar. The goal is to contrast the progress bar with the baseline taskbar, so you can see both clearly.

By formatting taskbars, you can help readers of your plan identify various elements, such as progress or milestones. If you make changes to individual taskbars, people who are accustomed to Project's standard formatting might have trouble reading your plan.

To make formatting settings for various types of taskbars, follow these steps:

1. **Right-click the chart area outside any single taskbar, and then click Bar Styles.**

   The Bar Styles dialog box appears, as shown in Figure 11-1.

Figure 11-1:
You can modify the look of taskbars and the text you display along with them.

2. **In the spreadsheet along the top in the Name column, click the type of task that you want to modify (Task, Split, Progress, and so on).**

   For example, if you want to modify the styles used for all summary tasks, click Summary. The choices in the Bars tab in the bottom half of the dialog box change based on the task type you click.

3. **Click in the Show For . . . Tasks column for the task type you want to modify and then select criteria for the task, such as Critical or Finished.**

4. **Click the Bars tab to display it, if necessary, and then do the following:**

   a. **Click any of the Shape lists to modify the shape of either end or the middle of the taskbar.**

      Shapes on either end might be an arrow, a diamond, or a circle. The shape in the middle consists of a bar of a certain width.

     b. Click any of the Color lists to modify the color used on either end or in the middle of the taskbar.

     The Automatic choice is the default color for this type of taskbar element.

     c. Click either of the Type lists to modify the type of formatting for the shape on either end of the taskbar.

     This setting controls how such a shape is outlined: framed with a solid line, surrounded by a dashed line, or filled in with a solid color.

     d. Click the Pattern list to select another pattern for the middle of the bar.

  5. Click the Text tab (shown in Figure 11-2), and then do the following:

     a. Click any of the text locations.

     An arrow appears at the end of that line.

     b. Click the arrow to display an alphabetical list of possible data you can include, and then click a field name to select it.

     c. Repeat Steps 5a and 5b to choose additional text locations.

  6. Click OK to accept all new taskbar settings.

Figure 11-2: You can place text in up to four locations around your taskbars.

The Gantt Chart Wizard

What would formatting be without a wizard to help you to make all your settings quickly? The Gantt Chart Wizard allows you to make formatting settings to the entire Gantt Chart, including what information to display (standard, critical path, baseline, or several combinations of these), one piece of information to include with your taskbars, and whether you want to display lines to show dependencies among tasks.

If you choose to make custom settings while using the Gantt Chart Wizard, you can specify many of the settings you see in the Bar Styles dialog box, but those choices affect *all* taskbar elements of that type *in the project*, not just individual taskbars. You access the Gantt Chart Wizard by selecting it from the Format menu.

If you want to make the same types of changes to an individual taskbar rather than to all taskbars of a certain type, right-click the taskbar and then click Format Bar. A Format Bar dialog box appears, offering the same Text and Bar tabs found in the Bar Styles dialog box.

Formatting Task Boxes

Network diagram task boxes use different shapes to help you spot different types of tasks — for example, these three:

- ✔ **Summary tasks** use a slightly slanted box shape and include a plus or minus symbol, depending on whether the summary task's subtasks are hidden or displayed. Click the symbol to hide or display subtasks.

- ✔ **Subtasks** show up in simple rectangular boxes.

- ✔ **Milestones** are shown in diamond-shaped boxes with blue shading.

You can change the formatting of each task box individually or by type. To change the formatting of task boxes displayed in the Network Diagram view, do this:

1. **Display the Network Diagram view.**

2. **Right-click the task box you want to change and then click Format Box, or right-click anywhere outside the task boxes and then click Box Styles to change formatting for all boxes of a certain style.**

   The Format Box or Box Styles dialog box appears (as shown in Figure 11-3).

Box Styles

Style settings for: Preview:

Critical
Noncritical
Critical Milestone
Noncritical Milestone
Critical Summary
Noncritical Summary
Critical Inserted Project
Noncritical Inserted Project
Critical Marked
Noncritical Marked
Critical External
Noncritical External
Project Summary

[Name]

Start: [Start]   ID: [ID]

Finish: [Finish]   Dur: [Duration]

Comp: [% Complete]

☐ Set highlight filter style   Show data from task ID: [   ] ⬍

Data template

[Summary   ▾]   [More Templates...]

Border

Shape: [▱ ▾]   Color: [■ Red ▾]   Width: [——— ▾]

☑ Show horizontal gridlines   ☐ Show vertical gridlines

Background

Color: [☐ White ▾]   Pattern: [■■■ ▾]

[Help]   [OK]   [Cancel]

Figure 11-3:
Change
styles for all
boxes in the
Box Styles
dialog box.

3. **To modify the border style, make your selection in the Shape, Color, and Width lists.**

4. **To modify the background area inside the box, make a selection in the Color list, Pattern list, or both (at the bottom of the dialog box).**

5. **Click OK to save your new settings.**

When you modify the formatting of individual boxes in the Network Diagram view, the standard settings of slanted summary tasks and shaded milestones no longer serve as a visual guide to *all* tasks. If you make changes and decide you'd like to put a task box back to its default setting, click Reset in the Format Box dialog box.

Adjusting the Layout

In addition to displaying particular columns and formatting taskbars, you can make certain changes to the layout of your view. These options vary a great deal depending on what view you're working with: The layout of the Calendar and Network Diagram views is quite different than the layout choices offered in the Gantt Chart view.

To display the Layout dialog box for a view, right-click the area (for example, the chart area of the Gantt Chart) or anywhere on the Calendar or Network Diagram view, and then click Layout. The appropriate dialog box appears. Figures 11-4, 11-5, and 11-6 show the various layout choices available in the different views.

Figure 11-4:
The Layout dialog box for the Calendar view.

Figure 11-5:
The Layout dialog box for the Network Diagram view.

In general, the settings in these Layout dialog boxes deal with how the elements on the page are arranged and how dependency link lines are displayed.

Figure 11-6:
The Layout
dialog box
for the Gantt
Chart view.

Table 11-1 shows you the layout settings. You could probably spend a week redoing all these settings to see what they look like, and I could spend a few days writing about the various options. The tools Project offers to modify the formatting of elements such as taskbars and task boxes provide wonderful flexibility.

Table 11-1		Layout Options
Layout Type	*Option*	*Use*
Calendar view	Use Current Sort Order	Project uses the latest sort order you've applied to tasks
	Attempt to Fit as Many Tasks as Possible	Ignores the sort order and fits as many tasks in a date box as possible
	Show Bar Splits	When a task includes a period of inactivity, that task can be shown as split into different parts over time
	Automatic Layout	Project modifies the layout in response to the insertion of additional tasks

Layout Type	Option	Use
Network Diagram view	Layout Mode area	Allows automatic or manual positioning
	Box Layout area	The settings in this section arrange and align boxes, adjusting alignment, spacing, and height and modifying how summary tasks are displayed
	Link Style area	Modifies the style for dependency link lines and labels
	Link Color area	Sets the color for links both on and off the critical path
	Diagram Options area	Controls the background color and pattern for boxes, and how page breaks and progress on tasks are indicated
Gantt Chart view	Links	Style of lines indicating dependency links
	Date Format	Modifies the format of the date used to label taskbars
	Bar Height	Sets the height of taskbars in points
	Always Roll up Gantt Bars	When checked, taskbar details roll up to the highest-level summary task
	Round Bars to Whole Days	When you have portions of days, allows bars to represent the nearest whole-day increment
	Show Bar Splits	When a task includes a period of inactivity, that task can be shown as split into different parts over time
	Show Drawings	When you've included drawings, they are displayed on the screen and in the printout

Now that you've seen the many options available for modifying view layouts, I have some advice: Stick with default settings unless you have a specific reason to make a change (such as when you want to highlight certain types of information for a project presentation). And when you don't need that layout change anymore, go right back to the default settings. Or, if you want to make changes, make them globally across your organization and stick to them. That makes it much easier for those reading your project plan to interpret the different kinds of information presented in views. Generally speaking, if you tinker too often with the way Project displays information, at this point it'll just make the learning curve steeper — and confuse those who know Project's default settings.

Modifying Gridlines

Just as phone numbers are broken up into several shorter sets of numbers to help you remember them, visual elements are often broken up to help you understand information in chunks. Tables use lines, calendars use boxes, football fields use yard lines, and so on.

Several views in Project include gridlines to indicate certain things, such as the break between weeks or the status date (that is, the date as of which progress has been tracked on a project). These lines help the reader of your plan discern intervals of time or breaks in information (for example, gridlines can be used to indicate major and minor column breaks). You can modify these gridlines in several ways, including changing the color and style of the lines and the interval at which they appear.

To modify gridlines, use the Gridlines dialog box, as follows:

1. **Right-click any area of a view that contains a grid (for example, the chart area of the Gantt Chart view or the Calendar view) and then click Gridlines.**

   The Gridlines dialog box appears, as shown in Figure 11-7.

Figure 11-7:
The possible lines you can change vary somewhat from one view to another.

2. **In the Line to Change list, click the gridline you want to modify.**

3. **Use the Normal Type and Color lists to select a line style and color.**

4. **If you want to use a contrasting color at various intervals in the grid to make it easier to read, do the following:**

   a. **Select an interval at which to include a contrasting line.**

   This setting is typically used with a different style or color from the Normal line setting to mark minor intervals for a grid. Note that not all types of gridlines can use contrasting intervals.

   b. **Choose the Type and Color of that line from the lists.**

5. **Click OK to save your settings.**

Note that you make choices for modifying gridlines one by one, and there is no Reset button to put these settings back the way they were. Also note that gridlines modified in one view don't affect gridlines in any other view.

Sample project: Spiffing up an IT project

Let's take a specific project — say one that involves setting up a corporate network. You have to bring a printout of the project to the next senior management meeting to give them some idea of current cost issues and upcoming tasks over the next several weeks.

What are some ways you might use all the formatting options Project offers to generate a color printout of a Network Diagram to help your management understand the project status? Here are some suggestions:

To help management understand the timing relationship between tasks, choose to show link labels in the Network Diagram Layout dialog box. When you do this, a label such as FS for a finish-to-start relationship is displayed along the lines that link the boxes in the diagram.

To break the diagram down into weeks so those reading the print out can easily identify what's

going on in the project over the next few weeks, choose the arrangement in the Layout dialog box that shows boxes top down by week. With this setting, all tasks that happen in a single week are arranged in one column.

To focus on what's happening with costs in the project, change the data template used in the Box Style dialog box to Cost. This modifies the data shown in each individual box to reflect baseline and actual costs to date.

Finally, to make the printout more colorful by using your company logo colors, consider changing the background from white to another color such as yellow (change this in the Layout dialog box), the box border color to a color such as blue (change this in the Box Styles dialog box), and the box background to yet another color, making sure it's not so dark that it makes the text in the boxes hard to read.

When a Picture Can Say It All

Words and numbers and taskbars and task boxes are fine, but what if you want to add something of your own? For example, you may want to draw attention to a task by drawing a circle around it, or you may want to include a simple drawing to show a process or working relationship in your plan.

You can use a Drawing toolbar to draw images in the chart area of the Gantt Chart view. Follow these steps to add a drawing:

1. **Display the Gantt Chart view.**

2. **Choose Insert ➪ Drawing.**

   The Drawing toolbar appears, as shown in Figure 11-8.

3. **Click the drawing tool that represents the type of object you want to draw, such as an oval or a rectangle.**

4. **Click at the location on the chart where you want to draw the object, and drag your mouse until the item is drawn approximately to the scale you want.**

5. **Release the mouse button.**

At this point, you have a few options:

✔ If you drew a text box, you can click in it and then type whatever text you like.

✔ You can resize any object you've drawn by selecting it and then clicking and dragging any of the resize handles (little black boxes) around its edges outward to enlarge it or inward to shrink it.

✔ You can move the mouse over the object until the cursor becomes a four-way arrow, and then click the object and drag it elsewhere on the chart.

✔ You can use the Cycle Fill Color tool to choose a color for a selected object. Each time you click this tool, it displays another color in the available palette. Just keep clicking the tool until the color you want appears.

✔ If you have several drawings or objects that you want to layer on your page, you can click the Draw button on the Drawing toolbar and choose an order for a selected object, bringing it to the front of other images or sending it behind them.

✔ Finally, you can attach a drawn object to any task by moving it next to a task and then clicking the Attach to Task drawing tool. If you should add or delete tasks to your task list or move the attached task, the drawing moves along with that task.

Figure 11-8:
This Drawing toolbar has some tools in common with other Office products you may have used.

Part IV
Avoiding Disaster: Staying On Track

The 5th Wave   By Rich Tennant

"You ever get the feeling this project could just up and die at any moment?"

In this part . . .

And behold, Murphy decreed: No project shall happen
the way you thought it would. To head off project
manager's frustration, this part shows you how to save a
baseline picture and to use it as you track the ongoing
struggle between actual activity and your ideal plan. You
get a look at reporting progress, pick up tips on how to
get back on track if the project strays from doing what it's
supposed to do, and get handy new tools for using past
data to make better future project plans.

Chapter 12

It All Begins with a Baseline

*W*hen you go on a diet (and I know you all have at one time or another!), you step on the scale the first day to check your weight. Then, as your diet progresses, you have a benchmark against which you can compare your dieting ups and downs.

Project doesn't have a weight problem, but it does have a method of benchmarking your project data so that you can compare the actual activity that takes place on your tasks to your original plan. This saved version of your plan data is called a *baseline,* and it includes all the information in your project — including task timing, resource assignments, and costs.

Project also provides something called an *interim plan* which is essentially a timing checklist. It includes only the actual start and finish dates of tasks and the estimated start and finish dates for tasks not yet started.

This chapter shows you when, why, and how to save a baseline and interim plan for your project.

All about Baselines

Saving a baseline is like freezing a mosquito in amber: It's a permanent record of your estimates of time, money, and resource workload for your project at the moment you consider your plan final and before you begin any activity. A baseline is saved in your original Project file and exists right alongside any actual activity you record on your tasks.

You can use baselines to debrief yourself or your team at any point in a project. This is especially useful at the end of a project, when you can compare what really happened against your best guesses those many weeks, months, or even years ago. You can then become a much better user of Project, making more accurate estimates up front. You can also use a baseline and the actual activity you track against it to explain delays or cost overruns to employers or clients using a wide variety of reports and printed views.

Finally, you can also save and clear baselines for only selected tasks. So, if one task is thrown way off track by a major change, you can modify your estimates for it and leave the rest of your baseline alone. Why throw out the baby with the bathwater?

What does a baseline look like?

After you've saved a baseline and tracked some actual activity against it, you get baseline *and* actual sets of data — as well as visual indications of baseline *versus* actual.

Figure 12-1 shows the Gantt Chart view for a project, displaying baseline and actual data. In the sheet area, you can display columns of data to compare baseline estimates and actual activity — for example, baseline finish and actual finish. In the chart area, the black line superimposed on the taskbar represents your baseline estimate. This black line indicates actual activity on that task.

Figure 12-2 shows the Network Diagram view. Here, progress on tasks is represented by a single slash for tasks where some activity has been recorded, and an *X* over tasks that are complete. A notation of percent completed is included in each task box not marked as complete.

You can change the way different graphic elements are represented by reformatting. (See Chapter 11 for more about formatting taskbars and task boxes.)

How do I save a baseline?

You can save a baseline at any time by displaying the Save Baseline dialog box. One setting in this dialog box requires a little explanation. The setting concerns how Project rolls up data to summary tasks when you set a baseline. By default, after you've saved a baseline the first time, a summary task's baseline data isn't updated if you make changes to a subtask below it, even if you delete a subtask. However, you can change that functionality by making a choice about how the baseline rolls up data. You can choose to have modifications rolled up to all summary tasks or only from subtasks for any summary tasks you've selected. This second option works only if you have selected summary tasks but not selected their subtasks.

Figure 12-1:
You can stay constantly aware of variations between your plan and reality with both data and graphics.

Figure 12-2:
You can also spot critical and noncritical tasks, which are color coded in the Network Diagram view.

You can save a baseline by following these steps:

1. **If you want to save a baseline for only certain tasks, select them.**

2. **Choose Tools ⇨ Tracking ⇨ Save Baseline.**

   The Save Baseline dialog box appears with the Save Baseline option selected, as shown in Figure 12-3.

3. **Click Entire Project or Selected Tasks.**

4. **Make selections for how the baseline rolls up, or summarizes, changes to task data.**

   You can have changed data summarized in all summary tasks or only for the summary tasks you've selected.

5. **Click OK to save the baseline.**

What if I want more than one baseline?

I know you love to hear about features in Project 2003 that you may never take full advantage of. (Who doesn't?) Here's one: You can now save your baseline up to 11 times during the life of your project. That's 11 potentially catastrophic events you can adjust for by resaving your baseline!

Multiple baselines can help you see the progress of your planning over the life of a longer project. They are also a sneaky but effective way of showing your boss that, yes, you really did anticipate that budget overrun — even though you didn't include it in your original saved plan. (I'm not advocating this, but it works as long as your boss didn't keep a copy of the original plan.)

The Save Baseline dialog box includes a list of these baselines, with the last date each was saved, as shown in Figure 12-4. When you save a baseline, you can save without overwriting an existing baseline by simply selecting another of the baselines in this list before saving.

Figure 12-4:
Each
baseline
to which
you've
saved
something
includes the
last saved
date in
this list.

Save Baseline	
○ Save baseline	
Baseline (last saved on Sat 4/26/03) ▾	

Baseline (last saved on Sat 4/26/03)
Baseline 1
Baseline 2
Baseline 3
Baseline 4
Baseline 5
Baseline 6
Baseline 7
Baseline 8
Baseline 9
Baseline 10

Help   OK   Cancel

If you save multiple baselines or interim plans, you can view them by displaying columns in any sheet view for those plans. For example, if you want to display information for a baseline you saved with the name Baseline 7, you would insert the column named Baseline 7 in your Gantt Chart view sheet.

You can view multiple baselines at one time by displaying the Multiple Baselines Gantt view.

How do I clear and reset a baseline?

Okay, if you read the first part of this chapter, you know that I said that a baseline is intended to be a frozen picture of your project plan that you keep sacrosanct and never change. Well, that's the theory. In practice, things can happen that make an original baseline so obsolete that it's less than useful. It's not even worth keeping as one of your 11 possible baselines.

For example, if you have a project that takes four years from beginning to end, you might want to save a new baseline every year because costs go up or resources change. Then you can see incremental versions of your estimates that reflect the changes you made based on changes in the real world. Or, what if you start your project with a wonderful, well-thought-out baseline plan, but a week later the entire industry shuts down with a massive strike that goes on for three months. All your original estimates of timing would be bogus, so it's better to make adjustments to your plan, save a new baseline, and move ahead after the strike is resolved.

To clear an existing baseline, follow these steps:

1. **If you want to clear the baseline for only certain tasks, select them.**

2. **Choose Tools ⇨ Tracking ⇨ Clear Baseline.**

   The Clear Baseline dialog box appears with the Clear Baseline Plan option selected by default, as shown in Figure 12-5.

Figure 12-5:
Use this to clear the baseline or interim plan.

Clear Baseline	☒
⦿ Clear baseline plan	Baseline (last saved on Sat 4/26/03) ▼
○ Clear interim plan	Start1/Finish1 ▼
For ⦿ Entire project ○ Selected tasks	
	OK Cancel

3. **In the Clear Baseline Plan box, select the baseline that you want to clear.**

4. **Click to clear the baseline for the entire project or for selected tasks.**

5. **Click OK.**

   The selected tasks or project baseline are cleared.

In the Interim

An *interim plan* is sort of like baseline lite. With an interim plan, you save only the actual start and finish dates of tasks that have had activity tracked on them as well as the baseline start and finish dates for all unstarted tasks.

Why save an interim plan rather than a baseline? An interim plan saves only timing information. If that's all you need, why save all the data about resource assignments and costs and so on? (Keep in mind that you'll end up with a huge file if you save ten baselines.)

Another issue with a baseline is that because there's so much data, the baseline can become obsolete at some point. An interim plan can be saved to record date changes but not overwrite your original baseline.

Finally, although you're allowed to save up to eleven baseline plans, if you need more than that, consider using some interim and some baseline data to expand the number of sets of data you can save.

Do not go baseline and interim plan crazy. Even in a long project, saving too many sets of plans can get confusing. When you do save a plan, print out a copy for your records and make a notation of when and why the plan was saved to help you keep track.

Saving an interim plan

Interim plans and baselines are saved using the same dialog box. The difference is that with an interim plan, you have to specify where the data is coming from. For example if you want to save the start and finish dates from your Baseline2 plan into the third interim plan, you'd copy from Baseline2 to Start/Finish3. If you want the current scheduled start and finish dates for all tasks, choose to copy from Start/Finish.

If you want currently scheduled start and finish dates changed in a baseline, but you don't want to change all the other data typically saved in a baseline, you can copy from Start/Finish to the baseline plan you want to change.

To save an interim plan, do this:

1. **If you want to save an interim plan for only certain tasks, select them.**
2. **Choose Tools ⇨ Tracking ⇨ Save Baseline.**

    The Save Baseline dialog box appears, as shown in Figure 12-6.

3. **Select Save Interim Plan.**
4. **In the Copy box, select the set of data that you want to copy to the interim plan.**
5. **In the Into box, select the fields in which you want to store the interim plan data.**
6. **Click to save the entire project or selected tasks.**
7. **Click OK to save the plan.**

By using the Copy and Into boxes in the Save Baseline dialog box, you can save up to ten interim plans based on baseline or actual data.

Figure 12-6:
You can
copy
settings
from any
saved
baseline to
an interim
plan.

Clearing and resetting a plan

Ten interim plans may seem like a lot now, but in the thick of a busy and ever-changing project, it may actually end up falling short of what you need. Because you have only ten interim plans to save, you may need to clear one at some point and resave it.

Project piggybacks the baseline and interim plan settings, so you actually choose a Clear Baseline menu command to clear an interim plan. This can be frightening to those who think that clicking a Clear Baseline command will send their baseline into oblivion. Don't worry — it won't!

To clear an interim plan, follow these steps:

1. **If you want to clear only some tasks in an interim plan, select them.**

2. **Choose Tools ⇨ Tracking ⇨ Clear Baseline.**

   The Clear Baseline dialog box appears, as shown in Figure 12-7.

Figure 12-7:
You can
clear and
reset interim
plans as
often as you
like during
the life of
your project.

3. **Select the Clear Interim Plan option, and then choose the plan you want to clear in the accompanying list.**

4. **Click to clear the specified interim plan for the entire project or for any tasks you have selected.**

5. **Click OK to clear the plan.**

You can now save a new set of information to that interim plan, if you like.

You may want to save a backup of various versions of your file with interim and baseline data. If you clear a baseline or an interim plan, remember: That data is gone forever!

Chapter 13

On the Right Track

*A*fter a project moves out of the planning stage and into action, it's like a constantly changing game in which there are rules, goals, and a general timeframe, but no one really knows which team will win (and sometimes where the ball is) until it's over.

Whether a task happens as planned or wanders off in an unexpected direction, your job at this stage of the game is to record that activity, which is referred to as *tracking*.

Tracking starts when your team reports their activity on the project. Then you (or someone else assigned to deal with tracking) must manage inputting that activity task by task.

When you have tracked activity, you'll be amazed at what data Project returns to you. Some of it will be good news, some bad, but all of it will be useful in managing your project throughout its lifetime.

Gathering Your Data

The first step in tracking progress on your project is to get information about what's been going on. The amount of data you collect will be determined by what you need to track, and at what level of detail. For example, some people don't even create and assign resources to tasks because they use Project only to create a timeline for their activities, not to manage resource time or tally costs. Others use resources and want to track their total work on tasks, but not to the level of detail that scrutinizes hourly work performed. For some people, simply marking one task 50 percent complete and another 100 percent complete — and letting Project assume all resources put in their estimated amount of work — is fine. Your tracking method is determined by the amount and type of information you need to monitor.

Therefore, the first thing you have to do is identify the best tracking method for you.

A method to your tracking madness

Microsoft has identified four tracking methods:

- ✓ **Task-total method**
- ✓ **Task-timephased method**
- ✓ **Assignment-total method**
- ✓ **Assignment-timephased method**

You can begin to understand these by looking at the difference between task and assignment tracking. You can track information at the *task* level, indicating total work or costs for the task up to the present or as of a status date you select. Or you can track costs by *resource assignment,* which is the more detailed way of tracking.

For example, suppose that the *Test Electrical Components* task is estimated to take 12 hours of work, according to your project baseline. Three human resources — Engineer, Electrician, and Assistant — are assigned at 100 percent of their time. Tracking by task, you can simply note that the task is 75 percent complete, which translates into nine hours of work finished.

Project assumes that the three resources split that work up equally. In reality, however, the Engineer put in one hour, the Electrician put in six, and the Assistant put in two. If you want more detailed tracking that shows you totals of work for each resource assignment and accurately tracks them, you would track the work at the resource-assignment level.

But here's where the timephased variable comes in: Whether you choose to track work on a task or the work done by individual resources on the task, you can also track by specific time increments — which Microsoft calls *timephased* tracking.

So, with our *Test Electrical Components* task, you can use a task approach of tracking nine hours of work to date or use a timephased approach to record those hours on a day-by-day basis. With a resource assignment approach, you can go to the very deepest level of tracking detail by tracking each and every resource's work hour by hour, day by day.

Finally, if you want Project to keep an eye on costs, be sure to track fixed costs and material usage that has been incurred on each task.

Going door to door

How do you get all the information about what work has been performed, by whom, and when? Well, the first method is the one you've probably been using for years: Hunt down the people on your project and ask them. Ask them in the hallway, in your weekly one-on-one meeting, or over lunch. Give each person a call, or have everyone turn in a form.

This is not rocket science, but you still have to determine up front what information you want, when you want it, and what form it should be in. The simpler you can keep manual reporting of progress on a project, the better, because people will actually do it. The more routine you can make it — such as every Friday, on a set form turned into the same person, and so on — the easier it will be.

If you need only a summary of where the task stands — say 25, 50, 75, or 100 percent complete — have the person in charge of the task give you that informed estimate. If you need total hours put into a task to date, that's what resources have to report. If you need a blow-by-blow, hour-by-hour, day-by-day report, you're likely to collect some form of timesheet from resources.

If your company is set up to use the Project Server feature, you can use that online work center to gather resource timesheets in one convenient location. (See Chapter 20 for more about how to do this.)

You can probably get information about fixed costs that have been incurred if you ask your accounting department for it, or by getting a copy of a purchase order or receipt from the human resource who spent the money.

Consider a third-party add-on product such as Timesheet Professional (http://timesheetprofessional.com) for reporting resource activity. You make Timesheet available to every resource on the project. The resources record their work time on it, and you can use Timesheet's tools to automatically update your project. If you're using Project Professional edition, Timesheet's features are incorporated into Project Server.

Let your project make the rounds

You can use the Send To feature on the File menu of Project to send your project to others and have them update their own activity. You can do this by either e-mailing a file or selected tasks as a file attachment, or you can route one file and have people make their changes in one place.

The challenge with the first method is that you need to manually incorporate the changes in the various files into a single file.

The challenge with the second approach is getting people to do the updating accurately and forward the file to the next person on the routing slip in a timely fashion. Generally, the best use of e-mail for updating projects is simply to have team members send an e-mail with their activity to the person updating the project, and let that person make all the changes in one central location.

Where Does All This Information Go?

After you've gathered information about task progress, fixed costs, and resource hours, you can input that information in several ways. You can use various views and tables to enter information in sheets of data; you can input information in the Task Information dialog box; or you can use the Tracking toolbar.

Doing things with the Tracking toolbar

Microsoft provides a toolbar for everything, so why should tracking be any different? The Tracking toolbar can be used to perform updates on selected tasks in any sheet view. Figure 13-1 shows the Tracking toolbar and the tools it has to offer.

Figure 13-1: Select a task and click one of these tools to update it.

Reschedule Work tool

Update as Scheduled tool

Percentage Complete tools

Add Progress Line tool

Update Tasks tool

The Tracking toolbar allows you to open the Project Statistics dialog box or display the Collaborate toolbar. You can use other tools to make specific updates to selected tasks:

✔ Selecting a task and clicking the **Update as Scheduled tool** automatically records activity to date as you anticipated in your baseline.

✔ The **Reschedule Work tool** reschedules all tasks that begin after the status date you set, or the current date if you didn't set a status date.

✔ The **Add Progress Line tool** turns on a kind of drawing tool. When you select the tool and then click the mouse cursor over a spot on the chart area, a progress line is placed at that point on the timescale. A progress line indicates visually to someone reviewing the project which tasks are ahead of schedule and which ones are behind schedule, by means of a line that connects in-progress tasks.

✔ The **Update Tasks tool** displays a dialog box containing tracking fields that you might recognize from the Task Information dialog box as well as some other fields you can use for updating your project.

✔ By clicking a **Percentage Complete tool** (0% to 100%), you can quickly mark a task's progress by the percentage of work completed.

You can also choose Tools ➪ Tracking ➪ Update Tasks to display the tracking fields from the Update Tasks dialog box; this is the same dialog box that the Update Tasks button on the Tracking toolbar displays.

For everything there is a view

By now, you probably know that Project has a view for everything you want to do. For example, the Task Sheet view and the Task Usage view (shown in Figures 13-2 and 13-3, respectively) allow you to update either task or resource information easily. So many variations are available, you might think Microsoft charged by the view!

Depending on the method of tracking you need (see "A method to your tracking madness," earlier in this chapter), different views serve different purposes. Table 13-1 shows the best view to use for each tracking method.

Table 13-1	Tracking Views	
Tracking Method	**Best View to Use**	**Table or Column Displayed**
Task	Task Sheet	Tracking table
Task timephased	Task Usage	Actual Work column
Assignment	Task Usage	Tracking table
Assignment timephased	Task Usage	Actual Work column

Figure 13-2:
The Task
Sheet view
is a great
place for
tracking
work, start,
and finish
dates.

	ⓘ	Task Name	Baseline Start	Start	Finish	Predecessors	Resource
1		⊟ **Product Localization Ten**	**Thu 1/1/04**	**Fri 1/9/04**	**Tue 8/3/04**		
2		⊟ **Scope**	**Thu 1/1/04**	**Fri 1/9/04**	**Mon 2/16/04**		
3	✓	Review business case	Thu 1/1/04	Fri 1/9/04	Mon 1/12/04		Project m
4		Estimate project unde	Mon 1/5/04	Thu 1/15/04	Wed 1/21/04	3	Project m
5		Prepare localization sp	Mon 1/12/04	Thu 1/22/04	Fri 1/23/04	4	Project m
6		Estimate costs	Wed 1/14/04	Mon 1/26/04	Wed 1/28/04	5	Project m
7		Identify risks	Mon 1/19/04	Thu 1/29/04	Fri 1/30/04	6	Project m
8		Secure project sponsc	Wed 1/21/04	Mon 2/2/04	Mon 2/2/04	7	Managen
9		Define preliminary resc	Thu 1/22/04	Tue 2/3/04	Mon 2/9/04	8	Project m
10		Define project commu	Thu 1/22/04	Tue 2/3/04	Thu 2/5/04	8	Project m
11		Secure core resources	Thu 1/29/04	Tue 2/10/04	Mon 2/16/04	9	Project m
12		Scope complete	Wed 2/4/04	Mon 2/16/04	Mon 2/16/04	11,10	
13		⊟ **Analysis/Planning**	**Thu 2/5/04**	**Tue 2/17/04**	**Thu 4/8/04**		
14		Identify localization res	Thu 2/5/04	Tue 2/17/04	Mon 2/23/04	12	Analyst
15		⊟ **Identify Components**	**Thu 2/12/04**	**Tue 2/24/04**	**Mon 3/1/04**		**Analyst**
16		⊟ **Software Compon**	**Thu 2/12/04**	**Tue 2/24/04**	**Mon 3/1/04**		
17		Setup	Thu 2/12/04	Tue 2/24/04	Mon 3/1/04	14	Analyst
18		User interface	Thu 2/12/04	Tue 2/24/04	Mon 3/1/04	14	Analyst
19		⊟ **User Assistance C**	**Thu 2/12/04**	**Tue 2/24/04**	**Mon 3/1/04**		
20		Online help, docu	Thu 2/12/04	Tue 2/24/04	Mon 3/1/04	14	Analyst

Figure 13-3:
The Task
Usage view
allows you
to enter
specific
resource
hours on
task day-by-
day on your
project.

	ⓘ	Task Name	Baseline Work	Work	Duration	Details	M	T	W
1		⊟ **Product Localization Te**	**3,472 hrs**	**3,504 hrs**	**148 days**	Work	8h	8h	
2		⊟ **Scope**	**240 hrs**	**272 hrs**	**27 days**	Work	8h	8h	
3	✓	⊟ Review business cas	32 hrs	64 hrs	4 days	Work			
		Management	16 hrs	32 hrs		Work			
		Project manager	16 hrs	32 hrs		Work			
4		⊟ Estimate project und	40 hrs	40 hrs	1 wk	Work	8h	8h	
		Project manager	40 hrs	40 hrs		Work	8h	8h	
5		⊟ Prepare localization s	16 hrs	16 hrs	2 days	Work			
		Project manager	16 hrs	16 hrs		Work			
6		⊟ Estimate costs	24 hrs	24 hrs	3 days	Work			
		Project manager	24 hrs	24 hrs		Work			
7		⊟ Identify risks	16 hrs	16 hrs	2 days	Work			
		Project manager	16 hrs	16 hrs		Work			
8		⊟ Secure project spons	8 hrs	8 hrs	1 day	Work			
		Management	8 hrs	8 hrs		Work			
9		⊟ Define preliminary res	40 hrs	40 hrs	1 wk	Work			
		Project manager	40 hrs	40 hrs		Work			
10		⊟ Define project comm	24 hrs	24 hrs	3 days	Work			
		Project manager	24 hrs	24 hrs		Work			
11		⊟ Secure core resource	40 hrs	40 hrs	1 wk	Work			
		Project manager	40 hrs	40 hrs		Work			

When you find the right view with the right columns displayed, entering tracking information is as simple as typing a number of hours, a dollar amount for fixed costs, or a start or finish date in the appropriate column for the task you're updating.

Tracking your work for the record

You need to input several types of information to track progress on your project. First, you have to tell Project as of when you want to track progress: By default, it records information as of the current date based on your computer's calendar settings, but if you want to record progress as of, say, Arbor Day, you can do that, too.

You can record actual start and finish dates for tasks, the percentage of a task that is complete (for example, a task might be 75 percent complete), and actual work performed (that is, the number of hours that resources put in on each task). If you think that the task will take less or more time than you anticipated, based on progress to date, you can modify the remaining duration for the task. You can also enter units of materials used, and fixed-cost information for expenditures incurred, such as equipment rental or consulting fees.

Progress as of when?

If you don't know what day of the week it is, you can't very well gauge whether you're making the right amount of headway through your week's work. Well, tracking is like that: The first thing you have to do is establish a *status date;* that is, the date as of which you are tracking progress.

By default, Project uses the calendar setting of your computer as the current date when you enter actual activity information. However, sometimes you'll want to time travel. For example, suppose that your boss asks for a report showing the status of the project as of the last day of the quarter, December 31. You gathered all your resources' timesheets up through that date, but you didn't get around to inputting those updates until three days after the end of the quarter. You can deal with this situation by setting the status date in Project to December 31 and then entering your tracking data.

After you've set the status date and entered information, Project uses that date to make calculations such as earned value (the value of work completed to date). Also, any task-complete or percentage-complete information records as of that date, and progress lines in the chart area reflect that timing. Any reports or printouts of views that you generate give a picture of the status of your project as of that date.

Here's how to set the status date:

1. **Choose Project ➪ Project Information.**

   The Project Information dialog box appears, as shown in Figure 13-4.

Figure 13-4:
When you
first open
this dialog
box, the
status date
is not set;
your project
is controlled
by the
current
date.

2. **In the Status Date box, click the arrow to display the calendar.**

3. **If you want to set the status date in another month, use the right or left arrow at the top of the calendar to maneuver to that month.**

4. **Click the date you want.**

5. **Click OK.**

Now you're ready to start inputting tracking data.

Percentage complete: How to tell?

When people ask me how to figure out whether a task is 25 percent, 50 percent, or even 36.5 percent complete, I usually refer them to their own intuition. If your boss asks you how things are coming on that report, you typically go through a quick internal calculation and come back with a rough estimate with no problem. A rough estimate, based on your experience and the information your resources provide you about their progress, is often good enough.

Can tracking get too detailed?

Does it make sense to track 2.25 percent of progress every other day on a two-month task? Probably not. Except on the lengthiest tasks, entering a percentage more finely broken down than 25, 50, 75, and 100 percent complete probably isn't worth it. That's partly because tasks longer than a few weeks should probably be broken down into subtasks for ease of tracking, and partly because one of the main purposes of tracking is reporting. If your boss or board or client could really care less about when you hit your exact 33.75 percent-complete point, why track it?

On the other hand, if (for some reason known only to you) your project must include a six-month task and you can't break it into subtasks, you might use percentages such as 10, 20, 30, 40, 50, and so on to prevent having to wait a month between updates with (apparently) no progress to show.

You can also calculate percentage complete in more precise ways. For example, if you estimate that a task should take ten hours of effort, and your resources report performing five hours of effort, you could say you're 50 percent there. But be careful. Just because people have spent half the allocated time doesn't mean that they have accomplished half the work.

You could go by costs: If your original estimates said that your four resources assigned to a four-day task would tally $4,000 of costs, and the time your resources report spending on the task add up to $3,000, you could *guess* that the task is 75 percent finished. But again, just because you've spent three quarters of the money doesn't mean you've accomplished three quarters of what you set out to do.

When a task's deliverable is measurable, that helps a lot. For example, if you have a task to produce 100 cars on the assembly line in four days and you've produced 25 cars, you might be about 25 percent finished with the task. Or if you were supposed to install software on ten computers in a computer lab and you've installed it on five of them, that's an easy 50 percent.

But not every task can be calculated so neatly. The best rule of thumb is to trust your instincts and review what your team is telling you about their progress.

The simplest and quickest way to update percent complete on a task is to click the task to select it in any view, and then click the 0%, 25%, 50%, 75%, or 100% button on the Tracking toolbar. Alternately, you can double-click any task to open the Task Information dialog box, and then enter the percent complete there. You can also select a task and click the Update Tasks button on the Tracking toolbar to open the Update Tasks dialog box and make the change there. If you want to enter a percentage in increments of other than 25 percent, you'll have to enter it in the Task Information or Update Tasks dialog box or the Percent Complete column in any sheet view.

When did you start? When did you finish?

If you note that a task is complete and don't enter an Actual Start date, Project (ever the optimist) assumes you started on time. If you didn't start on time and you want to reflect the actual timing, you should modify the Actual Start date. If you finished late, you should enter the Actual Finish date. However, be aware that if you don't modify the task duration and enter an earlier finish date, the start date will be calculated to have occurred earlier.

You have several options of where to track this information. You can use the Update Tasks dialog box, which appears when you click the Update Tasks button on the Tracking toolbar (shown in Figure 13-5). You can also display a sheet view with Actual Start and Actual Finish columns, such as the Tracking Gantt view with the Tracking table displayed or the Gantt View with the Tracking table displayed. Then use the drop-down calendar in the Actual Start or Actual Finish dates columns to specify a date.

Figure 13-5:
Click the
arrow in the
Start or
Finish boxes
and choose
a date from
a drop-
down
calendar.

Update Tasks	
Name: Secure executive sponsorship	Duration: 2d
% Complete: 0% Actual dur: 0d	Remaining dur: 2d
Actual	**Current**
Start: Wed 4/23/03	Start: Tue 7/13/04
Finish: NA	Finish: Wed 7/14/04
Help	Notes... OK Cancel

A few conditions could cause a warning message to appear when you enter an actual start or finish date: for example, if the actual start date falls before the start date for the project, or if it causes a conflict with a dependent task. When this warning message appears, you have the following options: cancel the operation or force the conflict to exist (or the task to start) before the project starts. If you want to cancel the change, correct what's causing the problem, and then go back and enter the actual information, you can. Or you can force the conflict, and let it stand.

John worked three hours, Maisie worked ten

If you want to get to the blow-by-blow level of tracking, you'll need to record exactly how many hours each resource put in on your tasks. This can be about as much fun as typing the New York City phone book into a database, but it has some benefits. After you've tracked actual hours, you can get tallies of total hours put in by each resource in your project by day, week, or month. If you have to bill clients based on resource hours (for example, if you're a lawyer), you have a clear record to refer to. If you're tracking a budget in detail, resource hours multiplied by their individual rates will tally an accurate accounting of costs as finely as day by day.

If you don't enter specific hours, Project just averages the work done on the task according to the total duration. For many people, that's fine; for others, more detail is better. If you're in the detail camp, specify actual resource hours as a total by task or day-by-day through the life of each task.

To enter resource hours, follow these steps:

1. **Display the Resource Usage view, which is shown in Figure 13-6.**

Figure 13-6: Track resource activity day-by-day in this view.

2. **In the Resource Name column, scroll down to locate the resource you want to track.**

    The tasks that each resource is assigned to are listed underneath the resource name.

3. **Enter the hours put in by the resource:**

    a. If you want to enter only total hours, locate the task name under the resource listing, and display the Actual Work column and enter the total hours there.

    b. If you want to enter hours on the task day by day, scroll in the chart pane to locate the timeframe for the task. Click the cell for a day that the resource worked and enter a number. Repeat this for each day that the resource worked on that task.

If the hours you enter for a resource total more or less than the baseline estimate for that resource on that task, here's what happens:

✔ When you enter an amount and press Enter, the Work column total recalculates to reflect the total hours worked on that task.

✔ The hour notation on that date is displayed in red, showing some variation from baseline hours.

✔ A little pencil symbol appears in the ID column for that task, indicating that the assignment has been edited.

✔ A yellow box with an exclamation point appears in the ID column to the left of the task's summary task, indicating a resource overallocation.

Note that you can easily look up the total hours put in by each resource on the project by checking the summary number of work hours listed next to the resource in the Resource Name column of the Resource Usage view.

Uh-oh, we're into overtime

When you enter 16 hours of work on a single day for a resource, even though that resource is based on a calendar with an 8-hour day, Project doesn't recognize any of those hours as overtime. This is one case where you have to lead Project by the hand and actually tell it to specify overtime work.

When you enter hours in the Overtime Work field, Project interprets that as the number of total Work hours that are overtime hours. So, if you enter 16 hours of work on a task in the Work column, and then enter 4 in the Overtime Work column, Project assumes that there were 12 hours of work at the standard resource rate and 4 hours at overtime rates.

To enter overtime hours, follow these steps:

1. **Display the Resource Usage view.**

2. **Right-click a column heading and then click Insert Column.**

   The Column Definition dialog box appears.

3. **In the Field Name box, click Overtime Work.**

4. **Click OK to display the column.**

5. **Click in the Overtime Work column for the resource and task you want to modify, and then use the spinner arrows to specify the overtime hours.**

Note that if you specify overtime, Project assumes that effort-driven tasks are happening in less time. After all, if the task was to take three 8-hour days (24 hours of work) to complete, and you recorded that the resource worked 12 hours for two days in a row, Project figures that all the effort got accomplished in less time. The duration for the task will actually shrink. If that's not what you want, you have to go in and modify the task duration yourself.

Specifying remaining durations

A lot of tracking information has a weird and wonderful relationship in Project. For example, Project tries to help you out by calculating durations based on other entries you make — such as actual start and finish dates. In that particular case, Project figures out task duration according to those dates. (This works in reverse, too: If you enter the task duration, Project recalculates the finish date to reflect it.)

Sometimes you'll want to enter a duration rather than have Project base it on other information you input. For example, you might have entered a start date and 20 hours of work on a task that had a baseline of 16 hours of work. What Project can't know is that the scope of the task changed, and now the task is not complete and will also take another 20 hours of work. You have to tell Project about that.

To modify the duration on a task in progress or completed, follow these steps:

1. **Display the Gantt Chart view.**

2. **Choose View ▷ Table ▷ Tracking.**

   The Tracking table is displayed.

3. **Click in the Actual Duration column for the task you want to modify, and then use the arrows to adjust the actual duration up or down.**

4. **If you want to enter a remaining duration, click in the Remaining Duration column and type a number as well as an increment symbol.**

For example, you might type **25d** (where *d* is the increment symbol for days).

If you enter a percentage-of-completion for a task and then modify the duration to differ from the baseline, Project automatically recalculates the percentage considered complete to reflect the new duration. So, if you enter *50% complete* on a 10-hour task and then modify the actual duration to 20 hours, Project considers that 5 hours (50% of 10 hours) as only 25% of the 20 hours.

Entering fixed-cost updates

Fixed costs are costs that aren't influenced by time, such as equipment purchases and consulting fees. Compared to the calculations and interactions of percentage completions and start and finish dates for hourly resources, fixed-cost tracking will seem like simplicity itself!

Here's how to do it:

1. **Display the Gantt Chart view.**

2. **Right-click in a column heading and then click Insert Column.**

The Column Definition dialog box appears.

3. **In the Field Name box, select Fixed Cost.**

4. **Click OK.**

5. **Click in the Fixed Cost column for the task you want to update.**

6. **Type the fixed cost, or a total of several fixed costs, for the task.**

That's it! However, because Project lets you enter only one fixed-cost amount per task, consider adding a note to the task itemizing the costs you've included in the total. Also, there is no baseline fixed cost column, so to compare how your actual fixed costs outstripped your baseline estimates, you'll have to do a little math to find the difference between baseline costs and actual costs: Deduct out non-fixed costs to get the variation in fixed costs.

Consider using some of the 30 customizable Text columns for itemized fixed-cost entry. Rename one Equipment Purchase, another Facility Rental, and so on and enter those costs in those columns. Of course these columns of data won't perform calculations such as rolling up total costs to the summary tasks in your project, but they'll serve as a reminder about itemized fixed costs.

Update Project: Sweeping Changes for Dummies

If it's been a while since you tracked activity and you want to update your schedule, Update Project might be for you. It allows you to track chunks of activity for a period of time. Update Project works best, however, if most tasks happened pretty much on schedule.

This is not fine-tuned tracking: It's akin to getting your bank balance, drawing a line in your checkbook, and writing down that balance as gospel rather than accounting for your balance check by check (if you're like most of us, you've done this at least once). Doing so assumes that all your checks and deposits probably tally with what the bank says as of that date; thus, going forward, you're back on track.

Here are the setting choices Update Project offers you:

✔ **Update Work as Complete Through.** You can update your project through the date you specify in this box in one of two ways. The Set 0% – 100% Complete setting lets Project figure out the percent complete on every task that should have begun by that time; by making this choice, you tell Project to assume that the tasks started and progressed exactly on time. The Set 0% or 100% Complete Only setting works a little differently. This setting says to Project, just record 100% complete on tasks that the baseline said would be complete by now, but leave all other tasks at 0% complete.

✔ **Reschedule Uncompleted Work to Start After.** This setting reschedules the portions of tasks that aren't yet complete to start after the date you specify in this dialog box.

To use Update Project, do this:

1. **Display the Gantt Chart view.**

2. **If you want to update only certain tasks, select them.**

3. **Choose Tools ⇨ Tracking ⇨ Update Project.**

   The Update Project dialog box appears, as shown in Figure 13-7.

4. **Choose the Update method you prefer: Set 0% – 100% Complete or Set 0% or 100% Complete Only.**

5. **If you want a status date other than the current date, set it in the box in the upper-right corner.**

Figure 13-7:
You can
update only
selected
tasks or
the entire
project.

Update Project

- Update work as complete through: Mon 4/28/03
  - Set 0% - 100% complete
  - Set 0% or 100% complete only
- Reschedule uncompleted work to start: Mon 4/28/03

For: Entire project   Selected tasks

Help   OK   Cancel

6. **If you want Project to reschedule any work rather than updating work as complete, select the Reschedule Uncompleted Work to Start option and then select a date from the list.**

7. **Choose whether you want these changes to apply to the entire project or only selected tasks.**

8. **Click OK to save the settings and have Project make updates.**

If you want, you can use Update Project to make some global changes, such as marking all tasks that should be complete according to baseline as 100 percent complete, and then go in and perform more detailed task-by-task tracking on individual tasks that are only partially complete.

Tracking Materials Usage

Tracking the amount of materials used on tasks involves tracking actual units at the material resource level. So, if you created a resource called *rubber*, and assigned it to the task *Manufacture Tires* at 500 tons, but you actually used only 450 tons (in other words, you made 450 tons of rubber stretch . . .) you would go in and enter the actual units used.

This situation is akin to the way you track work resource hours on tasks. To make it happen, just follow these steps:

1. **Display the Resource Usage view (see Figure 13-8).**

2. **Locate the material resource in the list and scroll in the right pane until the assignment timeframe appears.**

3. **Enter the actual units used on each task to which you assigned that resource.**

Just keep in mind that if you assigned the material resource of, say, 500 tons to a five day task, the Resource Usage view will reflect that Project spread the usage out, 100 tons for each of the five days of the task. If you don't care on what day of the task the materials were used, you can simply modify one of the settings to be higher or lower to make up any difference in actual usage.

Figure 13-8:
Change the
baseline
units here
and the
actual
usage will
change in
the Work
column.

Tracking More Than One: Consolidated Projects

Often you'll have either projects that are related in some fashion (such as sharing resources or having timing dependencies between them) or a series of smaller projects that make up a larger project. In that case you can consolidate those separate projects into one file, either as a series of summary tasks or with all summary and subtasks included.

When you consolidate projects, you can choose to link to the source file. When you do, any changes to the source file are represented in the consolidated file.

If it's your job to keep track of the big picture, then you have to understand how consolidated projects get updated.

Consolidating projects

Creating a consolidated project is sort of like going to a Chinese restaurant — one from Column A, one from Column B, and so on, until you've built yourself a tasty meal. In Project, you open a blank file, then insert existing projects to build a satisfying master project plan.

The neat thing about consolidated projects is that you have some choices about how the consolidated project and the source files you insert in it interact. For example, you can link to a source file so that changes made in the source file will be reflected in the consolidated project. This is a great tool for somebody who has to keep his or her eye on multiple phases or many smaller projects.

You can also create dependencies between inserted projects in the consolidated file. If you have (for example) one project that can't start until another one finishes, you can clearly see in the consolidated file how various separate projects in your organization have an impact on each other.

The other thing you can do to relate consolidated projects to their source files is to make your consolidated project a two-way street, allowing changes in it to be reflected in the source files. You can also make the choice to have the source files be read-only so your changes won't go mucking around with other people's files — whichever suits your purposes.

To create a consolidated file, follow these steps:

1. **Open a blank Project file and display the Gantt Chart view.**

2. **Click in the Task Name column.**

   If you're inserting multiple projects, click the row in which you want the inserted file(s) to appear. If you want to insert a project between existing tasks, click the task beneath where you want the project to be inserted.

3. **Choose Insert ⇨ Project.**

   The Insert Project dialog box shown in Figure 13-9 appears.

4. **Using the Look In list, locate the Project file you want to insert and select it.**

5. **Click the arrow on the Insert button if you want to change the default Insert setting to Insert Read Only.**

6. **If you want to link the project in this file to the source file, so that whenever you open the consolidated file it updates automatically, make sure the Link to Project check box is selected.**

7. **Click OK.**

   The project is inserted in your file with the summary task showing and all subtasks hidden. To display all tasks in the inserted project, just click the plus sign to the left of the summary task.

Figure 13-9: Make choices about how your projects interact in this dialog box.

Insert Project dialog box:

Look in: Projects

PROJOFF
PROJOFF3

My Rece...
Desktop
My Documents
My Computer
My Netwo...

File name:
Files of type: Microsoft Project Files
☑ Link to project
ODBC...
Insert
Cancel

Updating consolidated projects

There are two ways to skin the cat called *updating a consolidated project,* and the one you use depends on whether you linked to the source files when you inserted them. If you linked the files and you inserted without the read-only setting, changes in source files are reflected in the consolidated file (and vice versa). Updating is simply a matter of making sure all the files are available in their original linked location (for example, in a folder on your network) and then Project updates automatically.

If you haven't linked the files, changes in source files won't be reflected in consolidated files and the consolidated file information will have no impact on the source information. You might create such an unlinked consolidated file if you simply want to see a snapshot of how all projects are going at the moment, and you don't want to run the risk of having your settings changing the source information. In this case, however, if you want to track progress, you have to create a new consolidated project, or manually enter all updates.

After you've inserted projects in a file, you can move them around using cut and paste tools. When you do, the Planning Wizard may appear offering you options to resolve any conflicts that may occur because of dependency links you've created between inserted projects.

Changing linking settings

Changing your mind is a project manager's prerogative. So, if, after you have inserted a source file in a consolidated file, you find you didn't initially establish a link, you can go in and change that setting so the files update each other automatically.

Follow these steps to make changes to the inserted project:

1. **Open the consolidated file.**

2. **Display the Gantt Chart view.**

3. **Click the Task Name of the inserted project you want to update.**

4. **Click the Task Information button on the Standard toolbar.**

   The Inserted Project Information dialog box (shown in Figure 13-10) appears.

Figure 13-10:
Data on the
source file
is displayed
in this
dialog box.

5. **Display the Advanced tab.**

6. **Select the Link to Project checkbox, then click the Browse button.**

   An Inserted Project dialog box appears.

7. **Use the Look In feature to locate the file you want to link to and select the file.**

8. Click OK.

9. If you want the source file to be Read Only, select that check box.

10. Click OK to save the link.

Chapter 14

A Project with a View: Observing Progress

Some people use Project just to paint a pretty picture of what their project will entail, and then put the plan in a drawer. That's a mistake. After you've entered all your project data, saved a baseline, and then tracked actual activity on your project, you get an amazing array of information back from Project that helps you to stay on time and on budget.

When you have tracked some actual activity on tasks, Project allows you to view baseline estimates right alongside your real-time plan. Project alerts you to tasks that are running late, and shows how the critical path shifts over time.

Project also provides detailed budget information. In fact, the information you can get about your costs might just make your accounting department's heart sing. The information is detailed and uses terms accountants love (such as *earned value, cost variance,* and *budgeted cost of work performed,* all translated in a later section of this chapter).

So keep that project file close at hand — and take a look at how Project can make you the most informed project manager in town.

Look at What Tracking Did!

You've diligently entered resource work hours on tasks, recorded the percentage of progress on tasks, and entered fixed costs. Now what? Well, all that information has caused several calculations to go on — and updates to be reflected — in your project. Time to take a quick look at the changes all your tracking has produced in your Project plan.

Getting an indication

A lot of information in Project just sits there waiting for you to hunt it down in obscure views or tables. But one tool that Project uses to practically jump up and down and say, "look at this" is *indicator icons.* You've seen these icons in the Indicator column and probably wondered what the heck they were for. Well, these little symbols give you a clue to important facts about each task, sometimes serving to alert you to problems or potential challenges.

Figure 14-1 shows several of these indicators, some of which relate to the results of tracking your project.

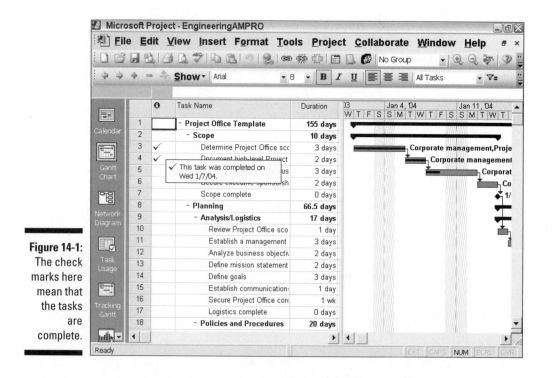

Figure 14-1: The check marks here mean that the tasks are complete.

If you see an unfamiliar indicator icon crop up in your project, hold your mouse cursor over the indicator. A box describing its meaning appears. To get a list of Project icons and their meanings, go to Help, click the Index tab, and type **icon** in the Type Keywords box. Click search, and then click About Indicators.

Lines of progress

Progress lines offer an additional visual indicator of how you're doing. As you can see in Figure 14-2, a progress line zigzags between tasks and forms, showing left-or-right-pointing peaks. These peaks indicate late or early tasks (calculated according to the status date you use when tracking). A progress line that points to the left of a task indicates that the task is running late. Progress lines that point to the right show that, wonder of wonders, you're running ahead of schedule. (Treasure these — they don't seem to appear often in most projects!)

Figure 14-2:
The circle indicator shows the direction of each progress line peak; here, we're behind schedule all the way!

		0	Task Name	Duration
	1		− **Project Office Template**	**155 days**
	2		− **Scope**	**10 days**
	3	✓	Determine Project Office sco	3 days
	4	✓	Document high-level Project	2 days
	5		Justify Project Office via bus	3 days
	6		Secure executive sponsorsh	2 days
	7		Scope complete	0 days
	8		− **Planning**	**66.5 days**
	9		− **Analysis/Logistics**	**17 days**
	10		Review Project Office sco	1 day
	11		Establish a management	3 days
	12		Analyze business objecti	2 days
	13		Define mission statement	2 days
	14		Define goals	3 days
	15		Establish communication:	1 day
	16		Secure Project Office cor	1 wk
	17		Logistics complete	0 days
	18		− **Policies and Procedures**	**20 days**

Displaying progress lines

By default, Project doesn't display progress lines. You have to turn them on — and while you're at it, you might as well specify when and how they appear. Here's how to make settings for and display progress lines:

1. **Display the Gantt Chart view.**

2. **Choose Tools ⇨ Tracking ⇨ Progress Lines.**

    The Progress Lines dialog box appears, as shown in Figure 14-3.

Figure 14-3: These two tabs allow you to control just about everything about progress lines.

3. **If you want Project to always show a progress line for the current or status date, select Always Display Current Progress Line and then select At Project Status Date or At Current Date.**

4. **If you want progress lines to be displayed at set intervals, do the following:**

    a. **Select Display Progress Lines at Recurring Intervals, and then select Daily, Weekly, or Monthly.**

    b. **Specify the interval settings.**

    For example, if you select Weekly, you can choose every week, every other week, and so on, as well as which day of the week the line should be displayed on the timescale. Figure 14-4 shows a project with progress lines at regular intervals.

Figure 14-4:
Multiple
progress
lines can
get rather
busy, but do
show you
clearly how
delays grew
over time.

5. **Choose whether you want to display progress lines beginning at the Project Start or on another date.**

   To use the Project Start date, simply select the Project Start option to the right of Begin At. To select an alternate start date, select the second option and then select a date in the calendar drop-down list.

6. **If you want to display a progress line on a specific date, click Display Selected Progress Lines and then choose a date from the Progress Line Dates drop-down calendar.**

   You can make this setting for multiple dates by clicking subsequent lines in this list and selecting additional dates.

7. **Finally, you can choose to display progress lines in relation to actual or baseline information.**

   If a task has been tracked to show 50 percent complete and you choose to have Project display progress lines based on actual information, the peak appears relative to the 50 percent *actual* line, not the complete baseline taskbar.

8. **Click OK to save your settings.**

You can use your mouse to add a single progress line quickly. On the Tracking toolbar, click the Add Progress Line tool button. Then click the Gantt Chart at the location on the timescale where you want the line to appear in the chart. To delete the line, right-click it and select Progress Lines. In the Progress Lines dialog box, click the item you want to delete in the Progress Line Dates list, then click Delete and OK.

Formatting progress lines

In keeping with the almost mind-boggling array of formatting options Project makes available to you, you can modify how progress lines are formatted.

As with any changes to formatting, you're tampering with the way Project codes visual information for readers. You should be cautious about formatting changes that will make your plan difficult to read for those who are used to Project's default formatting.

To modify progress line formatting, follow these steps:

1. **Choose Tools ⇨ Tracking ⇨ Progress Lines.**

2. **Click the Line Styles tab, if necessary, to display the options shown in Figure 14-5.**

3. **In the Progress Line Type display, click a line style sample.**

4. **In the Line Type box, click a style from the samples shown.**

   There are two settings you can make here: one for the Current Progress Line and one for All Other Progress Lines.

5. **You can change the line color, progress point shape, and progress point color by making different choices in those boxes.**

6. **If you want a date to appear alongside each progress line, select the Show Date for Each Progress Line option, and then select a date in the Format box.**

7. **If you want to change the font used for the displayed date, click the Change Font button and make your changes.**

8. **Click OK to save your settings.**

When worlds collide: Baseline versus actual

One of the most obvious ways to view the difference between your baseline estimates and what you've tracked in your project is through taskbars. When you've tracked some progress on tasks, the Gantt Chart shows a black bar superimposed on the blue taskbar that represents your baseline. For example, in Figure 14-6, Task 3 is complete; you can tell this by the solid black bar that extends the full length of the baseline taskbar. Task 5 is only partially complete; the black, actual task line only partially fills the baseline duration for the task. Task 6 has no recorded activity on it — there is no black *actual* line at all, only the blue baseline taskbar.

Figure 14-5:
Select line styles and colors with these settings.

Figure 14-6:
The solid line on taskbars represents actual activity in your project.

Learn by the Numbers

Visual indicators such as taskbars and indicator icons are useful to alert you to delays or variances between estimated and actual performance, but they don't provide any detailed information. To get the real lowdown on how far ahead (or behind) you are, down to the day or penny, you need to give the numbers a scan. The numbers that Project provides reveal much about whether you're on schedule and within your budget.

Two tables you can display in the Gantt Chart bring your situation into bold relief. The Cost and Variance tables provide information about dollars spent and variation in timing between baseline and actual activity.

The Cost table is shown in Figure 14-7. Here you can review data that compares baseline estimates of fixed costs and actual costs. These two sets of data are presented side-by-side in columns. In the project shown in Figure 14-7, so far you've spent $131,994 and your baseline estimate was $97,994, giving you a variance of $34,000 over your budget.

To display the Cost table, choose View ⇨ Table ⇨ Cost.

Figure 14-7:
The Variance column shows the difference between the total cost and the baseline.

	Fixed Cost Accrual	Total Cost	Baseline	Variance
1	Prorated	$131,994.00	$97,994.00	$34,000.00
2	Prorated	$49,400.00	$15,400.00	$34,000.00
3	Prorated	$29,320.00	$4,320.00	$25,000.00
4	Start	$5,380.00	$3,880.00	$1,500.00
5	Prorated	$5,820.00	$4,320.00	$1,500.00
6	Prorated	$5,380.00	$2,880.00	$2,500.00
7	Prorated	$3,500.00	$0.00	$3,500.00
8	Prorated	$58,210.00	$58,210.00	$0.00
9	Prorated	$10,930.00	$10,930.00	$0.00
10	Prorated	$0.00	$0.00	$0.00
11	Prorated	$240.00	$240.00	$0.00
12	Prorated	$4,320.00	$4,320.00	$0.00
13	Prorated	$0.00	$0.00	$0.00
14	Prorated	$2,980.00	$2,980.00	$0.00
15	Prorated	$480.00	$480.00	$0.00
16	Prorated	$720.00	$720.00	$0.00
17	Prorated	$240.00	$240.00	$0.00
18	Prorated	$1,950.00	$1,950.00	$0.00

Figure 14-8 shows the Variance table. This table is to your scheduling what the Cost table is to your budget. It shows the variance between baseline start and finish dates and task durations, as well as the timing that actually occurred on tasks after your project got going.

If you created a slack task to help you deal with delays that might come up, the total variance shown here will tell you how many days you may have to deduct from the duration of the slack task to get back on track. Read more about making adjustments in your plan to deal with delays and cost overruns in Chapter 15.

		Start	Finish	Baseline Start	Baseline Finish	Start Var.	Finish Var.
1		Fri 1/9/04	Fri 8/27/04	Thu 1/1/04	Wed 8/4/04	6 days	17 days
2		Fri 1/9/04	Tue 1/27/04	Thu 1/1/04	Wed 1/14/04	6 days	9 days
3		Fri 1/9/04	Mon 1/12/04	Thu 1/1/04	Mon 1/5/04	6 days	5 days
4		Fri 1/16/04	Mon 1/19/04	Tue 1/6/04	Wed 1/7/04	8 days	8 days
5		Thu 1/22/04	Fri 1/23/04	Thu 1/8/04	Mon 1/12/04	10 days	9 days
6		Mon 1/26/04	Tue 1/27/04	Tue 1/13/04	Wed 1/14/04	9 days	9 days
7		Tue 1/27/04	Tue 1/27/04	Wed 1/14/04	Wed 1/14/04	9 days	9 days
8		Thu 2/5/04	Tue 5/11/04	Thu 1/15/04	Fri 4/16/04	15 days	17 days
9		Thu 2/5/04	Tue 3/2/04	Thu 1/15/04	Fri 2/6/04	15 days	17 days
10		Thu 2/5/04	Wed 2/11/04	Thu 1/15/04	Thu 1/15/04	15 days	19 days
11		Thu 2/12/04	Mon 2/16/04	Fri 1/16/04	Tue 1/20/04	19 days	19 days
12		Fri 2/13/04	Mon 2/16/04	Wed 1/21/04	Thu 1/22/04	17 days	17 days
13		Tue 2/17/04	Wed 2/18/04	Fri 1/23/04	Mon 1/26/04	17 days	17 days
14		Thu 2/19/04	Mon 2/23/04	Tue 1/27/04	Thu 1/29/04	17 days	17 days
15		Tue 2/24/04	Tue 2/24/04	Fri 1/30/04	Fri 1/30/04	17 days	17 days
16		Wed 2/25/04	Tue 3/2/04	Mon 2/2/04	Fri 2/6/04	17 days	17 days
17		Tue 3/2/04	Tue 3/2/04	Fri 2/6/04	Fri 2/6/04	17 days	17 days
18		Wed 3/3/04	Tue 3/30/04	Mon 2/9/04	Fri 3/5/04	17 days	17 days

Figure 14-8: Use this table to see what delays are doing to your schedule.

Acronym Soup: BCWP, ACWP, EAC, and CV

In any view, you can insert several columns of data to give you some calculated analyses of what's going on in your project budget. Much of this data will mean more to an accountant than to most in-the-trenches project managers. But if only to make your accountant feel more comfortable, you should become familiar with some of the most common calculations. Also, many organizations require information on these specific numbers in project reports:

- **BCWP (budgeted cost of work performed).** Referred to in some circles as earned value, BCWP is essentially a calculation of the value of the work that you've completed expressed in dollars. For example, if a task has $2,000 of costs associated with it and you record that the task is 50 percent complete, the earned value for that task is $1,000 (50 percent of the baseline estimated costs).

- **ACWP (actual cost of work performed).** This calculation looks at actual costs, including tracked resource hours or units expended on the task plus fixed costs. Where BCWP looks at the baseline *value* of work, ACWP looks at actual tracked *costs*.

- **EAC (estimate at completion).** This is a total of all costs on a task. For a task in progress, EAC calculates the actual costs recorded to date plus the remaining baseline estimated costs.

- **CV (cost variance).** This represents the difference between planned costs (that is, costs included in the baseline for a task) and the combination of actual costs recorded to date plus any remaining estimated costs. This number is expressed as a negative number if you're under budget and as a positive number if you're like the rest of us (over budget).

Studying these numbers can help you see what it has cost to get where you are today on your project.

You can use the Euro Currency Converter to show your cost figures in another currency. Choose View➪Toolbars➪Euro Currency Converter to display the toolbar which includes an Add New Currency wizard for defining new cost fields.

Calculations behind the Scenes

While you're happily entering resource hours and fixed costs into your project, Project is busy making calculations that can shift around task timing and resource workload in your plan. These calculations relate to how tasks are updated, how the critical path is determined, and how earned value is calculated. If you're a control freak, you'll be happy to know that you can, to some extent, control how Project goes about making these calculations.

Going automatic or manual

By default, Project is on automatic as far as calculations go. When you make a change to your plan, Project recalculates totals, the critical path, and so on without your having to lift a finger. However, you can change that default setting and have Project wait for you to initiate calculations manually. You do so in the Calculation tab of the Options dialog box (Tools ⇨ Options). Figure 14-9 shows the settings available there.

If you change the Calculation mode to Manual, you must click the Calculate Now button in this dialog box any time you want Project to perform all its calculations. You also have the choice here of setting different modes for only the current project or for all open projects.

So why would you choose to use manual calculation? You might want to make a lot of changes and not have Project take the milliseconds required to recalculate between each change, slowing down your entry work. You can put things on manual, make all your changes, and then use the Calculate Now button to make all the changes at once.

In addition, because it's not always easy to spot all the items that have been recalculated when you make a series of changes, it might be easier to make all the changes in manual mode, print your Gantt Chart view, and *then* recalculate and compare the two. This approach shows you the cumulative calculations that occurred when all your changes were made so you can see whether you're happy with the revised plan. (This feature is especially useful for trying out what-if scenarios.)

Another calculation setting that you can arrange to occur automatically or manually is resource leveling. Choose Tools ⇨ Level Resources, and you can make settings in the Resource Leveling dialog box for automatic calculation. With this active, Project automatically runs the leveling calculation whenever a resource becomes overallocated in your project.

Earned-value options

Your first question about earned value probably is, "Why does Project use *BWCP* in its column names but *earned value* in the Options dialog box?" Don't ask. Just be glad I taught you both terms in a previous section ("Acronym Soup: BCWP, ACWP, EAC, and CV").

The second question you probably have is, "What do the settings you can make to the earned-value calculation do to your project?" Well, start by looking at Figure 14-10, which shows you what's behind the Earned Value button on the Calculation tab of the Options dialog box.

The Default Task Earned Value Method setting provides two choices:

✓ **% Complete.** This setting calculates earned value using the percent complete that you record on each task. This assumes that for a task that's halfway complete, half the work has taken place.

✔ **Physical % Complete.** Use this setting if you want to enter a percent of completion that is not based on a straight percent-complete calculation. For example, if you have a four-week task to do a mail survey, 50 percent of the effort might happen in the first 25 percent of the duration of the project — designing, printing, and mailing the survey. Nothing happens for two weeks while you wait for responses, and then there's a flurry of activity when the responses come back. So a straight calculation that 50 percent of the task is completed 50 percent of the way through wouldn't be accurate. If your projects have a lot of tasks like this, you might consider changing your settings to use this method. Then, you can display the Physical % Complete column in your Gantt Chart sheet, and enter what you consider more accurate percent-complete information for each task.

The second setting in the Earned Value dialog box indicates which baseline to use for calculations. Remember, *earned value* is the value of work completed, expressed in dollars, according to the baseline: A $2,000 task at 50 percent complete (for example) has a $1,000 earned value of work performed. Therefore the baseline against which you calculate this value is hugely important. Choose any of the 11 possible baselines you may have saved in your project here. When you've made these two choices, click Close to close the Earned Value dialog box.

You should explore one more option in the Options dialog box that concerns earned value calculation. The Edits to Total Task % Complete Will Be Spread to the Status Date option, which is not selected by default, affects how Project distributes changes in your schedule. If this option is left deselected, calculations go to the end of the duration of tasks in progress, rather than up to the status date or the current date. If you do select this option, calculations spread changes across your plan up to the status date or the current date, and no farther. Selecting this choice helps you see changes to your project in increments of time, rather than across the life of tasks in progress.

If I were you, I'd leave the Edits to Total Task % option not selected for the most accurate reflection of progress on your project.

How many critical paths are enough?

The last group of settings on the Calculation tab of the Options dialog box concerns critical path calculations.

The Inserted Projects Are Calculated Like Summary Tasks option is straightforward. If you insert another project as a task in your project, having this setting selected allows Project to calculate one critical path for your entire project. If you don't select it, any projects you insert are treated like other projects — that is, they're not taken into account in the master project's critical-path calculations. If an inserted project won't have an impact on your project's timing, you may want to clear this option.

If following one project's critical path is too tame for you, try getting critical with multiple paths. By selecting the Calculate Multiple Critical Paths option, you set up Project to calculate a different critical path for each set of tasks in your project. Doing so can be helpful if you want to identify tasks that, if delayed, will cause you to miss your final project deadline or the goals of a single phase in your project.

Finally, you can establish what puts a task on the critical path by specifying the number of days of slack critical tasks might have. By default, tasks with no slack are on the critical path. But you can change this situation if you want to be alerted that tasks with only one day of slack are critical — figuring that one day isn't much padding and that these tasks are still in jeopardy.

If you want all the settings on the Calculation tab to pertain to all projects, click the Set as Default button before clicking OK to save the new settings in the Options dialog box.

Chapter 15

You're Behind: Now What?

There comes a time in almost every project when you feel like the floor dropped out from under you. Suddenly — and this one just snuck up on you — you're $20,000 over budget. Or you're going to miss that drop-dead deadline by two weeks. All the aspirin in the world isn't going to solve this one.

Of course, you have a general idea of what happened because you're smart, you kept in touch with your team, and you have Project and all its columns of data. Still, somehow things are off track and you need to take action at this point. First, you have to justify what occurred (abbreviated CYA), and then you have to fix things so that you can go forward and just maybe save your project, your job, or both.

How do you save the day when things go off track? What you have to do at this point involves analyzing your options and making some tough choices. This is stuff you did before you ever heard of Microsoft Project. But Project can help you try out some possible solutions and anticipate the likely results. After you decide what to do, you have to implement your solutions in Project.

Justifying Yourself: Notes, Baselines, and Interim Plans

If you've kept interim plans, multiple baselines, and task notes in Project, it's much easier to explain how you got into this mess to the powers-that-be.

Interim plans and multiple baselines demonstrate how you made adjustments when major changes or problems occurred. Using these two items indicates to your boss that you were on top of things all the way and probably kept him or her in the loop by generating printouts or reports reflecting major changes as they occurred. (If you didn't, print them now from the interim plans or baselines you saved along the way — and watch them paint a picture of what happened.)

A *baseline* saves all project data; an *interim plan* saves only the start and finish dates of tasks in the project. Chapter 12 deals with interim plans and baselines.

To view or print information from various baselines or interim plans, follow these steps:

1. **Display the Gantt Chart view.**

2. **Right-click the column heading area of the sheet pane and then click Insert Column.**

   The Column Definition dialog box appears, as shown in Figure 15-1.

Figure 15-1:
Use this
dialog box
to insert
as many
columns as
you like in
any view
with a sheet
pane.

Column Definition	☒
Field name:	ID ▼
Title:	
Align title:	Center ▼
Align data:	Right ▼
Width:	10 ⬍ ☑ Header Text Wrapping
	Best Fit OK Cancel

3. **In the Field Name box, click a column name.**

   For example, you might choose Start 1-10 and Finish 1-10 for any one of your interim plans (or choose Baseline through Baseline 10 for baseline data).

4. **Click OK to display the column; if you need to, repeat Steps 1 through 3 to display additional columns.**

In addition to interim plans and baselines, task notes should include information about resource performance on a task, vendor problems, or late deliveries. Notes that are especially important to add are those you make when someone in authority over you has asked for a change and okayed more money or time to make that change (don't worry, this hardly ever happens).

To add a note to a task, either display the task note column in a sheet pane or double-click a task and add the note on the Notes tab of the Task Information dialog box.

What If?

Just as you can get too close to a problem to see a solution, you can get too close to your project to recognize what you need to do. Using Project's filtering and sorting features, you can slice and dice various aspects of your project a little differently to get a fresh perspective.

You can also use tools such as resource leveling to solve resource conflicts. Resource leveling might not always solve problems to your taste, but it's a good way to let Project show you one what-if scenario that will solve most resource problems instantly.

Sorting things out

Sometimes when things won't sort themselves out, it's time to sort your tasks. Project allows you to sort tasks by several criteria, including start date, finish date, priority, and cost.

How can sorting help you? Well, here are a few examples:

- ✔ If you're trying to cut your costs, consider sorting tasks by cost. Then you can focus on the most expensive tasks first to see whether there's room to trim nice-to-have-but-pricey items.

- ✔ If you want to delete some tasks to save time, display tasks by priority and then look at the low-priority tasks as the first candidates for the waste bin.

- ✔ To review task timing, sort by duration in descending order to see the longest tasks first.

If you want to apply a preset sorting order, simply choose Project ⇨ Sort and then click an option in the submenu, such as by Start Date or by Cost.

If you want to see additional sort criteria — or sort by more than one criterion — follow these steps:

1. Choose Project ⇨ Sort ⇨ Sort by.

The Sort dialog box appears, as shown in Figure 15-2.

Figure 15-2:
This dialog
box allows
you to sort
by three
criteria in
ascending
or
descending
order.

2. **In the Sort By list, select a criterion.**

3. **Click either Ascending (to sort from lowest to highest) or Descending (to sort from highest to lowest).**

   With a date field, the sorting order would be soonest to latest and latest to soonest, respectively; with a text field, alphabetical would be the order.

4. **If you want a second criterion, click the first Then By box and make a selection.**

   For example, if you choose to sort first by Cost and then by Type, tasks are sorted from least expensive to most expensive, and then (within each cost level) by type (Fixed Duration, Fixed Units, and Fixed Work).

5. **If you want to add a third criterion, click the second Then By box and make a selection.**

6. **Click Sort.**

To return to your original task order, choose Project ⇨ Sort ⇨ by ID. Tasks are now back in *task ID number* order, Project's standard sorting criterion.

Filtering

Chapter 10 deals with how you create and apply filters in Project. Now's a good time to call on your knowledge of those features. Especially in larger projects, where it's not always easy to scan hundreds of tasks and notice which are running late or over budget, filters can hone in on exactly where your trouble lies.

You can choose to have tasks that don't meet filter criteria removed from your display or simply highlighted on-screen.

Table 15-1 lists some filters that are useful when you're trying to identify and solve problems with your schedule.

Table 15-1	Filters to Isolate Problems
Filter Name	*What It Displays*
Critical	Tasks in the project that must be completed according to schedule to make your final deadline (critical path)
Cost Overbudget	Tasks that exceed budgeted expenditures
Incomplete Tasks	Tasks that haven't been marked as complete
Late/Overbudget Tasks	Tasks that are running later than their baseline estimate and are over budget
Should Start by	Tasks that should have started as of a specified date
Slipped/Late Progress	Tasks that are running late and have no progress recorded
Update Needed	A task that should have had progress tracked by now
Overallocated Resources	Tasks that have resources assigned who are over booked at some point during the life of the task
Slipping Assignments	Tasks that involve resource work that should have begun by now
Work Incomplete	Tasks that should have had all their work recorded by now
Work Overbudget	More work hours have been put in on the task than you had estimated

Don't see all these choices in the More Filters dialog box? Remember, when you use this dialog box (Project➪Filtered for➪More Filters), you have to click the Task option to see task-related filters and the Resource option to see resource-related filters.

You might also consider exporting your Project information to a program such as Excel so you can use analysis tools such as Pivot tables to figure out what's going on.

Examining the critical path

One of the most useful filters is the one called Critical. This displays or high-lights all tasks that are on the critical path. If you're running late, knowing which tasks can't slip helps you identify where there is no room for delay and, conversely, where you can delay noncritical tasks and still meet your deadline. You might use the Critical filter to help you determine how to free up overallocated resources or get a task that's running late back on track.

You can look at the critical path in any Gantt Chart or Network Diagram view. Figure 15-3 shows the Gantt Chart view of a project with the critical path highlighted. Figure 15-4 shows the Network Diagram view with the same filter applied.

If you need a closer look at task timing, consider modifying the timescale display to use smaller increments of time, such as days or hours. To do so, right-click the timescale itself and then click Timescale.

Use resource leveling one more time

If you performed manual resource leveling earlier in your project to solve resource conflicts, consider trying it again. With changes to tasks and tracked activity, resource leveling may give you some new options to solve conflicts.

If resource leveling is set to automatic, Project automatically performs this calculation every time you modify your schedule. To see whether this is set to automatic or manual, choose Tools ➪ Level Resources (as in Figure 15-5). If it's set to manual, click the Level Now button to run resource leveling.

Figure 15-3: The Gantt Chart view shows you columns of data and a more precise timescale for each task.

	Task Name	Duration
128	Rough-in mechanical in mas	4 wks
129	Rough-in mechanical in dryw	2 wks
130	Install duct in building chase	3 wks
131	Set HVAC trim and test and	4 wks
132	− **Final Clean-up and Occupar**	**60 days**
133	Install hard tile flooring in coi	1 wk
134	Clean hard tile floors	4 days
135	Remove debris from building	4 days
136	Substantial completion date	1 day
137	− Complete Final Inspections	6 days
138	Complete elevator inspectio	3 days
139	Perform architect's inspectio	1 day
140	Perform local building agenc	1 day
141	Perform fire marshal's inspec	1 day
142	Complete punch list items from	2 wks
143	Obtain certificate of occupancy	2 days
144	Issue final completion documer	1 day
145	Issue final request for payment	1 day

Figure 15-4:
The
Network
Diagram
view gives
you a
feel for
workflow
and depen-
dencies
among
tasks.

Figure 15-5:
Here's
where you
determine
whether you
or Project
will control
resource
leveling.

Using the Analysis Toolbar

Though your project woes might make you feel like entering analysis with an expensive shrink, save some money and just use the Analysis toolbar instead.

The Analysis toolbar allows you to use the Program, Evaluation, and Review Technique (PERT — cute, huh?) to figure out a task's duration based on information you enter about optimistic, pessimistic, and expected scenarios. Getting information about these three possible futures can help you analyze where your project is headed if you don't make some changes.

The default settings for pessimistic, optimistic, and expected durations of a task suggest that the expected outcome is most likely, and both the optimistic and pessimistic outcomes are equally likely. You can change that by modifying the weight you give to each task scenario. For example, the default probability for expected is 4 out of 6; pessimistic and optimistic are each 1 out of 6. If you adjust the pessimistic setting to 3 out of 6, you're saying it's more likely than the optimistic outcome. Project then performs a calculation to create a weighted average of the three. This weighted average will provide a likely task duration, pessimistic task duration, and optimistic task duration.

To display the Analysis toolbar, right-click on the toolbar area and click on Analysis on the toolbar list. Once the Analysis toolbar is displayed, click on the PERT Analysis button to display the PERT analysis toolbar, shown in Figure 15-6.

To perform an analysis, first you have to enter the three categories of durations. Then you can perform the calculation and display three possible futures in your Gantt Chart. Follow these steps to use the PERT analysis:

1. **Select the task you want to analyze.**

2. **Display the PERT Analysis toolbar and click the PERT Entry Sheet button.**

   The PERT Entry Sheet is displayed.

3. **Enter the optimistic, expected, and pessimistic durations for the task in the appropriate fields.**

4. **Click Calculate PERT.**

Project estimates a task duration based on the average of the three durations you entered. You can click the Optimistic Gantt, Expected Gantt, and Pessimistic Gantt buttons on the PERT Analysis toolbar to see what each scenario does to your project timing.

Microsoft Project - COMCONST

File   Edit   View   Insert   Format   Tools   Project   Collaborate   Window   Help

No Group

Show ▾   Arial   8   B I U ≡ ≡ ≡   All Tasks

PERT Analysis | Visio WBS Chart Wizard ▾ | XML Reporting Wizard

Figure 15-6:
You can
view
your Gantt
Chart
from an
expected,
optimistic,
or pes-
simistic
viewpoint
using these
tools.

		ⓘ	Task Name	Duration	April 1 3/27 4/3	April 11 4/10 4/17	April 21 4/24
	1		**Three-story Office Building (76,**	**344 days**			
	2		− **General Conditions**	**12 days**			
	3		Receive notice to proceed ar	3 days			
	4		Submit bond and insurance	2 days			
	5		Prepare and submit project s	2 days			
	6		Prepare and submit schedul	2 days			
	7		Obtain building permits	4 days			
	8		Submit preliminary shop dra	1 wk			
	9		Submit monthly requests for	1 day			
	10		− **Long Lead Procurement**	**70 days**			
	11		Submit shop drawings and o	2 wks			
	12		Submit shop drawings and o	2 wks			
	13		Submit shop drawings and o	2 wks			
	14		Submit shop drawings and o	2 wks			
	15		Submit shop drawings and o	2 wks			

Ready   EXT CAPS NUM SCRL OVR

If you want to change the default weights for each scenario, click the Set PERT Weights button on the PERT Analysis toolbar and enter new values. Remember that the sum of all three numbers has to be equal to 6, so you'll have to change at least two fields to make things jibe.

How Adding People or Time Affects Your Project

It's part of corporate human nature to want to throw money and people at problems, and in some cases that instinct is on target. But you don't always have the ability to draw on endless supplies of resources or an endless amount of time to play with. Because of this, you may have to play around with a combination of options involving time and resources.

Hurry up!

Saving time in Project means doing things faster or adjusting the timing of things to suck up slack. But you'll find that making this adjustment can be like an intricate puzzle: Correct one thing and something else pops up to cause you aggravation.

To accomplish work faster, you have two options: Get more people to help out on tasks or modify the scope of tasks. Adding people adds money. So you might get back on track time-wise but it will cost you. Modifying the scope of the task might have an effect on its quality. If you do two inspections instead of three, or shorten your Q&A cycle by a week, you may run the risk of other types of problems down the road.

Changing the timing of tasks and shifting dependencies uses up slack to make up for delays but may leave you with no wiggle room. Next time a problem comes up, you'll be up against the wall with no slack to save you.

In reality, it's often a combination of small modifications in both areas of time and money that help you save the day.

Throwing people at the problem

With effort-driven tasks, things get accomplished when the specified amount of effort is expended. So, a task with a duration of 3 days based on a standard calendar will require 3 days times 8 hours a day to be completed, or 24 hours of effort. One resource performing this task working full time will take three days to complete it. Three resources working full time will take one day to complete 24 hours of work. When you add resources to such a task, Project automatically recalculates its duration.

But beyond simply adding resources to a task, you can also make modifications to existing assignments.

Changing how resources are assigned

On any given project, you might have dozens (or even hundreds) of resources working on tasks. All those people are working according to their working calendars, the percentage of resource time you assigned to particular tasks, and their ability to do the job. Take a look at how you assigned folks to begin with, and see whether you could save some time or money by modifying those assignments.

You can modify assignments in several ways:

- If someone is working at, say, only 50 percent of capacity on a task, consider upping the person's assignment units.
- If you have someone available who could perform a given task more quickly, switch resources on a task and then shorten its duration.

✔ Consider having some people work overtime or be overbooked at various points during the project. You may have modified an overbooked resource's assignments earlier to get rid of a conflict, but now you find that there's no choice but to have the resource work that occasional 12- or 14-hour day!

Remembering the consequences

Before you get carried away making changes to resources, think a minute. Adding resources to effort-driven tasks can shrink them, helping your project get back on track. But depending on the resources' hourly rates, it may cost you more.

Remember that three people working on a task won't necessarily geometrically shrink the duration of the task. That's because three people have to coordinate their efforts, hold meetings, and generally do the things people do when they interact that make their work a tad less efficient than when they work alone. If you add resources, Project shrinks the task geometrically: Consider going in and adding a little time to the task to accommodate the inefficiencies of multiple resources.

The other concern about adding resources to tasks is that it could cause more resource conflicts, with already busy people getting overbooked on too many tasks that happen in the same timeframe. But if you have the resources and they have the skills and the time, beefing up the workforce is definitely one way to perform some tasks more quickly.

To add resources to a task, you can use the Resources tab in the Task Information dialog box or choose the task and click the Assign Resources tool button on the Standard toolbar.

Shifting dependencies and task timing

Time is a project manager's greatest enemy. There's never enough, and what there is gets eaten up like a bag of Quarter Pounders in a room full of hungry Little Leaguers.

Here are some ways you can modify task timing to save time:

✔ **Delete a task.** You heard me. If a task represents a step that could be skipped, just get rid of it. This doesn't happen often, but sometimes — on rethinking your project — you realize that a few things aren't necessary or have already been handled by someone else.

✔ **Adjust dependencies.** Couldn't the revision of the manual start a few days before *all* the feedback comes back? Could the electrical and plumbing go on at the same time instead of one after the other (assuming that the electrician and the plumber can stay out of each other's way)? Use the Predecessors tab of the Task Information dialog box shown in Figure 15-7 to modify dependencies.

✔ **Modify constraints.** Perhaps you set a task to start no earlier than the first of the year because you don't want to spend money on it until the new fiscal year budget kicks in. To save time, consider whether you could allow it to start a week before the end of the year — and just bill the costs in January. Examine any constraints such as this — specifically, those created to verify the timing logic.

✔ **Check external dependencies.** If you've inserted a hyperlinked task to represent another project and set dependencies with tasks in your project, check with the other project manager to see whether he or she can hurry up some things. Or if the timing relationship isn't absolutely critical, delete the hyperlink to the other project — it could be slowing you down more than you know.

Figure 15-7:
Review a
task's
depen-
dencies
here, and
modify the
Lag column
to include a
negative
number to
allow tasks
to overlap.

Task Information					
General	Predecessors	Resources	Advanced	Notes	Custom Fields

Name: Rough grade site (cut and fill)   Duration: 1w   ☐ Estimated

Predecessors:

26

ID	Task Name	Type	Lag
26	Stone site access and temporary parking area	Finish-to-Start (FS)	0d
23	Prepare site - lay down yard and temporary fenc	Finish-to-Start (FS)	0d

Help   OK   Cancel

If you've set resource leveling to automatic, Project may be delaying some tasks until overbooked resources are freed up. Choose Tools⇨Level Resources and change the setting to manual.

When All Else Fails

Okay. You've monkeyed with resource assignments and shifted task dependencies around to save time, and deleted tasks and assigned cheaper workers to save money. But it's still not enough. This is the scenario where you have to say to your boss, "You can have it on time, you can have it on budget, or you can have quality work: Choose two."

If your boss throws money at you, go ahead and add resources to tasks, as discussed in the section of this chapter called "Throwing people at the problem." If she opts for time or quality, read on.

All the time in the world

If your boss is willing to give you more time, grab it. When you do, you have to update your project in a few ways:

- ✔ **Add to slack.** If you have a Slack task, you can simply add to its duration, giving more waffle room to all other tasks.

- ✔ **Modify task durations.** Take tasks that are running late and give them more time to be accomplished. In Project, this means increasing their durations or pushing out their start dates to a later time.

- ✔ **Review your task constraints.** If you specified that some tasks couldn't finish any later than a certain date but now you're moving your deadline out three months, you may be able to remove or adjust those original constraints accordingly.

After you've worked in the extra time provided to you, make sure that the new timing of tasks doesn't cause new resource conflicts, review the Resource Graph view, and then reset your baseline to reflect the new schedule. You reset a baseline by choosing Tools ➪ Tracking ➪ Save Baseline. When asked whether you're sure that you want to overwrite the existing baseline, reply Yes. Or choose Baseline 1-10 in the Save Baseline dialog box to save to a different baseline and preserve the original.

Don't forget to inform your team of the new timing and provide them with an updated version of your plan.

And now for something completely different

If your manager tells you to cut some corners and sacrifice quality, you have license to modify the scope of the project. You can cut out some tasks that might ensure higher quality, such as a final proofreading of the employee manual. You can hire cheaper workers. You can use cheaper paper or computer equipment.

In Project, this means you have to do the following:

Goal	*Action*
Take less steps	Delete tasks (click the ID of the task in the Gantt Chart view and press Delete).

Use less expensive resources   Delete one set of resource assignments and assign other resources to tasks in the Assign Resources dialog box.

Use less expensive materials   Change the unit price for materials you've created in the Resource Sheet view, as shown in Figure 15-8.

Figure 15-8: Use the Resource Sheet to quickly modify unit prices.

You can also take a more sweeping approach: Just redefine the goal of the project. If your goal was to launch a new product line, perhaps you can modify your goal to simply manage the design of the new product, and leave the launch to a later date or another project manager. If you were supposed to produce 10,000 widgets, could your company get along with 7,500? To make such changes, you may have to slice-and-dice entire phases of your project — or even start from scratch and build a new plan.

Consider saving your current project plan with a new name to give you a head start. Clear the baseline (Tools⇨Tracking⇨Clear Baseline), make your modifications, and then save a new baseline.

What Does Project Have to Say About This?

One final word of caution: When you take certain steps, such as deleting tasks or modifying dependency relationships, your action might just cause Project to alert you to a potential problem you hadn't thought of. If that happens, Project shows you a Planning wizard dialog box like the one in Figure 15-9. If you make changes on your own instead of using the Planning wizard, you may be more apt to back yourself into a problem situation.

Figure 15-9:
Here the wizard wants to be sure that you know that deleting a summary task takes all its subtasks with it.

> **Planning Wizard**
>
> 'Long Lead Procurement' is a summary task. Deleting it will delete all its subtasks as well.
>
> You can:
>
> ⦿ Continue. Delete 'Long Lead Procurement' and its subtasks.
>
> ◯ Cancel. Don't delete any tasks.
>
> [OK] [Cancel] [Help]
>
> ☐ Don't tell me about this again.

These dialog boxes offer you options — typically to go ahead and proceed, to cancel, or to proceed but with some modification. Read these alerts carefully and consider the pros and cons of what will happen if you proceed.

Chapter 16

Spreading the News: Reporting

· ·

In This Chapter

▶ Generating standard reports

▶ Creating custom reports

▶ Using the XML Reporting wizard

▶ Using graphics and formatting in reports

▶ Making printer settings

▶ Working with report legends

· ·

*H*ere it is. The big payoff. The reward you get for inputting all those task names, entering all those resource hourly rates, and tracking activity on dozens of tasks during those late-hour sessions in the first hectic weeks of your project. You finally get to print a *report,* getting something tangible out of Project that you can hand out at meetings and impress your boss with.

Reports help you communicate about your project, conveying information about resource assignments, how costs are accumulating, and what activities are in progress or coming up soon. You can take advantage of built-in reports or customize those reports to include the data that's most relevant to you.

Knowing that you'll want to impress people, Project has also made it possible to apply certain formatting settings to reports and add drawings to help get your point across. There's even a new XML Reporting wizard to help you generate polished-looking online reports.

Off the Rack: Standard Reports

Standard reports are already designed for you, offering a lot of choices regarding the information you can include. You don't have to do much more than click a few buttons to generate them. Essentially, you select a category of report, choose a specific report, and print it. If the plain-vanilla version of a report isn't quite right, you can modify standard reports in a variety of ways.

You can also print any view in Project; just display the view and click the Print tool button. The entire project is printed in whatever view you have on the screen at the time. Or you can choose File➪Print; in the Print dialog box, you can choose to print only certain pages of your project or only a specific date range from the timescale. Any filters or grouping you've applied will pertain to the printed document.

What's available

Project has five categories of standard reports: Overview, Current Activities, Costs, Assignments, and Workload. Each category contains several pre-designed reports, as you can see in the dialog box for Overview Reports shown in Figure 16-1, for a total of 22 standard reports.

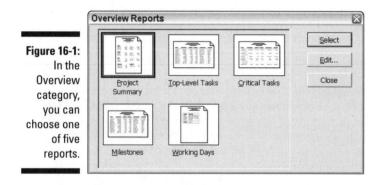

Figure 16-1: In the Overview category, you can choose one of five reports.

Standard reports vary in content, format (for example, a table versus a columnar report), and sometimes in page orientation (landscape or portrait). You can edit each report to change its name, the time period it covers, the table of information it's based on, and filters applied to it. You can also sort information as you generate the report and add formatting such as borders or gridlines.

Going with the standard

The standard report is simplicity itself. You could practically do this one in your sleep.

Or better yet, you could create a macro to generate your reports with a single-keystroke shortcut (more about macros in Chapter 17).

Follow these steps to generate any standard report:

1. **Choose View ⇨ Reports.**

   The Reports dialog box appears, as shown in Figure 16-2.

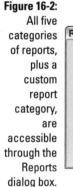

2. **Click the category of standard report you want, and then click Select.**

   A dialog box named after the category of report you selected appears, as shown in Figure 16-1.

3. **Click one of the standard reports shown here, and then click Select.**

   A preview of the report appears, like the one of Unstarted Tasks shown in Figure 16-3.

4. **To print, click the Print button.**

Clicking Close will return you to the Reports dialog box, which lists the category of reports. You'll have to start all over again if you do this.

When you click Print, with some reports an additional dialog box appears, asking for a date range or other data specific to that report.

A standard report, with a twist

Some people are happy with the cookie-cutter standard reports that Project provides. But even though standard reports are prebuilt, you can still get in under the hood and tinker a little.

Figure 16-3:
You may
have to click
a report
preview to
zoom in so
you can
read its
details.

You can edit three categories of things about a standard report:

- **Definition.** This includes the report name, the time period, the table of information, any filters applied, and whether or not summary tasks should appear.

- **Details.** Details can be included for tasks (such as notes or predecessors) and for resource assignments (such as notes or cost). You can also choose to show totals and add a border around the report, or gridlines between details.

- **Sort.** You can sort by up to three criteria in ascending or descending order.

When modifying standard reports, you'll encounter some variations. For example, when you try to edit a Project Summary report, all you get is a text formatting dialog box. But the majority of reports are edited through one dialog box, as shown in the procedure that follows.

To edit a standard report, follow these steps:

1. Choose View ⇨ Reports.

The Reports dialog box appears.

2. **Click a category of report, and then click Select.**

3. **Click a specific report, and then click Edit.**

   Depending on the type of report you chose, the Resource Report, Task Report, or Crosstab Report dialog box appears. The settings in these dialog boxes are the same, except for some default choices (for example, which filter is applied). Figure 16-4 shows a Task Report dialog box.

Task Report

| Definition | Details | Sort |

Name: Top Level Tasks   OK

Period: Entire Project   Cancel

Count: 1   Text...

Table: Summary

Filter: Top Level Tasks   ☐ Highlight   Help

☑ Show summary tasks

☐ Gray bands

Figure 16-4:
You can
make three
tabs' worth
of settings.

4. **Click the Definition tab, if it's not already displayed, and make your selections:**

   a. **If you want a new name for the report, type the name in the Name box.**

   b. **In the Period box, click the period of time you want the report to reflect.**

      If rather than choosing Entire Project, you choose an increment of time in the Period box, such as week, you can set the Count counter to reflect the number of increments (for example, **3** for three weeks, which prints the report on the project in three-week increments).

   c. **If you'd like a different table of information to be included, make a selection in the Table box.**

      If you don't change this setting, the table currently displayed in the project will be used.

   d. **If you want to apply a filter to tasks, select one in the Filter box.**

      To highlight tasks that match the filter's criteria, rather than simply exclude those tasks that don't meet the criteria from the report, simply select the Highlight option.

5. **Click the Details tab (shown in Figure 16-5) and make your selections:**

    a. **Select various check boxes to include different types of information, such as task notes or resource assignment costs.**

    b. **If you want a border around these elements, select the Border Around Details option.**

    c. **If you want gridlines in the report, select the Gridlines Between Details option.**

        This gives your report more of the appearance of a table.

    d. **To include totals of dollar amounts or hours, select Show Totals.**

Figure 16-5:
Some of
these
options may
be selected
already,
depending
on the
standard
report
you're
editing.

6. **Click the Sort tab, and make your selections:**

    a. **In the Sort By box, click a sort criterion, and then click either Ascending or Descending to choose a sort order.**

    b. **If you want to sort by additional criteria, repeat Step 6a with the Then By boxes.**

7. **Click OK to save your settings.**

8. **In the Reports dialog box, click Select to generate the report preview.**

You can find more details about sorting in Chapter 15.

Crosstabs: A different animal

Certain reports, called Crosstab reports, present slightly different settings when you edit them. Figure 16-6 shows the Definition tab of the Crosstab Report dialog box. A *crosstab report* tabulates a unique piece of data relative to column and row definitions. Essentially, the cell formed by the column and row intersection represents the unique data.

Figure 16-6:
Here you
have to
choose
which three
elements
define the
crosstab.

For example, you might have columns that list days and rows that list resources. The piece of information where the column and row intersects is resource work on a particular day. The report would show the hours of work by each resource, by day.

When you edit a crosstab, you define the column, the row, and the piece of data being compared. On the Details tab for the crosstab, you can make settings to include row or column totals, to insert gridlines, and to display values of 0.

A Custom Job

Not impressed with the standard reports? Or perhaps none of those reports quite fits your information needs? That's okay. You can create as many custom reports as your heart desires.

A custom report starts out with a report type, which can be task, resource, monthly calendar, or crosstab. After you choose that basic category, you simply work with the same Reports dialog box that you use to edit a standard report.

Follow these steps to begin the process of creating a custom report:

1. **Choose View ➪ Reports.**

   The Reports dialog box appears.

2. **Click the Custom category, and then click Select.**

The Custom Reports dialog box appears, as shown in Figure 16-7. You have two options: You can edit an existing report, or you can create an entirely new custom report.

Figure 16-7:
The Custom Reports dialog box lets you start with an existing set of data.

Custom Reports

Reports:

Base Calendar
Budget Report
Cash Flow
Completed Tasks
Critical Tasks
Crosstab
Earned Value
Milestones
Overallocated Resources
Overbudget Resources
Overbudget Tasks

New...
Edit...
Copy...
Organizer...

Preview   Setup...   Print   Cancel

3. **Decide whether you want to base your custom report on an existing report or create a new report, and proceed accordingly.**

    a. **If you want to base your custom report on an existing report, select a report in the Reports list, and then click Edit.**

    b. **If you want to create a report, not based on any other report, click New. Click one of the categories in the dialog box that appears, and then click OK.**

4. **In the Report dialog box, make choices to define your new report, and then click OK.**

The choices in this dialog box are discussed in detail previously in this chapter, in the section titled "A standard report, with a twist."

If you create a custom report based on an existing report, be sure to give it a unique name.

Going Online with the XML Reporting Wizard

Everybody's online these days, and why should you be left out? Wouldn't it be nice to generate reports in nice, neat Web format to post online? If that sounds good to you, then you'll be glad to hear that Project 2003 offers a new feature that makes it possible: an XML Reporting Wizard.

The wizard works with templates. There are only a few built-in templates, but you can also build your own.

To create your own templates, you save a Project file in XML format.

To run the wizard, follow these steps:

1. **Choose View➪Toolbars➪XML Reporting Wizard.**

   The XML Reporting Wizard dialog box appears.

2. **Click Next. In the dialog box that appears, specify one of two options:**

   a. **Choose to generate a New File, which will be based on the currently active Project file.**

   b. **Specify an existing HTML report you want to work with.**

3. **Click Next.**

4. **The Save Project as XML File dialog box appears.**

   The file is saved to the Office templates file by default, in XML format.

5. **Enter a different name for the file if you like in the File Name box.**

6. **Click Save.**

7. **In the dialog box that appears, click Browse to select the XSL/T template to apply.**

   The Select XSL/T Template dialog box appears.

8. **Click on a template, then click Open.**

9. **Click Next.**

   To complete the HTML report, choose one of two options in the final wizard dialog box:

   a. **Click Preview to preview the report in your browser.**

   The report appears in Web format. Close your browser to return to the wizard.

   b. **Click Save to save the report to a file.**

   The Save As dialog box appears. Give the file a name and click Save to return to the wizard.

10. **Click Finish to finish the wizard and close the final dialog box.**

Spiffing Things Up

These days, image is everything. You and your project may be judged to some extent by how professional your printed information looks. Even if your project is a million dollars over budget and four months behind, making your reports or other printouts look good can make delivering bad news easier.

To create impressive documents, make sure you cross the *t*'s of formatting text and dot the *i*'s of visual design.

Using graphics in Project

Wouldn't your company logo look spiffy in the header of your report? Or what about including a picture of the new product box in the Gantt Chart view of your New Product Launch project?

Graphics can add visual information or just plain make your plan look nicer. You can insert graphics in your project file by using three methods. You can

✔ Cut and paste a graphic from another file.

✔ Insert a link to an existing graphics file. Linking keeps your Project file smaller.

✔ Embed a graphic. Embedding lets you edit the graphic's contents in Project, using the tools of an image program such as Paint.

You can't add graphics willy-nilly, however. You can add graphics in only a few places: the chart pane of any Gantt Chart view, a task note, a resource note, or a header, footer, or legend used in reports or printouts of views.

You might put pictures of resources in the resource note field so that you can remember who's who. Or you might include a photo of your corporate head-quarters in the header of your report, for example.

Remember, graphics files swell your Project file like a sponge in a pail of water. If you're thinking of using a lot of graphics, be sure they don't detract from the main information in your printouts, or try linking to them instead of inserting them in the file.

Follow these steps to begin the process of inserting a graphic in your Gantt Chart, using the capability of object linking and embedding:

1. **Display the Gantt Chart view.**

2. **Choose Insert⇨Object.**

    The Insert Object dialog box appears, as shown in Figure 16-8.

If you want to insert an existing graphics file, do the following:

1. **In the Insert Object dialog box, select Create from File.**

   The choices in the dialog box change to those shown in Figure 16-9.

Insert Object

Object Type:

⦿ Create New:

○ Create from File:

Bitmap Image
CA Default RequestDenial Control
Calendar Control 11.0
CDDBControl Class
eDTWinSock Control
LEAD Main Control (12.0)
Media Clip
Microsoft Drawing 1.01

OK

Cancel

☐ Display As Icon

Result

Inserts a new Bitmap Image object into your document.

2. **Type the file name in the File box or click Browse to locate the file.**

3. **If you want to link to the file, select the Link option and then click OK.**

   If you don't select this option, the object will be embedded in your file.

4. **If you want to insert the object as an icon, select Display As Icon.**

   When you display the object as an icon, those viewing your project on a computer can click the icon to view the picture.

5. **Click OK.**

   The image appears in the Gantt Chart pane.

6. **You can then use the resizing nodes on the corners of the image to expand or shrink it, or click the image to move it around the pane.**

Insert Object

○ Create New:

⦿ Create from File:

File:

c:\documents and settings\owner\my d

Browse...   ☐ Link

OK

Cancel

☐ Display As Icon

Result

Inserts the contents of the file as an object into your document so that you may activate it using the application which created it.

If instead of inserting an existing graphics file, you want to insert a blank graphics file, follow these steps:

1. **Click Create New.**

2. **In the Object Type list, click the type of object you want to insert.**

   For example, you might select Bitmap Image, Microsoft Word Picture, or Paintbrush Picture.

3. **If you want to insert the object as an icon, select Display as Icon.**

   When you display the object as an icon, those viewing your project on a computer can click the icon to view the picture.

4. **Click OK.**

   You see a blank object box, along with tools, similar to the one in Paintbox (shown in Figure 16-10.)

5. **Use the tools of the program from which you inserted an object to make, draw, insert, or format the new graphic object.**

To insert an object into a notes field, open the Task or Resource Information dialog box, and then click the Insert Object tool. The Insert Object dialog box appears. Then just proceed as shown in the preceding steps. A similar tool is available in the Page Setup dialog box, where you can use the Header, Footer, or Legend tabs to insert objects.

Figure 16-10:
When you close this window you'll be back in your Project file; double-click on the object to open this editing environment any time you like.

Formatting reports

You probably cut your computing teeth by formatting text in word processors, so formatting reports will be a breeze. You have all the usual formatting options available to you whenever you generate a report in Project.

To edit report text, just follow these steps:

1. **Choose View ⇨ Reports.**

   The Reports dialog box appears.

2. **Click a report category, and then click Select.**

3. **In the Reports category dialog box that appears, click the specific report that you want to generate.**

4. **Click Edit.**

   The specific report dialog box opens. With some reports, the Text Styles dialog box opens at this point, because there are no other settings you can change in those reports. If this happens, skip Step 5 and proceed with Step 6.

5. **Click the Text button.**

   The Text Styles dialog box appears, as shown in Figure 16-11.

Figure 16-11: This dialog box contains many familiar text settings.

6. **In the Item to Change box, click the item that you want to format.**

7. **Make your selections in the Font, Font Style, Size, or Color boxes.**

8. **If you want to format another item, select it in the Item to Change box and repeat Step 7.**

9. **When you're finished, click OK.**

10. **To view the report in preview, click Select.**

As with any other business document, your goal in formatting text should be readability. Remember, in addition to dealing with neat columns of data, you also might be dealing with labels of dates or resource names wedged alongside taskbars in the chart pane. Keep the following points in mind when formatting Project text:

- Choose simple sans-serif fonts, such as Arial.

- If you're publishing your project on the Web, consider using Verdana, a font created for readability online.

- Consider your use of color. Will the printout be in color or black and white? Will the use of too many colors become confusing for the reader? Will certain colors, such as yellow, be difficult to read?

- Use a font size that is readable, without making it so big that the taskbar labels become too crowded.

- Avoid text effects that can make some text difficult to read (such as bold, italic, or underlining). Use such effects only to call attention to a few elements of your project.

Call the Printer!

The proof of the report is in the printing, but you should see to several adjustments before you click that button to print. With Project, it's not just margins or page orientation that you need to set (though you do have to set those, too). You can also put useful information in headers and footers, and set legends that help your reader understand the many bars, diamonds, and other graphic elements many Project views and reports display.

Working with Page Setup

The Page Setup dialog box can be used to control printouts of both reports and any currently displayed Project view. You get to this dialog box in slightly different ways:

✔ To make settings for printing the current view, choose File ➪ Page Setup.

✔ To modify the page setup for a report, you have to select Page Setup from the preview of the report. Choose View ➪ Reports, then click a report category, and then click a specific report. When you click Select to generate a specific report, the print preview appears. Click the Page Setup button that appears there.

The Page Setup dialog box, shown in Figure 16-12, contains six tabs. In the case of reports, all tabs might not be available to you. For example, reports don't contain graphic elements such as taskbars, so you can't set a legend to appear on them. Also, you have access to the View tab only when you're printing the currently displayed view.

Figure 16-12:
You can
control
how your
document is
laid out and
is printed.

When size is important

The Page tab contains some basic page settings that determine the orientation, the paper size, and the way the contents are scaled to fit the page. By making these settings, you are influencing how much can fit on each page and how many pages long your document will be.

Here are the choices you have on this tab (shown previously in Figure 16-12):

✔ **Portrait or Landscape orientation:** No doubt you've dealt with these before. Portrait is set up like the Mona Lisa; Landscape is like . . . well, having the long edge of the paper running across the top instead!

✔ **Scaling:** You can use the Adjust To or Fit To settings. The Adjust To setting works by a percentage of the original size. The Fit To setting gives you some control over scaling to fit to the width of a single page or the height of a single page.

✔ **Other:** This area is a catchall for two options: Paper Size and First Page Number. All the standard choices for paper size are available in the Paper Size list, including index cards and envelopes. First Page Number can be left as Auto (in which case the first page is numbered 1, the second page, 2, and so on), or you can enter another number there yourself.

Keeping things within the margins

I won't bore you by defining what a margin is. However, I will remind you that margins serve the dual purpose of controlling how much information can fit on each page and creating a border of white space that frames your document, making it cleaner looking and easier to read.

To set margins using the Page Setup dialog box, follow these steps:

1. Click the Margins tab, which is shown in Figure 16-13.

Figure 16-13:
As you modify margin settings, the preview shows you where they will appear on your page.

2. Use the arrows to set the Top, Bottom, Left, and Right margins.

Click the up arrow for a wider margin and the down arrow for a narrower margin.

3. **If you'd like a border representing the margin, use the Borders Around settings.**

   Here you can choose to print a border on Every Page, on only Outer Pages (this prints a border on the first and last pages only and is available only when printing a Network Diagram view), or None.

Setting margins to be less than 1/2 inch (.5) could cause your printed output to be cut off because printers can only print so close to the edge of a page.

Putting all the right stuff in headers and footers

Throughout the life of a project, you'll print many versions of your project, many reports, and many types of information using various tables. Headers and footers are a great feature to help you and your readers keep track of all this information.

You can use the Header (shown in Figure 16-14) and Footer tabs of the Page Setup dialog box to set and preview header and footer contents.

Figure 16-14:
The Header
and Footer
tabs are
identical:
One
controls
what
appears at
the top of
your page,
the other
what
appears at
the bottom.

You can get to this area of the Page Setup dialog box also by choosing View ➪ Header and Footer.

Here are the settings you can make on these tabs:

✔ Specify that the text you enter is to appear on the Left, at Center, or to the Right of the header or footer by clicking on one of those tabs and then typing the text.

✔ Format text using the tool buttons, or quickly insert such things as the page number, the date, or a picture file.

✔ Select additional standard text to insert by using the General and Project Fields lists. The General list includes such things as Total Page Count, Project Title, and Company Name. The Project Fields list includes all the fields available in Project. You might use these to alert the reader to key fields to review or the nature of the printout. To add General or Project Field items, select them from their respective lists and then click Add to add them to the Left, Center, or Right tab.

Working with a legend

A *legend* acts as a guide to the meanings of various graphic elements, as shown in Figure 16-15. The Legend tab bears a striking resemblance to the Header and Footer tabs, except that the legend is generated automatically, so all you can specify here is the text that fits in the box to the left of the legend.

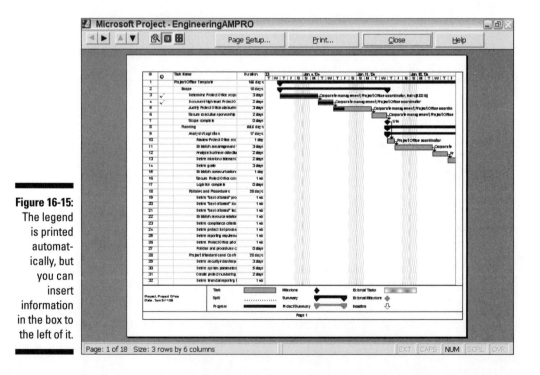

Figure 16-15:
The legend is printed automatically, but you can insert information in the box to the left of it.

The Legend tab of the Page Setup dialog box has only two settings that differ from the Header and Footer tabs:

- ✔ You can print the legend on every page or on a separate legend page — or you can decide to not print a legend.
- ✔ You can establish the width of the text area of the legend (the area where you can insert elements such as the page number or the date).

Unlike a header or footer, where you have to enter something to have anything appear, a legend prints by default. If you don't want a legend to print, choose this tab and then set the Legend On setting to None.

What to print?

If you're printing a currently displayed view, the View tab of the Page Setup dialog box is available to you, as shown in Figure 16-16.

Page Setup - Gantt Chart

| Page | Margins | Header | Footer | Legend | View |

☐ Print all sheet columns
☑ Print first `3` columns on all pages
☐ Print notes
☐ Print blank pages
☑ Fit timescale to end of page
☐ Print row totals for values within print date range
☐ Print column totals

Print Preview... | Options... | Print... | OK | Cancel

Figure 16-16: This tab is not available if you're printing a report.

You can make the following settings here:

- ✔ **Print All Sheet Columns:** Prints every sheet column in the view, whether or not it's currently visible on your screen. With this not selected, only the columns that show in your view will print.
- ✔ **Print First # Columns On All Pages:** Allows you to control a specific number of columns to print.

✔ **Print Notes:** Prints every task, resource, and assignment note. These items are printed on a separate notes page.

✔ **Print Blank Pages:** Choose this setting if you want blank pages, for example, a page that represents a time in your project when no tasks are occurring, to print anyway. If you want to view inactive as well as active periods for your project, choose this setting. If you want a smaller number of pages in your printout, don't choose this setting it.

✔ **Fit Timescale to End of Page:** Scales the timescale to allow you to fit more of your project on the page.

✔ **Print Row Totals for Values Within Print Date Range:** Adds a column containing row totals. Pertains to printouts of Usage views.

✔ **Print Column Totals:** Adds a column containing column totals. Pertains to printouts of Usage views.

Get a preview

There are movie previews, fall fashion previews, and in software, print previews. The Print Preview feature is accessible from many places in Project:

✔ Choose File➪Print Preview (to preview the current view).

✔ Click the Print Preview button on the Standard toolbar.

✔ Click Print Preview on any tab of the Page Setup dialog box.

✔ Generate a print preview when you select a specific report to print.

Figure 16-15 shows a print preview. You can use the tool buttons here to do the following:

✔ Move around the pages of the report by using the Page Left, Right, Up, and Down arrows on the toolbar, as well as the horizontal and vertical scroll bars.

✔ Read more detail by clicking the Zoom tool button and then clicking the report.

✔ Focus on a single page or all the pages of your report by using the One Page and Multiple Pages tool buttons.

✔ Modify margins and the orientation of the printout by displaying the Page Setup dialog box.

✔ Display the Print dialog box by clicking Print.

✔ Close the preview by clicking Close.

So Let's Print!

Last but not least, here's how to actually print that document for which you've made all the wonderful settings discussed in this chapter. For this, you need to deal with the Print dialog box, which you've seen a million times in almost any other Windows program on the planet (see Figure 16-17 for a quick refresher).

Figure 16-17:
Control the
printer, the
number of
copies, and
what prints.

Here are the settings you encounter in this dialog box:

- ✔ The first area of this dialog box concerns the printer you will use. You can choose a printer in the Name list, and click the Properties button to control printer settings such as color quality and paper source.

- ✔ The Print Range area allows you to print All pages or to select a page range From one page number To another.

- ✔ The Copies area contains one simple setting: Click the up arrow here to print more copies, or the down arrow to print fewer (but no less than 1).

- ✔ The Timescale settings are unique to Project's Print dialog box: Here you can choose to print the entire timescale (the entire length of your project) or only a range of dates within your project. Along with Print Range, this setting helps control how much of your Project will print.

✔ If you want the leftmost column of the page to print on every page, select Print Left Column of Pages Only. For example, you may want the task ID number column to print on both pages when a printout width stretches over two pages.

✔ Finally, if you've inserted manual page breaks in your project, you can click the Manual Page Breaks option to include these breaks in your printed report. Leave this option blank if you want the Print feature to control where pages break.

After you make all your settings and you're ready to print, just click OK.

Chapter 17

Getting Better All the Time

In This Chapter

▶ Reviewing your successes and failures

▶ Creating a template for future projects

▶ Developing macros to make things easier

*H*ave you ever finished a project, and then wondered how the heck everything came together at the end? The total budget numbers mystically appear to be several thousand dollars too much, you missed your final deadline by three weeks, and somewhere along the line you lost track of three people who were supposed to be working on tasks. But you delivered your deliverable (somehow), and you can finally stuff your project file in the bottom of your drawer. Or can you?

Microsoft Project is not just a giant electronic to-do list; it's a way to manage your projects. But the by-product of that management is a fantastic tool that you can use to become a better Project user — and a better project manager.

When you've sent out the last memo on your project and accepted your last kudos or criticism from your boss, take a moment to look over your Project plan one more time.

Learning from Your Mistakes

When I teach classes in using project-management software, people are often a bit overwhelmed at all that a product such as Project can do. They're reeling from all the data that they have to input — and all the information that Project throws back at them. They can't see straight for all the views, reports, tables, and filters that they can use to access information on their projects.

Here's the secret I tell them: You won't understand every nuance of your Project plan on your first project. You won't even uncover all Project can do on your second project. But gradually, as you learn the ins and outs of

Project and understand what you can get out of it, you'll become better at absorbing all that information — and at understanding how it can help you avoid mistakes on your future projects.

The best way to make that benefit happen is to review every project to see what you did right and what you did wrong. Then do it all better in your next project.

It was only an estimate

You know what they say: If you don't study history, you're doomed to repeat it. And that's the last thing you want to do, at least where mistakes in project management are concerned.

Consider these strategies to debrief yourself on what happened in the course of your last project:

- ✔ **Compare your original baseline plan against the final actual activity (as illustrated in Figure 17-1).** Even if you have interim baseline plans that adjusted for drastic changes, looking at the widest gap between what you expected to happen and what did happen can be the best way to see the areas where you tend to underestimate most.

- ✔ **Review the notes you made on your tasks to remind yourself of changes or problems that came up along the way.** Insert the column named Notes on your Gantt Chart sheet and read through all the notes at one time.

- ✔ **Note which resources delivered on their promises and which didn't; if you manage some of them, provide them with constructive feedback.** For those you don't manage, keep some notes on hand about how well or how fast they worked and make future assignments with those notes in mind. Also note which outside vendors performed and which didn't (and consider crossing the latter off your vendor list).

- ✔ **Assess your own communications to others in saved e-mails or memos.** Did you give your team enough information to perform effectively? Did you keep management informed about changes or problems in a timely way?

Debrief your team

No project is the province of a single person. Even if no one else ever touched your Project plan, still your team provided input for that plan through the hours of activity they reported and the information they provided to you during the course of your project.

Figure 17-1:
Baseline and actual figures, displayed side by side, paint an interesting picture of your planning strengths and weaknesses.

Consider these suggestions for refining your communications process:

✔ **Ask people how the process of reporting actual activity worked.** Did you use e-mail, schedule notes, route files, or use the Project Server and SharePoint collaborative tools to get resource information? Should you consider the use of a third-party product such as Timeslips for automated resource activity tracking on the next project?

✔ **Would your team rate your communications as frequent and thorough enough?** Did you share enough of your project with resources, or did you inundate them with too much information? Did you send an entire Project file to people regularly when a simple report on a specific aspect of the project would have served you and them better? Did your management team feel your reporting on the project was sufficient for their needs?

✔ **Did you integrate activity on various projects successfully so that resources weren't overbooked or underutilized?** If people on your team reported that there were conflicts with other projects, consider using some special Project tools such as hyperlinking to tasks in other project plans, or developing a master project (which involves inserting several projects into a master plan so you can view resource conflicts across them).

Debrief yourself?

Don't forget to sit down and have a good talk with yourself about what went on during your project. Did your team give you the kind of information you needed to operate efficiently, or should you lay down more stringent ground rules for reporting in the next project? Were you overbooked throughout the project, and would it be wise to find someone to make updating entries for you the next time around? Did management give you information about company changes in a timely way so that you could make adjustments to keep your project on schedule?

It's often the case that in the heat of the project battle, many of us don't have time to stop and change processes or get the help we need. Review the notes you kept in the Project notes areas to see what types of snafus made you pull your hair out — and institute changes before you begin the next project.

Building on Your Success

Although it's human nature to focus on all the things that went wrong with a project, the fact is that you probably did many, many things right. So before you start planning your next project, take the good stuff and put it in a place where you can find it easily later.

Create a template

One option is to create a template. *Templates* are simply files you save that contain certain settings. When you open a template, you can save it as a Project document with a new name and have all those settings already built in.

Project contains its own templates for common projects, but you can save any of your projects as templates. If you often use the same set of tasks in your projects — as people in many industries do — you'll save yourself the time of creating all those tasks again. In addition to any tasks in the project, templates can contain any or all of the following information for those tasks:

- All the information for each baseline
- Actual values
- Rates for all resources
- Fixed costs
- Notations of tasks that you have published to Microsoft Project Server

You can save all this information or only selected items. So, for example, if you created a lot of fixed costs, such as equipment, and resources with associated rates, and will use those again in most of your projects, you could save a template with only fixed costs and resource rates.

To save a file as a template, follow these steps:

1. **With the file you want to save open, choose File ➪ Save As.**

   The Save As dialog box appears, as shown in Figure 17-2.

Figure 17-2: Microsoft saves templates in a central file called Templates.

2. **In the Save As Type list, click Template.**

   Project selects the Templates folder as the Save In location.

3. **Click Save.**

   The Save As Template dialog box appears, as shown in Figure 17-3.

4. **Select the check boxes for the information you want saved in the template.**

5. **Click Save.**

   The file is saved in the template format with the MPT extension. When you open a new project, click General Templates in the New Project task pane. The Templates dialog box appears, and any templates you've saved will appear in the list on the General tab. Just open the template, and then save it as a Project file with a new name.

Figure 17-3:
Choose
which
information
about
values and
resource
rates will be
saved with
all the tasks
in the
project in a
template
format.

Save As Template

You are about to save a file as a template. If you wish, you can choose not to save certain data from your file in the template.

Select the type of data that you do not want saved in the template:

- ☐ Values of all baselines
- ☐ Actual Values
- ☐ Resource Rates
- ☐ Fixed Costs
- ☐ Whether tasks have been published to Microsoft Project Server

Save   Cancel

Master the Organizer

Project has this marvelously flexible nature that allows you to customize a lot of things. For example, you can create your own tables of data to display in views that contain sheet panes. You also can create your own filters, reports, and calendars. If you have any kind of a life, you don't want to spend your evenings recreating all that stuff for your next project. So, use the Organizer to copy them to other Project files instead.

The Organizer allows you to take information in one file and copy it to another file. You can also rename the items. Some of the most commonly used types of items you can copy with Organizer include these:

- ✔ Calendars
- ✔ Forms
- ✔ Tables
- ✔ Reports
- ✔ Views
- ✔ Fields
- ✔ Groups
- ✔ Toolbars
- ✔ Filters

Follow these steps to use the Organizer:

1. **Open the project that you want to copy things from and the project that you want to copy things to.**

2. **In the file you want to copy to, choose Tools ⇨ Organizer.**

   The Organizer dialog box appears, as shown in Figure 17-4.

Figure 17-4:
You have
eleven
sheets'
worth of
stuff you
can copy
here!

3. **Click the tab for the type of information you want to copy.**

4. **If necessary, choose other files to copy to or from.**

   By default, Project uses the Global template as the file to copy from; the file you used to open the Organizer becomes the file to copy to. To use other files, select another file in the Views Available In box on the left (copy from) or right (copy to) of the dialog box. These boxes contain the Global.MPT file and any other files you currently have open.

5. **Click an item in the list on the left that you want to include in the file on the right, and then click Copy.**

   The item appears in the list on the right.

6. **If you want to rename an item, click it and then click Rename. In the Rename dialog box that appears, enter a new name and then click OK.**

7. **To copy additional items on the same tab, repeat Step 5.**

8. **To copy an item on a different tab, repeat Steps 3 to 7.**

9. **When you've finished copying items from one file to another, click the X in the upper-right hand corner.**

    All the items have now been copied.

Handy little timesavers: Macros

If you were paying attention, you may have noticed that there were a lot of activities in your project that you did again, and again, and again. No, I'm not talking about all those cups of coffee you downed in the wee hours. I'm talking about things such as generating a weekly report, or inserting your five department projects into a single master schedule, once every quarter, to review resource allocations.

You don't have to reinvent the wheel to perform actions such as these. Instead, you can create a *macro* — a combination of keystrokes, text entries, and so on that you can record and play back any time you like.

For example, suppose you generate and print a report on current activities every week. Doing so requires the following keystrokes and entries:

1. **Choose View ➪ Reports.**

2. **Click Current Activities.**

3. **Click Select.**

4. **Click Tasks Starting Soon.**

5. **Click Select.**

6. **Type a unique date for tasks that start or finish after a point in time.**

7. **Click OK.**

8. **Type a unique date for tasks that start or finish before a point in time to complete the specified range.**

9. **Click OK.**

10. **Click Print to print the report.**

If you record all those keystrokes, you go through a ten-step process. But once recorded, that process is reduced to three steps when you play back the macro (you start your macro, enter the first part of the date range, and then enter the last part of the date range).

One great use I've seen for macros is to copy a range of tasks that's repeated again and again in your project — for example, a Q&A procedure that's repeated five times throughout a project. In recording the macro, just select the absolute range and copy it, go to the first blank task and paste it, five times. While the macro's running, you can go get yourself another cup of coffee.

Recording a macro

Recording a macro is a simple process: You just start recording, do whatever you usually do to perform the action, and then stop recording. You run macros by selecting them from a list of macros or use a keystroke shortcut. You also can edit them if you need a slightly different series of keystrokes at a later date.

Here's how you record a macro:

1. **Choose Tools ⇨ Macro ⇨ Record New Macro.**

   The Record Macro dialog box appears, as shown in Figure 17-5.

Figure 17-5:
Macros you record are played back using a shortcut key that you designate here.

2. **In the Macro Name box, type a name.**

   Make the name descriptive of what the macro does.

3. **In the Shortcut Key box, type a letter.**

   Pressing Ctrl plus that key will play back the macro.

4. **If you like, edit or add to the description of the macro.**

   This is especially useful if you think others will use it.

5. **Select whether row and column references will be relative or absolute.**

   With *relative references,* if you select (say) the task in the third row displayed in a sheet and perform an action on it, then Project selects the task in the third row whenever you run the macro. With *absolute references,* Project selects a specific, named task, no matter what row it occupies.

6. **Click OK to begin recording.**

Remember that every keystroke you make during this time becomes part of the macro.

7. **When you've completed your keystrokes, choose Tools ⇨ Macro ⇨ Stop Recorder.**

Here are some points to keep in mind about recording macros:

✔ Macro names have to start with a letter and can't contain spaces. Use the underscore to separate words in a macro name (Weekly_Report, for example).

✔ Several keystroke shortcuts are already reserved by Project for use with built-in functions (Ctrl+K, for example, inserts a hyperlink). Project displays a message telling you this if you choose such a shortcut and gives you an opportunity to choose another letter or number.

✔ If what you record includes entering specific information (such as a name or a date range), you're presented with a blank box into which you enter new information when you run the macro — even if you entered information while recording the macro.

Running and editing macros

To run a macro, your best bet is the shortcut key you entered when you created it. This two-keystroke combination runs the macro, pausing for you to fill in any requested information.

Alternately, you can choose Tools ⇨ Macro ⇨ Macros, click a macro in the list of macros shown in the Macros dialog box in Figure 17-6, and then click Run.

To edit a macro, you might want to simply re-record (this is sometimes the quickest way to do it). Or you can choose Tools ⇨ Macro ⇨ Macros. In the Macros dialog box, click the macro you want to modify and then click Edit. The Microsoft Visual Basic editor opens; your macro is displayed in Visual Basic code, as shown in Figure 17-7.

You can edit this code much as you edit text in a word-processed document. Although you have to be familiar with the Visual Basic programming language to make most changes, you can make some edits without being a programmer. For example, any items in quotes are text entries or names of things such as reports. For example, it's pretty easy to change a macro that generates the report named Tasks Starting Soon so it generates the report Tasks in Progress — just replace the existing report name (within the quotation marks) with the new report name.

Figure 17-6:
The Macros
dialog box
lists all
available
macros in
any open
projects.

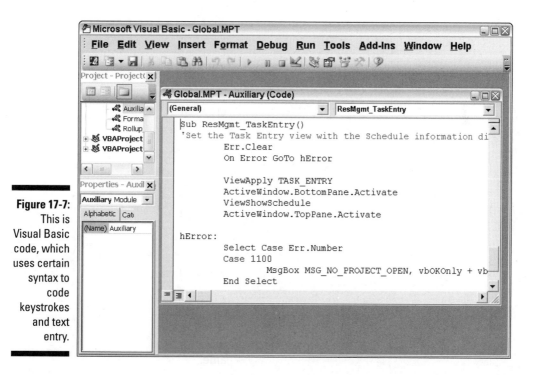

Figure 17-7:
This is
Visual Basic
code, which
uses certain
syntax to
code
keystrokes
and text
entry.

If you want to delete a piece of the process, you can usually figure that out from the code. For example, if you see the line `'If project is empty, alert the user and end the macro'` and you don't want the macro to include that step, just select it and press the Delete key.

But monkeying around with Visual Basic for anything much more complex could mess up your macro. Because I don't want to write another book on Visual Basic at this point, I suggest that you keep your life and mine simple: Delete the first macro and walk through the procedure again, re-recording it as a new macro.

Part V

Working with Enterprise Projects

The 5th Wave   By Rich Tennant

"We can monitor our entire operation from one central location. We know what the 'Wax Lips' people are doing; we know what the 'Whoopee Cushion' people are doing; we know what the 'Fly-in-the-Ice Cube' people are doing. But we don't know what the 'Plastic Vomit' people are doing. We don't want to know what the 'Plastic Vomit' people are doing."

In this part . . .

Here's where Project Professional comes into its own: Serving the enterprise via Project Server and SharePoint, you can get some real online collaboration going. You can share documents online with your team, get your human resources report their work time, and integrate Project information into Outlook. This part gives you a glimpse of what Project Server can do, how to set it up, and how to get it going.

Chapter 18

Getting Ready to Use Project Server

● ●

In This Chapter

▶ Determining whether Project Server is right for you

▶ Using Project in an enterprise environment

▶ Jumping in the Enterprise Resource Pool

▶ Understanding the benefits of online reporting of resource time

▶ Setting organizational standards

▶ Identifying enterprise roles for projects

● ●

*A*n important feature set in Microsoft Project 2003 Professional Edition
includes the enterprise tools you access through Microsoft Project
Server 2003. These features allow you to share and update information across
an *enterprise* (a fancy word for an organization).

If you used Project 2000, you'll recognize much of the Project Server
functionality — it used to be built into the product and was called Project
Central. But times move on, and now you have to learn a new name for an
old — but improved — feature.

You'll have to fork over more money to buy Project Server — it's not built
into Project. But after you do, you'll find a wealth of features available to you.
With Project Server you can use commands on the Project Collaborate menu
to publish projects to the Web, allow team members to update their progress,
analyze your project status, and generally communicate in one central, online
location.

Is Project Server for You?

Just as you don't need a Hummer to run to the corner grocery store for milk once a week, Project Server can be too high-powered a solution for some organizations. Implementing Project Server involves not only money for product licenses, but also some other specific commitments:

- ✔ Time to install and configure it
- ✔ Effort to standardize how Project is used across your organization
- ✔ Time and money to train people to use the tools
- ✔ Ongoing maintenance of the Project Server database

Therefore, before you jump in with both feet to the Project Server world, you should be sure that the benefits of using it outweigh the effort required.

Project Server is useful to organizations that have an enterprise orientation. That means they make the effort to centralize information online in some fashion so it's standardized and available throughout the company.

Typically, Project Server is worthwhile for mid- to large-size companies that manage several projects at once across departments or disciplines. Project Server provides the managers of these companies with a way to orchestrate resources more efficiently, and get a broad perspective on the efficiency and success of their project-management efforts across the organization.

Another plus to using Project Server is that it can make all project information for the company available online through a company intranet that can be accessed from anywhere in the world.

The benefits of using Project Server include:

- ✔ Standard formats, reports, and resource information that can be accessed and shared by all project managers for consistency among multiple projects
- ✔ The ability to see, on an enterprise-wide level, how resources are being utilized (as in Figure 18-1, where you can assign resources with an eye to the big picture)
- ✔ A perspective on all the projects in the company, which can help management prioritize and strategize overall enterprise efforts
- ✔ A greater capability to collaborate among projects
- ✔ More efficient methods of having resources track their time on project tasks without anybody having to reenter the information in Project

Figure 18-1:
The Enterprise Resource Pool feature of Project Server helps you build a project using all the resources in your organization at a glance.

If you have a company LAN or intranet, you can set up Project Server to deliver all these benefits and more.

Not every member of your team has to have Project installed to interact with it, as long as they have access to your LAN or intranet, a Web-browser product called Project Web Access, and appropriate network permissions.

The downside to Project Server includes some tough stuff to chew on:

✔ The cost for licenses.

✔ The time to install and maintain the server, as well as training users.

✔ The need to ensure that projects are handled in a uniform way across your enterprise. (If you don't do this, the information you receive through Project Server may be inaccurate and out of date.)

What Can Project Server Do?

Way back when there was no Internet, companies had to share information by passing around memos. The guy in Manufacturing had no idea what the people in Sales were up to until a handwritten purchase order was hand-delivered to his desk and he realized they didn't have enough products on hand to fill the order.

Computer networks and the Internet changed all that. Suddenly information could be shared in centralized online repositories. People could communicate instantly through e-mail. An action in one part of the company could instantly be seen in another, and that group could respond and act accordingly.

In a sense, Project Server is to Project what the Internet is to standard business operations. Project Server works with Microsoft Project Professional to provide the centralized information and communications that can keep projects on track in our I-need-it-now world.

Server sets up an online project-command central that can be used by people in your project to

✔ Communicate online, exchanging updates on progress and sending suggested new tasks to project managers.

✔ Make, view, and accept or decline task assignments from a standardized resource pool.

✔ Update activity on tasks using a timesheet interface (shown in Figure 18-2).

✔ Send and request status reports and review project information.

✔ Manage project documents, creating and comparing multiple versions of projects and setting up document libraries.

✔ Attach important documents to a project; for example you might include a goal statement or Excel budget file with your project for others to view online.

✔ Use analysis tools to model what-if scenarios, and determine risks and progress on projects.

Who's who?

As with most network-oriented computing, everybody has a role to play and has to be set up to use features on the network based on that role. Project Server provides a user model with three types of participants, and provides various information and access requirements accordingly:

✔ Managers, who oversee the day-to-day operations of a project

✔ Team members, who perform the work on the project

✔ Shareholders, such as clients and senior management, who require regular updating on project progress, often across several projects in an organization

Figure 18-2:
The timesheet entry form provides a handy way for resources to enter time spent on projects.

You should analyze the way these roles relate to the functions in your project teams and work with your IT person to set up Project Server permissions accordingly.

What's Involved in Setting Up Project Server?

Well, I wish I could tell you that Project Server is a plug-and-play solution, but it's a little more complicated than that. Actually, it's a *lot* more complicated than that. Well, okay, it's a pain in the neck.

But I'll give you an overview, just so you can say I told you so.

Here's where I tip my hat to my colleague Elaine Marmel, who worked with me through my installation of Project Server. Elaine gives you some marvelous detailed help with it in her book, *Microsoft Project Bible 2003* from Wiley Publishing. If you really have to get into the nuts and bolts of installing and setting up Project Server, buy her book and read it, or give it to your favorite IT person to snuggle up with.

How it works

Here's the thumbnail version of how this technology works (in other words, all you really need to know about the techie side of things) as well as some of the things you'll have to do to use Project Server.

Somebody from your IT group gets to be the administrator for Project Server. This lucky soul gets to work through the pages of documentation for Project Server to actually install the software on a company server.

At some point early in this process, somebody in your organization has to line up a lot of information — such as enterprise resource names, hourly rates, availability, and so on — to set up a common Enterprise Resource Pool in the Project Server database. You should also determine custom fields you may need to add to the Project Server Enterprise Global Template (shown in Figure 18-3). This information can then be set up on Project Server so that all those with the proper permissions can access these tools company-wide.

Once Project Server is implemented, project managers can create Web-based projects in Project 2003 and publish those projects in the Project Server database. The administrator sets up viewing rights for individuals; anybody with viewing rights can access the project information using Internet Explorer 5.5 or later and even interact with each other through tools such as status reports or timesheets used to update project progress.

Tools built right into the Project Collaborate menu will become available to you when Project Server is installed so you can perform much of your work with Project Server right from your copy of Microsoft Project.

Planning to use Project Server

Before your administrator begins the process of installing Project Server, you have to sit down and do some thinking about how you'll use it in your organization. That's because during the installation process there are some design choices that will vary based on how you want to use the product.

Get a team together

First figure out who at your organization should be part of this process. For example you'll probably need senior management input, end user (the people on your project teams) input, the experience and expertise of all the project managers in your company who will use the enterprise features, and somebody (or three or four somebodies) from your IT department who actually has to set the thing up.

Figure 18-3:
The
Enterprise
Global
Template
provides a
standard-
ized starting
point for
every
project in
your organi-
zation.

Gather information

Next, set up a process to research and come to an agreement on all the enterprise-wide information you'll need to enter into Project Server, such as resources, their rates, their calendars of availability; WBS code structure; standard report formats; custom fields you'd like to include in the Project Server Enterprise Global Template (kind of like the Global Template in Project 2003, but available online); and filters, views, tables, and so on.

The keyword in this planning process is standardize. By standardizing the information in your projects and making that information available online, you increase efficiency in building projects, and provide mechanisms for comparing projects in an apples-to-apples way.

Standardize processes

Pay special attention to the reporting process that different people use on their projects. Standardizing reporting processes and formats will ensure that those reading reports about multiple projects will easily and quickly under-stand what they're looking at. Also, determine how project performance will be assessed. For example the way in which earned value is used in creating tasks will produce different measures of progress on projects.

Coordinate with IT

Finally, work with your IT people to identify the Project Server features that you want to use in your organization. For example, if document sharing is an important thing to your company, Windows SharePoint Services will have to be installed so you can create document libraries.

Getting Your Project Server ducks in a row

Okay, I hope you're sitting down. Here's what you have to do to start using Project Server through a company intranet or the Internet:

1. Buy Microsoft Project Server and Microsoft Web Access licenses for the number of people in your organization who will use them.

2. Project 2003 itself must be installed on each project manager's computer.

3. Install and set up the Server product on a server computer that uses Internet Information Server (IIS) 5.0 or later as well as Microsoft Windows Server 2000 or later and SQL Server 2000 with the Service Pack 3 update.

4. The server computer must also have one of these Windows operating systems installed: Windows 98, Millennium, NT 4.0 (Service Pack 6), 2000 Professional, XP Home, or XP Professional.

5. If you want to use shared workspaces and document libraries (you can learn more about these in the next section), set up SharePoint Team Services Server and a subweb.

6. Make sure all team members have Internet Explorer 5.5 or later and access to the server where Project Server is installed.

7. Create accounts for all your team members, which may include setting up authentication (passwords) for greater security. On an intranet, everyone must have network access — and appropriate network privileges.

Did your eyes glaze over around Step 3? I don't blame you. There are several pieces of software and several network setup details that have to be just right to get Project Server installed and working. Because every network is configured a little bit differently, getting all these things set up just right can be challenging.

Bottom line: Don't try this at home. Leave it to your professional IT guy or gal to set this up for you. Once IT has handled Steps 1 through 7, you'll be able to use the tools outlined in the next section.

Don't forget the training!

Project Server requires that different people in your organization learn new tricks. Your IT people will need time to get up to speed on setting up and maintaining the Project Server database. Project managers will have to learn to use the Enterprise Global Template and Enterprise Resource Pool to build projects. Team members will require some training on the status report and timesheet features in Project Server. Build in time and money to your implementation process to make effective training happen.

Project Server's Tools

So what goodies become available to you to use once you've been through the daunting task of getting it in place? It's time for a little closer look at how you'll use specific Project Server features in your projects.

Chapter 19 goes into more detail about how to use these features.

Sharing workspaces

The newest addition to Project that allows you to share work with your project team is the Shared Workspaces feature. This feature lets you store your project-related files in one spot using document libraries through Windows SharePoint Services. With this approach to sharing documents, users don't have to have access to Project Server to access your information.

After your document libraries such as those shown in Figure 18-4 are set up, you can publish documents to the libraries and assign permissions to regulate who can access what. You can even allow some users to create sublibraries for your project. But you're not limited to Project documents in these libraries: You can include memos, spreadsheets, organization charts, or whatever you like in this centralized repository.

You can also use a feature called Issue Tracking. *Issues* are like big red flags that display an indicator on the document, project, or task that you attach them to. You can also set up Project Server to send e-mails alerting everyone that such a flag has been posted.

The Shared Workspace feature does require a server running Windows SharePoint Services. You then create a workspace and establish permissions for those you want to access it. With that set up, you can save your Project to the workspace through the Save As dialog box (you save it to the URL associated with the workspace).

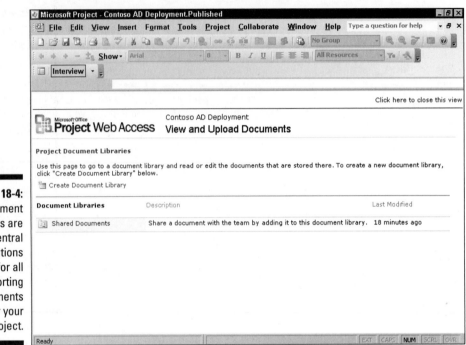

Figure 18-4:
Document
libraries are
central
locations
for all
supporting
documents
for your
project.

Once SharePoint Services is set up (which is again best handled by your IT guy or gal), several menu commands you couldn't use before are usable, such as Check In and Versions on the File menu and the Shared Workspace command on the Tools menu to access the workspace. There's also a Shared Workspace task pane where you can view documents created with any Office 2003 application and stored in the workspace, and view your team members' to-do tasks (versus Project tasks), documents, and lists.

You can also manage different versions of documents with the Versions dialog box. Here you can open and view comments in a particular version of a document, delete a version, or create a new version.

Make assignments and delegate tasks

Because the main focus of Project Server is to help you interact with your team members, one of its most useful features is the capability to post resource assignments and delegate work on tasks.

Members of a project team can interact and access data on Project Server using Microsoft Project Web Access, shown in Figure 18-5. Think of Web Access as being like all those views you can look at in Project — essentially it's an online browser interface for Project Server.

When you make assignments to projects, you can do so using the Enterprise Resource Pool. This central repository of resources ensures consistency of resource calendars, rates, and so on across your company's projects. Assigning resources from this pool to your project tasks also lets you see where resources are overbooked on multiple projects.

Once you've made assignments, the folks on your team can access timesheets, such as the one shown in Figure 18-6, for their specific assignments and can get e-mail notification of those assignments. Team members can delegate assignments to others on the team. Then the team member can review and approve status reports on work performed on the task before sending those reports on to the project manager.

Of course, you don't want everyone on a project to be able to pass the buck when it comes to assignments: The project manager has control over who can — and can't — delegate tasks in a project.

Figure 18-5:
Web Access is like a browser used to view your online project data.

Figure 18-6:
Timesheets
can be
automat-
ically ported
over to your
Project file
for easy and
fast
updating.

Track your progress

In Chapter 13 of this book, I tell you all about gathering resource-activity information and entering it in your Project file to track progress. This can be a somewhat tedious process. Wouldn't it be nice if your resources could just enter their work in timesheets that could be automatically imported into Project to do your tracking for you? Well, I've got a surprise for you. . . .

One huge perk to using Project Server is the functionality it gives your team members to track their activity on tasks and report their progress to you online. Project managers can request updates or send reminders shortly before updates are due.

Team members can use the Microsoft Project Web Access interface to enter actual activity into a timesheet. Web Access communicates directly with Project on the project manager's computer. As the project manager, you can then make manual updates to your project plan or let Project make its own updates automatically.

You can learn how to use features such as the tracking sheet in Chapter 19.

Figure out what's going on with status reports

Status reports, such as the one shown in Figure 18-7, are essentially forms that the people on your project can complete to explain the status of their tasks. These aren't used to track and record actual work performed. Instead, they help team members describe various issues that come up and what's going on with the progress of tasks.

One of the nice things about status reports for you, as a project manager, is that you can assemble all the individual reports into a complete status report for the project. Then you can make that report available to shareholders to update them on the latest news.

Figure 18-7:
Consistent
status
report
formats help
company
manage-
ment assess
progress
across
enterprise
projects.

Planning for Problems

One final word about implementing Project Server at your organization. Because you will now be sharing resources and information with others on a daily basis, put a little thought into how you'll deal with problems when they come up. What would happen if you want to use a resource, but another project manager already has that resource assigned to a project? How do various project managers make use of tools such as resource leveling to resolve resource conflicts?

Make sure everybody understands the rules of etiquette involved in working in a more enterprise-wide fashion, sharing people, equipment, and information.

Chapter 19

Getting Your Project Virtual with Project Server

*I*f you think Project Server is like an add-on applet (tiny application) that works with Project, you'd be wrong. It's actually a full-fledged software product that enables you to take your project — and all its accompanying resources, tracking, and reporting — into the world of the Internet.

Project Server comprises two main components: the Project Server database where project data is stored, and Project Web Access, the browser-like interface that connects you and others to that database.

Note: Before you can actually perform the steps in this chapter, somebody must have installed Project Server on your company network and configured it for your company's standards and requirements. This usually requires that IT type people stay up nights installing and configuring software, and another team of people design the implementation. After all that is accomplished, you can actually do the steps listed here and not just read about them.

With Project Server (which works only with the Professional edition of Microsoft Project), you can enhance communications, interactions, and documentation for each and every project you undertake.

But is Project Server for you? Find out by reviewing its features in this chapter.

Who Does What — and Why?

If you want to understand how useful a tool is, it helps to know who will use it and for what type of work, right?

Project Server serves three major groups:

- ✔ **Users** can view project information, use Timesheet features to track their work, work with related documents, and communicate with the project manager.

- ✔ **Project managers** gain the capability to publish projects online, assign and communicate with resources, and adjust work according to user tracking data.

- ✔ **Senior management members** find risk-analysis and modeling tools included with Project Server that help them make strategic decisions about multiple projects across their organization.

How you set up Project Server is a study in itself, involving options, settings, and choices about who has the appropriate permissions — and capabilities — to access information and perform actions. (As such, it's beyond the scope of this humble chapter.) To use Project Server, your IT people must set up the software (which requires that certain versions of the Windows Server, SQL, and other software be in place). As the project manager, you must have access to Project Server software, as well as have Project Professional edition installed.

In order to perform certain tasks online, users and senior managers can do without Project Server as long as they have Project Web Access, which is kind of a browser for viewing information on Project Server. My advice is to get together with your IT people and Project Server documentation and map out a strategy for settings and implementation up front based on your specific circumstances.

I recommend you look at the *Microsoft Project 2003 Bible* by Elaine Marmel from Wiley Publishing for a more advanced discussion of these setup issues.

In this chapter, I focus on the two major groups who use Project Server on a day-to-day basis: Project managers and users.

The Project Manager Gets Things Rolling

When it comes to a project and how it will be used on Project Server, the project manager is the head honcho. Therefore, the project manager is the logical starting point for using Project Server, because it's the project manager who sets up Project Server and posts a Web-based project to it, long before a single user logs on. Project managers can also call on an Enterprise Resource Pool feature to assign resources, making resource management across all the projects in an organization more efficient.

After a project gets posted, project managers and users can then begin to interact with activities such as tracking, adjusting actual work data, and sending status reports.

Getting ready to use Project Server

You can't just jump into using a project online willy-nilly. You have to get your ducks in a row, which involves a few relatively simple steps.

The first step in using Project Server (once it's been installed and configured by your IT department) is to set up a Project Server account for yourself with appropriate permissions and access. Then, you can create a project and store it in the Project Server database. Then you can connect to Project Server using Project Professional to create a new project or import an offline project into Project Server.

Setting up a Project Manager Account

If you're technology challenged, feel free to ask your IT person to set up an account for you. But honestly, setup isn't hard after your IT guy or gal provides the Project Server URL (online address), so I've included the steps here for the do-it-yourself project manager.

Follow these steps to create your own account:

1. **Choose Tools⇨Enterprise Options⇨Microsoft Project Server Accounts.**

   The Microsoft Project Server Accounts dialog box, as shown in Figure 19-1, appears.

Figure 19-1:
Use this
dialog box
to add a
Project
Server
logon
account and
specify
connection
options.

2. **Click the Add button. You'll see the Account Properties dialog box, as shown in Figure 19-2.**

3. **In the Account Name box, enter a name for the account.**

   You have to use a name that is relatively unique, such as your first initial and last name.

4. **In the Microsoft Project Server box, type the URL for the location of your Project Server database.**

   To be sure that you entered the URL correctly, click the Test Connection button; if you did things right, a dialog box appears telling you that Project has successfully connected to the server.

5. **In the When Connecting section, choose the type of connection that your company uses:**

   • Use your Windows login information by choosing Windows User Account.

   • Use your Microsoft Project Server account, which uses Project Server authentication. In the User Name box, enter your name. Note that your administrator must have granted access to you before you try to log on in order for you to access Project Server.

6. **(Optional) If you intend to create more than one account and you want the current account to be your default logon account, check the Set As Default Account box.**

   Why would you bother to create another account? Well, if your company uses more than one database in Project Server, perhaps one for each department, you have to have an account to access each database.

Figure 19-2:
Use this
dialog box
to create a
new Project
Server
account.

7. **Click OK.**

   The Microsoft Project Server Accounts dialog box reappears.

8. **In the bottom area of the dialog box, choose whether you want to log on automatically or control the connection manually.**

   If you choose the manual option here, you'll next see the dialog box shown in Figure 19-3. If you choose to automatically detect the connection state, you *won't* see the dialog box shown in Figure 19-3 (in which you choose the account that you want to use to log on); instead, Project simply attempts to detect the Project Server when you start it up.

   You may also see the Microsoft Project Server Accounts dialog box if you lose your connection to Project Server.

Figure 19-3:
You only see
this box
if you
choose to
control the
connection
manually.

Creating a Web-based project and storing it in the database

I hope you're being patient because you can't yet use Project Server's features — but we're getting closer. The next step is to create a Web-based project by setting up a project's options to work with Web-based communication features.

First, you have to be logged onto the Project Server database. If you specified automatic login as you set up your account in the previous section, and if your computer is connected to the network where Project Server lives, then you get connected automatically when you start Project. If you chose the manual option, you're given the option of logging on to Project Server every time you start up Project.

Open the project you want to become a Web-based project. Then follow these steps to set options for a Web-based project:

1. **Choose Tools⇨Options.**

2. **Click the Collaborate tab, shown in Figure 19-4.**

Figure 19-4:
To set a project's options for Web communication, use the Collaborate tab of the Options dialog box.

3. **In the Collaborate Using drop-down list, select Microsoft Office Project Server.**

4. **In the Microsoft Project Server URL dialog box, enter the URL that users would enter in their Web browsers to display Project Web Access.**

   This Internet address points to a Web server or your organizational server and a folder that contains the Project Server database. It's the same URL that you used to create your Project Server logon account in the previous section.

5. **Specify a method of identification:**

   - Use Windows login information by choosing Windows User Account.

   - Use Microsoft Project user names, which you can set on the General tab of the Options dialog box.

The name on the General tab is unavailable when you are logged on to Project Server. To change the user name on the General tab, you have to open Project Professional without logging on to Project Server.

6. **In the E-mail Address box, enter your e-mail address (assuming you're the person who wants to receive notifications about assignment updates; that is, that you're the project manager).**

7. **Choose your collaboration settings.**

   At the bottom of the Collaborate tab, you can choose whether resources can delegate tasks in Project Web Access, what updated information is sent to the Project Server database when you save a project, and the types of changes that cause updates to resource assignments.

8. **Click OK to save all your settings.**

9. **Choose File ➪ Save As.**

   The Save to Microsoft Project Server dialog box appears, as shown in Figure 19-5.

10. **Enter a file name, then click Save.**

Publishing project information

When you finally get to the point where you can store a project you created on your computer in the Project Server database, hang in there: Once you've performed this step, you can actually get some project work done online.

Make sure you're logged on to Project Server before you do this one; then you can follow these steps:

1. **Open the project you want to work with.**

2. **Choose File ➪ Save As.**

   The Save to Microsoft Project Server dialog box appears, as shown in Figure 19-5. Choose File ➪ Open to open the project you want to work with. Because you're logged on to Project Server, you see the projects that have been saved to the server (but only the ones your administrator has rights to see). Select your project.

   This dialog box might look a little different if you chose some custom fields for your project in the Enterprise Global template that you can attach to online projects.

3. **Choose Collaborate ⇨ Publish to update the project to Project Server.**

   A menu of commands appears, including the following choices:

   - **All Information:** Publishes both new and changed assignments and a project plan.

   - **New and Changed Assignments:** Publishes changes to tasks, such as new start or finish dates. Resources receive notification in Project Web Access and via e-mail if your organization has set up Project Server to provide those notifications and reminders.

   - **Project Plan:** When you choose this command, you get the option to publish the entire plan or a summary of the plan. The summary includes only task and scheduling information; the complete plan includes assignments. If you publish the summary only, the project will appear in the Project Center, but you won't be able to take a look at project details because they simply won't be there.

   - **Republish Assignments:** This command causes Project to publish assignments — even if they've been published before. You do have some control here: You can republish all or only selected assignments.

   When you choose one of these commands, Project publishes the project information to the Project Server database.

That's it!

Working with the gang online

Now, finally, you can get to work with resource assignments, communicating with status reports and updates, and making changes to your project based on tracking data your team members submit online.

Assigning resources

One of the really cool things about Project Server is how it empowers project managers to make resource assignments in a way that takes into account one set of shared resources across a whole organization. The Enterprise Resource Pool, which the Project Server administrator from your IT group can set up, offers this sort of "resource central" where you can go to make assignments without having to recreate entries for all your resources every time you create a project.

You can also use the Team Builder feature to replace generic resources in your project with resources from the Enterprise Resource Pool, and use the Resource Substitution wizard to help you to figure out how best to make use of limited resources across multiple projects.

Here are the steps involved in adding an enterprise resource to a Project plan:

1. **Choose Tools ➪ Build Team from Enterprise.**

   Project displays the Team Builder dialog box shown in Figure 19-6. The Enterprise Resources are listed in the lower-left portion and the resources assigned to the project are shown on the right.

2. **Select the Enterprise Resource you want to add to your project team and then click the "Add >" button.**

Figure 19-6:
The dialog box used to assign enterprise resources to a project.

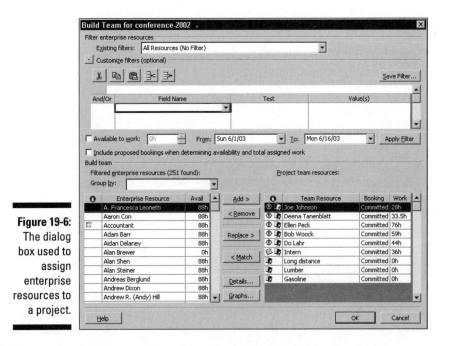

3. **Click OK.**

   These resources now appear on the Resource Sheet view of your project. Project Server updates the Enterprise Resource Pool to show that these resources are involved in your project.

You can adjust which resources are shown in the dialog box in Figure 19-6 by using filters to choose which fields to filter out of the list.

Notifying resources of assignments

Now that the resources have been added to the project team, you can use the Assign Resources option to make task assignments. As project manager, you're the one who doles out the work to the resources working on your project. Whether more work is good or bad news to these folks, it's your job to deliver the news.

Resources will get a notification in Project Web Access when there's a new or changed assignment; Project Server can also send them an e-mail if you set it up to do that.

Here's how you send work assignments to resources after you've made assignments to your project:

1. **Select the tasks you want to notify resources about.**

   This is an optional step because you can make choices about which tasks to update in the next step.

2. **Choose Collaborate⇨Publish.**

   At this point, you have two options:

   • You can choose New and Changed Assignments to send notifications only about those assignments.

   • You can choose Republish Assignments; this will cause Project to update all assignments.

   If you choose Republish Assignments, Project displays the Republish Assignments dialog box shown in Figure 19-7. From here you can set the following options for updating assignments:

   • Send e-mail messages to all affected resources. The e-mail message is sent in addition to the notification that the resource sees in Project Web Access. Figure 19-8 shows the standard e-mail notification Project sends; you can change this text by clicking the Edit Message Text button.

- Tell Project to overwrite actual work entered by resources.

- Become the manager for the assignments.

Now hear this: Status reports

In an ideal world, every resource on your project would report to you faithfully on his or her progress (and the news would all be good). In reality, the news is often not so good, but there's nothing Project or I can do about that. However, Project Server does provide a way for you to design status reports — and regularly nudge your team to submit them to you.

Figure 19-7: Use this window to send notice of work assignments to resources.

You can design a status report, and request that your team submit these reports at intervals by using a handy wizard. To start the wizard, click the Status Reports link at the top of the Project Web Access main page. In the Actions pane, click the Request a Status Report link and the wizard opens.

Figure 19-8: Standard e-mail notification text that Project sends.

As you follow the wizard steps, you can choose to create a status report or edit one. When you have designed a report using the wizard's settings, you can click Set up a new status report for your team to respond to, and then click OK. Project Web Access then displays a series of four screens, where you enter titles and information about how often you want the report to be submitted, and who should report, the topics you'd like covered. The first of these screens is shown in Figure 19-9.

Figure 19-9: Here's where you enter overview information for the report you're designing.

On the final screen that appears, you can click Send and the report form goes out to your team, ready for them to fill in the blanks with good news — and not so good.

Seeing Project Server from the User's Perspective

Project Server is a two-way street. That is, project managers post projects, notify resources of assignments, and request status reports, but the members of your project team can also initiate actions. They can record their time spent on tasks, take a look at project information, send updates to managers, and attach related documents for other team members to view online.

The main Project Web Access home page is shown in Figure 19-10. On the various tabs here (Home, Tasks, Projects, Status Reports, and so on) you can view a wealth of project information. You can also use the links in the Actions Pane along the left side of the screen to move around the site.

Working with Timesheet

Okay, put aside your project manager hat (if you have one), and imagine for a moment that you're working on a project team. Your project manager — we'll call him Milt — has assigned you to tasks and you have deadlines (way too many in your humble opinion) to meet.

The Timesheet feature (which you can access through Project Web Access) is the way you view your tasks and enter information about the actual time you spent on them. Milt can check your timesheet (shown in Figure 19-11) and use it to track progress automatically.

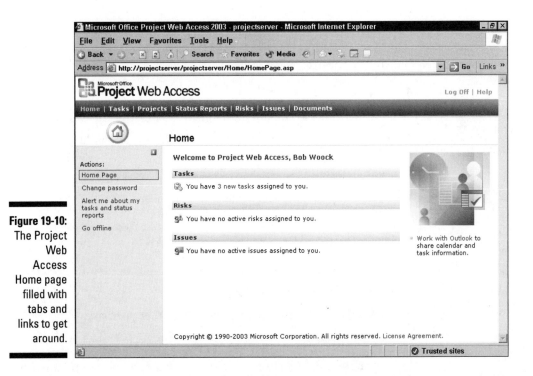

Figure 19-10:
The Project Web Access Home page filled with tabs and links to get around.

Figure 19-11:
The
Timesheet
view of a
Task page
can be
opened
using
Project Web
Access.

Here's how get to the Timesheet view:

1. **Display the main Project Web Access page.**

2. **Click the Tasks tab at the top of the page or click the Tasks link.**

   All tasks assigned to you appear in a Gantt Chart view, as shown in Figure 19-12.

3. **Click the Timesheet View link.**

   The Timesheet View shown in Figure 19-11 appears.

As you can see in Figure 19-11, the Timesheet view has two parts and looks something like a spreadsheet. To enter work on tasks, follow these steps:

1. **Scroll to locate the timeframe for a task you want to view or update.**

2. **Click in the cell you want to update.**

3. **Enter the actual time you spent on a task on that particular day.**

   Use a number (such as 3 for three hours) in the Actual Work field or a percentage (such as 75) in the % Work Complete column. Note that the tracking method you can use for tasks determines whether updates are made to percent complete, actual hours and remaining hours, or to hours of work done per day or week. The Project Server administrator or the Project Manager determines what tracking method will be used.

Figure 19-12:
The Gantt
Chart view
of the Task
Page.

4. **When you've entered all updates, click the Save Changes button at the top of the Project Web Access page.**

What you see in the Timesheet view may differ slightly, depending on the options you chose in Project Server for updating data on projects. For example (if you've been given the proper permissions), you might have a Delegation tab where you can delegate tasks to others and view those tasks.

Notifying managers of changes

When you save the changes you make in the Timesheet, those changes get stored in the Project Server database, but they haven't been used to update the project yet. That's up to Milt, your faithful project manager.

To notify your project manager that you've done something on one or more tasks in the project, you have to click the Update All button or the Update Selected Rows button (after selecting some rows on the Timesheet). That causes Project Web Access to send an e-mail to your manager who can accept or reject the updates in the project.

Okay, switch hats for a second: As a project manager you can log on to Project Web Access, then click the Update link. All task changes are displayed. You can accept or reject these by clicking the Accept column and making your choice from a drop-down list.

Working with project documents

You've endured information about Project Server and Project Web Access admirably. But there's one more component to this online enterprise solution you should know about: SharePoint Services. (This one works pretty much the same no matter whether you're wearing the project manager or team member hat.)

Windows SharePoint Services offers you a way to attach documents of various kinds to a project, task, or to-do list. These document libraries make a variety of information available to your project team without having to send out files or paper copies ad nauseam.

To view a document attached to a project (for example, an Excel budget, RFP, or memo), follow these steps:

1. **Display the Project Web Access page.**

2. **Click the Documents tab (shown in Figure 19-13).**

   All the projects you are working on and associated documents are displayed.

Figure 19-13:
This tab shows all the projects that you have access to, and lists any documents attached to those projects.

Microsoft Office Project Web Access 2003 - projectserver - Microsoft Internet Explorer

File   Edit   View   Favorites   Tools   Help

Back   Search   Favorites   Media

Address http://projectserver/sample/Library/WssMain.asp?list=doc&_oid=-1   Go   Links »

Microsoft Office **Project** Web Access   Log Off | Help

Home | Tasks | Projects | Status Reports | Risks | Issues | Documents

View and upload documents in all projects

Go to selected project workspace

Actions:

View and upload documents in all projects

View and upload public documents

Click the project name to view and upload documents in that project.

▲ Project Name	Project Manager
☐ **My Projects**	
Contoso AD Deployment	Eva Corets
☐ **Public**	
Public Documents	Administrator

Print Grid   Export Grid to Excel

Done   Trusted sites

3. **Click on the link for the project to which you want to attach a document.**

4. **Click the Shared Documents link to see any documents posted there, as shown in Figure 19-14.**

   This is known as a Shared Documents library.

5. **To view a document, click on its link.**

   A prompt appears asking you to save the file to your hard drive or view it from this location.

6. **Make your selection in the prompt box, and then click OK.**

   The document is displayed.

To post a document to a Shared Documents library, from the screen shown in Figure 19-14, click on the New Document or Upload Document button. Browse to locate the document you want to upload. Click on a link at the bottom of the screen to attach the document to a particular task. When you click Save and Close, Project Web Access refreshes the Share Documents page and your document will be listed.

Figure 19-14: View all the documents attached to a project in a library of documents.

Part VI
The Part of Tens

The 5th Wave   By Rich Tennant

"We're not sure what it is. Rob cobbled it together from paper clips and stuff in the mail room, but MAN wait till you see how scalable it is."

In this part . . .

Ten fingers, ten toes, lists of ten items — how traditional can you get? This part gives you two handy lists
of ten: Ten Golden Rules of Project Management and Ten
Project-Management Software Products to Explore. The
first of these chapters offers new users of Project (as well
as seasoned veterans) some pointers on getting your
project to perform. The second chapter looks at add-on
products and supplemental software to enhance Microsoft
Project.

Chapter 20

Ten Golden Rules of Project Management

In This Chapter
▶ Putting good project-management practices to work using Microsoft Project
▶ Creating and tracking Project schedules more efficiently
▶ Learning from your mistakes

*Y*ou've heard this one: You can have your deliverable on time, on budget, or done right — choose two. That's an example of some traditional project management wisdom. But how does that wisdom translate to the use of project-management software?

Well, it's simple: If you assign additional resources to a Project schedule, you add costs and time to your schedule. That's because resources have costs attached and can work only according to their work calendars. So, clearly, making changes that might improve quality — such as adding more or higher-priced resources — affects the time and money needed for your project. That adage about time being money is still true; it's just that now you can clearly see the effect one action has on other aspects of your project (especially if something you do tinkers with time or money) — it's all visible in Project's many views and reports.

So what project management adages should you be aware of as you begin to use Project? Here are ten to tack up on your office wall.

Don't Bite Off More Than You Can Manage

As I've mentioned elsewhere in this book (see Chapter 1), you must have an understanding of the goal of your project as well as the scope of its activities before you start to build a Project schedule. Don't plan a full marketing campaign if all you can anticipate at this point is what the market-research phase will look like. Because the additional elements of an actual marketing campaign hinge on that market research, do first things first; build your project in phases. That way you'll have less reworking of later tasks that simply couldn't be anticipated when you began. You'll also have less need to manipulate the baseline for those later tasks — if they're too far in the future, then by the time you get there, their time demands won't look anything like what you originally set aside for them. Moral: Don't set them in stone too early in the game.

Here are some Project features that help you with this process:

- ✔ The capability to combine subprojects into a master project with linking
- ✔ The Network Diagram view, which helps you visualize phases of your project graphically
- ✔ The flexible nature of Project outlines, which allows you to hide or display different phases of a project

Get Your Ducks in a Row

Before you start creating your project, you would be wise to do your homework. If you don't have all the information you need when you sit down at your computer to work with Project, you'll find yourself constantly stopping in midplanning and running off to find that information. This isn't a very efficient way to work.

Here are some things to research before you sit down to build a project schedule:

- ✔ **Resource information.** This includes the full name, contact information, manager and manager's contact information, skills, cost, schedule, and timing conflicts. For equipment or facilities, find out their availability and cost.

✔ **Team structure.** Will everyone do his or her own tracking, or will someone else on the team input everyone's progress? Who will update the schedule for changes that might occur? Who should get copies of which reports? Should your team have access to the master schedule online? Does everyone on the team have the technology to communicate using collaborative features such as Project Server?

✔ **Management expectations.** Does management expect to see standard reports on a regular basis? Do you need to get budget approval at various phases in your project planning, and from whom? Are cross-divisional interests involved that require you to report to or get approval from multiple sources?

✔ **Company policies.** These include company work policies regarding resource hours and overtime, the holiday calendar, how your company charges overhead costs or markups to projects, and what information can — and can't — be shared with clients or vendors.

The Enterprise resource features in Project 2003 help you call on company information stored on your server, such as enterprise resources, for consistency across projects.

Now you're ready to sit down and start inputting a Project project! (Is there an echo in here?)

Plan for Murphy

You know he's out there: Murphy and his darn law! The fact is that most projects don't happen on time or on budget. This is especially true of lengthier and more complex projects. Your job is to do the most accurate planning you can — and make prudent adjustments whenever a wrench is thrown into the works. Project gives you lots of tools to do that. But beyond all the automated features of Project, you can anticipate change by planning for it.

As described in Chapter 6, the *critical path* in a project is indeed critical. Every wise project manager builds extra time, even extra money, into schedules. When the project comes in only a week late and only $5,000 over budget, only the project manager knows that it was really four weeks later and $25,000 costlier than what the first schedule — the one with no allowance for Murphy — reflected.

Add time to the duration of every task if possible to account for shifts in schedule, and add a resource to every phase of your project that pads your budget just a bit to help you deal with overages. You can even name the extra resource *Murphy,* if you like!

Don't Put Off Until Tomorrow

Project-management software can make many aspects of your life easier, but the thing that overwhelms most people when they begin to use Project is the amount of time you have to spend actually inputting data and keeping it up to date. True, those tasks can be cumbersome, but what you can get back from those automated updating and reporting capabilities more than makes up for the work.

However, if you don't tend to the task of tracking progress on a project, you can wind up behind the proverbial eight-ball. Track just as often as you can — at least once a week. This not only saves you from facing a mountain of tracking data to be entered, but also means that you and your team are seeing the true picture of your project at any point in time. That way, you can promptly spot disaster coming — and make adjustments accordingly.

Delegate, Delegate, Delegate!

Don't try to do everything on a project yourself. Although creating and maintaining your Project file on your own may seem to give you more control, doing so is just about impossible in larger projects. Of course, you don't want dozens of people going in and making changes to your plan, because you'd run the risk of losing track of who did what and when. But a few simple practices make a few fingers in the project pie helpful, not harmful:

- ✔ Designate one person whose mission is to enter all tracking data into the master file for you — or you can automate tracking by using the Request Progress Information feature.

- ✔ Break your project into a few subprojects and assign people you trust to act as managers of those phases. Let them deal with their own tracking and adjustments, and then assemble the phase projects into a master project so you can monitor their changes.

- ✔ Enlist the help of your IS/IT person(s) in setting up Project Server to provide enhanced collaborative features to your team.

- ✔ Set uniform procedures for your team up front. Don't have one person report time on an inter-office memo sheet, somebody else e-mail you his progress, and let others stick the work they did on tasks into the Timesheet willy-nilly. Work up a strategy that uses Project features to communicate consistently.

CYA (Document!)

Everyone knows the project-management adage to CYA, but Project makes it a lot easier. Try using these features to document the details of your project:

- ✔ Use the Notes area for tasks *and* resources to make a record of background information, changes, or special issues.

- ✔ Use the routing feature of Project to route schedules to people for review. This builds an electronic paper trail of where information went and who responded.

- ✔ Customize reports to incorporate all pertinent information and help you document trends and changes.

- ✔ Save multiple versions of your project, especially if you make changes to your baseline in later versions. This provides a record of every step in your project planning, which you can refer to when questions arise down the road.

- ✔ Share updates to your plan through Project Server (as shown in Figure 20-1) so nobody can say he or she was out of the loop when some important change came down.

Figure 20-1:
You can make many Project Server settings from the Options dialog box.

Keep Your Team in the Loop

I've worked in offices where I spent more time wrestling with who to keep informed about what than I did working. If I didn't include marketing and finance in every e-mail on a new product launch, I'd be called on the carpet the next day, or — worse — some vital action step would fall through the cracks because someone didn't know he or she was supposed to take action. Try these methods of keeping communication channels open:

- ✔ Use the Project features that allow you to integrate with Outlook or other e-mail programs to route Project files or other communications.

- ✔ Build address lists in your e-mail program specific to your project team so that every message goes to everyone, every time.

- ✔ Review progress with your team by meeting regularly, whether in person, over the phone, online in a chat area, or by using meeting software. Make sure each team member has the latest version of the Project schedule to refer to during these meetings.

- ✔ Use the Send to: Exchange Folder command to post the latest version of a project in a folder on your network so others know what's going on.

- ✔ If you run SharePoint Services, you can use the integrated task pane in Project to work with the Shared Workspace feature. Shared Workspace is a great centralized place to post and exchange project-related documents created in any Office 2003 application.

- ✔ Display the work-breakdown structure code on reports so you can easily refer to specific tasks in large projects without confusion.

Take advantage of the new Printing wizard in Project Guide. This feature helps you find the best way to print various views of your project to share hard-copy updates with your team.

Measure Success

When you begin your project, you should have an idea of what constitutes success and a way to measure that success. Success can involve attaining many goals, such as

- ✔ Customer satisfaction
- ✔ Management satisfaction

✔ Being on budget

✔ Being on time

When you start your project planning, know how you'll measure your success. Will success in budgeting mean that you don't exceed your original estimates by more than 10 percent? Will your project be considered on time if you worked the estimated amount of weeks on it minus a two-month period when you went on hold for a union strike, or is the total working time less important than meeting a specific deadline? How will you measure customer satisfaction? Will management satisfaction be a done deal if you get a promotion or your division receives more funding? Does a successful product launch include high sales figures after the launch, or was your project successful merely because you got it out the door?

Place milestones in your project (as in Figure 20-2) that reflect the achievement of each type of success. When you reach each milestone, you can pat your team on the back. Knowing what success looks like helps you motivate your team to get there.

Figure 20-2: Milestones provide markers along the way that give your team a feeling of achievement.

Have a Flexible Strategy

Stuff happens. There hasn't been a project in the world that didn't require accommodations for surprises along the way. The mark of a good project manager is that he or she is alert to these changes and makes adjustments to deal with them quickly.

This isn't always easy: It's really, really hard to be the messenger of bad news. But avoiding a problem in your project, hoping it will go away, has a nasty habit of snowballing. The following tools can help you stay alert to changes and make adjustments:

- ✔ The Resource Substitution wizard helps you make changes when the one resource you'd counted on suddenly wins the lottery and disappears.

- ✔ Use the Portfolio Modeling feature (shown in Figure 20-3) to try what-if analyses on your project to anticipate how possible changes might affect you.

- ✔ Use various views to see the critical path on your project and track how much slack you have left. Adjusting tasks to efficiently use up their slack may keep you on schedule in a crisis.

Figure 20-3:
Critical path can be seen in several ways using Project's views and filters.

Learn from Your Mistakes

One of the greatest gifts Project offers you is the capability to look back when you've completed a project — so you can learn from your mistakes. You can review your original schedule and every version after that to see how well you estimated time and money, and learn to do it better.

By using records of your project, you can spot trends. Where do you always seem to miss on timing? Do you always allow way too little time on market research and way too much time for Q&A? Do you always forget to budget in temporary help during rush times, or do you overstaff early on when you could get by with fewer people?

Use the wealth of information in Project schedules to educate yourself on your own strengths and weaknesses as a project planner and manager and to get better with each project you take on.

Chapter 21

Ten Project-Management Software Products to Explore

In This Chapter

▶ Looking at add-on software

▶ Discovering software that integrates with Project-generated plans

▶ Reviewing separate software products that help project managers with project-related tasks

*Y*ou've probably figured out by now that project-management software — just like a project manager — wears a lot of hats. Project does everything from allowing you to create tasks and assign resources, to tracking progress, analyzing cost overruns, and analyzing scheduling conflicts. It can handle graphics, complex calculations, and interactions with the Web.

Software designers always have to make trade-offs among features, deciding which ones to include and how much functionality to give each feature. Most of Project's features do everything you need, but others are less complete. Some features may not quite get the job done as well as a more specialized tool you can use in addition to Project. Third-party software partners work with Microsoft to create add-on software to provide Project with that greater functionality — for example, generating more graphic reports. In other cases, software handles specialized functions that Project doesn't incorporate, such as managing the hundreds of drawings involved in construction projects.

Consider this the when-two-heads-are-better-than-one chapter. This chapter describes ten interesting software tools you can use with Project. Most of their makers offer some kind of free demo of their product on company Web sites. Plenty of products are out there, so use this chapter as a starting point as you consider ways to extend Project's functionality.

AMS Real Time Helps Keep Resources in Line

AMS Real Time, from Advanced Management Solutions (www.amsrealtime. com), is billed as an "enterprise project and resource management suite." Features that make this an interesting add-on to Project include the Workforce Browser, which helps you define and share information about resources across various projects and project managers. Also included are timesheets that people on your project can use to report their activity on multiple projects that you're tracking in Microsoft Project.

Another nice feature of this software is that it enables integration with *enterprise resource planning* (ERP) systems such as those manufactured by PeopleSoft and Oracle. In fact, when you use AMS Real Time with Project, an Enterprise menu is added to your standard Project menus so you can work from your familiar Project interface. Advanced Management Solutions even offers seminars on how to integrate Project with their software.

Cobra Squeezes the Most from Cost/Earned Value

WST Corporation (www.welcom.com), which makes its own complete project management package called Welcom, also produces Cobra, a cost/earned value management software package that you can use with Project plans. Tools offer functionality in estimating, what-if modeling of costs, and budget forecasting based on information in your Project schedule. An easy-to-use Integration wizard helps you combine Project data with Cobra's costing software.

Cobra allows you to define certain budget calculations yourself — and it offers more flexibility than some of Project's costing features. In addition, the Chart Template Designer lets you play around with a variety of 3-D charts, which you can manipulate and rotate in several ways, expanding your options for presenting Project data in three dimensions.

Inspiration Helps Planning with Visual Thinking Tools

Inspiration is an interesting product, though it's not an add-on to Microsoft Project. Inspiration is a visual learning and visual thinking software package from Strategic Transitions (www.strategictransitions.com). It's used in educational and corporate settings to help you create visual models of ideas and processes. In some ways, it resembles the Network Diagram view in Project, providing a visual view of processes. But Inspiration is more robust and flexible. You can use collections of graphic symbols, photos, and animated symbols to create diagrams.

Templates make getting started with the product fairly easy. Try the checklist feature in Inspiration to help you start planning your task list in Project.

The software has a variety of uses. Novelists can map out book ideas; corporate types can brainstorm their project goals. Use the Webbing feature to map project phases and work processes before you start to build your Project schedule. You can use it for online brainstorming with your team to get their ideas, as well. Although there's no direct integration with Project, you can place links to Inspiration diagrams in your Project file, and cut-and-paste notes you've created here into Project task or resource forms. Think of the various forms and captions in Inspiration as an efficient way to make your project brainstorming visible.

Innate Integrates Projects Large and Small

Innate Timesheets and Innate Resource Manager from Innate Management Systems (www.innateus.com) are especially helpful if you're juggling multiple projects that range from small to large. You can use Innate to manage the human resources who work on smaller projects in your organization and are also busy on larger projects that you plan in Microsoft Project. Timesheet can group resources in various useful ways.

The Innate Resource Manager helps you scope out resource availability and prioritize resource assignments. Innate Timesheets is tracking software, but it offers more than Project does in this area. You can do productivity comparisons across several tasks or projects. You can also tap into sophisticated billing systems and integrate your project information with accounting and payroll systems.

PlanView Models Your Workforce Capacity

PlanView, Inc. (www.planview.com) produces a software product that helps you sort through the various players in your project. This role-modeling feature in PlanView is intriguing. This feature creates three project roles:

✔ Stakeholders, such as clients and business partners who have a need to know. PlanView offers a scoreboard feature to help stakeholders see the overall productivity in a project.

✔ Managers, who must make decisions and manage people and processes. These people can use PlanView's tools to figure out the best deployment of resources in a project.

✔ Contributors are those working on the project who track their actual work on tasks. PlanView connects contributors' data into expense and billing features.

You can also define your own roles for people in your project.

PlanView is closely integrated with Microsoft Project, so you can share information about processes and people on a project between the two products. PlanView templates can also be used to give you a head start on your next Project plan.

Projeca Streamlines Business Processes

Projeca, from Tenrox (www.projeca.com), puts the focus on business processes, such as performance analysis, resource planning, purchasing, and revenue and cost accounting. One of the best uses of this software for the Microsoft Project user is as a bridge to various enterprise and accounting packages such as SAP and ADP Payroll.

Projeca is a Web-based solution that can be very useful in a geographically diverse project team setting. You should take a look at this package also if you have a need for RFI, quotation, and evaluation functions in your projects. Projeca offers a set of proposal-management tools to help you get the project off the ground in the first place.

Project KickStart Gives Your Project a Headstart

Project KickStart from Experience In Software (www.experienceware.com) is a simple-to-use program with a wizard-like approach to helping you lay the groundwork for small to midsize projects. If you need a little help getting started with a project, you can create your plan here in 30 minutes or less, and then use their hot link to port information over to Microsoft Project.

Project KickStart is designed to help you figure out your project strategy as you come up with a list of tasks. Planning icons remind you to map out the goals of your project and plan for obstacles. Libraries of typical goals and challenges make building them into your plan simple, and you can add your own specific company or industry phrases to the libraries. Links to Outlook, Word, and Excel also offer you some flexibility in sharing information among the Office family of products, which includes Project.

Project Manager's Assistant Organizes Drawings for Construction Projects

Originally created for the construction industry, Project Manager's Assistant from Crestsoft (www.crestsoft.com) is useful for any industry that uses a lot of drawings.

Essentially, this is a database product that helps you track drawings, issue copies, and manage changes over the life of the project. Although the product doesn't integrate directly to Project, it's an additional software product that might prove useful to many project managers. For example, graphic designers and new product designers who generate drawings can catalogue them here. If you manage scientific or engineering projects, you might also find this software useful for managing schematics or diagrams. By placing links to this database in your Project plan, you can make this information available to your project team.

TeamTrack Solves Mission-Critical Issues

TeamTrack from TeamShare (www.teamshare.com) offers "Web-architected workflow management solutions." In English, that means that the software helps you identify problems and defects that may crop up in your processes — and find solutions. The software allows you to create visual maps for your processes and share that data among your team. The Web focus here means that people can get to the process data online without having Project running.

One nice feature of this software is that it notifies you when a problem occurs or deadlines have passed without activity. TeamTrack even helps you identify issues that may arise when "non-talking" systems communicate. In other words, if you integrate two pieces of software to share data, and data comes into Project that causes a problem, you won't even know it — because you're not inputting it. TeamTrack flags such problems to help you avoid missing a critical situation before it's too late.

TeamShare's Web site offers a live online demo.

TimeSheet Professional Makes Tracking a Piece of Cake

Microsoft integrated some of TimeSheet's features into Project a few years ago. However, the fullest functionality comes from buying the TimeSheet Professional software package and using it with Project. The TimeSheet interface is simple to use, and the software is seamlessly integrated with Project for automated updating of your schedule.

This is a great product for gathering resource information on work performed on tasks. If every member of your team doesn't have access to Project, provide them with this much less expensive product for inputting their work time; then you can easily download all their data to update Project. In addition, you can get useful information on total project effort and estimates of what the costs will be by the time your project is complete.

Part VII
Appendixes

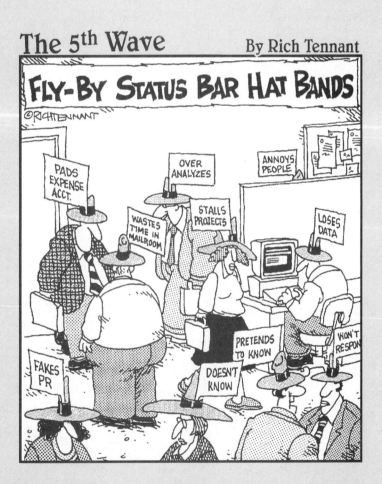

The 5th Wave   By Rich Tennant

FLY-BY STATUS BAR HAT BANDS

PADS EXPENSE ACCT.

OVER ANALYZES

ANNOYS PEOPLE

WASTES TIME IN MAILROOM

STALLS PROJECTS

LOSES DATA

PRETENDS TO KNOW

WON'T RESPOND

FAKES PR

DOESN'T KNOW

In this part . . .

This part of the book dives into the incredibly useful companion CD (chock-full of project-management goodies, software, and project templates). You get the lowdown on what's on the CD and you make use of it.

Then — by way of the last word(s) — you get a handy glossary that will have you talking like a project manager in no time.

Appendix A

On the CD

. . . .

In This Appendix

▶ System requirements

▶ Using the CD with Windows

▶ What you'll find on the CD

▶ Troubleshooting

. . . .

Microsoft Project has always engendered a slew of third-party software products that boost its productivity. That makes sense because Project itself has many facets — from performing complex calculations to organizing data about resources and tasks and generating graphical representations of project data. Because Microsoft couldn't possibly cram every possible feature of sophisticated spreadsheet, database, and graphics software into Project, the available third-party products available can help you do maximize those capabilities.

The CD accompanying this book contains several demo and trial versions of third-party programs. Take a look at their features so you can begin to build a Project third-party software library that fits your needs.

System Requirements

Make sure your computer meets *at least* the minimum system requirements shown in the following list. If your computer doesn't match up to most of these requirements, you may have problems using the software and files on the CD. (For the latest and greatest information, please refer to the ReadMe file located at the root of the CD-ROM.)

- ✔ A PC with a Pentium or faster processor.

- ✔ Microsoft Windows 98 or later.

- ✔ At least 32MB of total RAM installed on your computer; for best performance, I recommend at least 64MB

- ✔ A CD-ROM drive.

If you need more information on the basics, check out these books published by Wiley Publishing, Inc.: *PCs For Dummies,* by Dan Gookin; *Windows 95 For Dummies, Windows 98 For Dummies, Windows 2000 Professional For Dummies, Microsoft Windows Me Millennium Edition For Dummies,* all by Andy Rathbone.

Using the CD

To install the items from the CD to your hard drive, follow these steps.

1. **Insert the CD into your computer's CD-ROM drive.**

2. **Click Start ➪ Run.**

3. **In the dialog box that appears, type** D:\Start.EXE.

   Replace *D* with the proper drive letter if your CD-ROM drive uses a different letter. (If you don't know the letter, see how your CD-ROM drive is listed under My Computer.)

4. **Click OK.**

   A license agreement window appears.

5. **Read through the license agreement, nod your head, and then click the Accept button if you want to use the CD — after you click Accept, you'll never be bothered by the License Agreement window again.**

   The CD-interface Welcome screen appears. The interface is a little program that shows you what's on the CD and coordinates installing the programs and running the demos. Using the interface, you can click a button or two to make things happen.

6. **Click anywhere on the Welcome screen to enter the interface.**

   Now you're getting to the action. The next screen lists categories for the software on the CD.

7. **To view the items within a category, just click the category's name.**

   A list of programs in the category appears.

8. **For more information about a program, click the program's name.**

   Be sure to read the information that appears. Sometimes a program has its own system requirements or requires you to do a few tricks on your computer before you can install or run the program. This screen tells you what you might need to do before you can run the software.

9. **If you don't want to install the program, click the Back button to return to the previous screen.**

   You can always return to the previous screen by clicking the Back button. This feature allows you to browse the different categories and products and decide what you want to install.

10. **To install a program, click the appropriate Install button.**

    The CD interface drops to the background while the CD installs the program you chose.

11. **To install other items, repeat Steps 7 through 10.**

12. **When you've finished installing programs, click the Quit button to close the interface.**

    You can eject the CD now. Carefully place it back in the plastic jacket of the book for safekeeping.

What You'll Find on the CD

The following sections provide a summary of the software you'll find on the CD. If you need help with installing the items provided on the CD, refer back to the installation instructions in the preceding section.

Shareware programs are fully functional, free, trial versions of copyrighted programs. If you like particular programs, register with their authors for a nominal fee and receive licenses, enhanced versions, and technical support.

Freeware programs are free, copyrighted games, applications, and utilities. You can copy them to as many PCs as you like — for free — but they offer no technical support.

GNU software is governed by its own license, which is included inside the folder of the GNU software. There are no restrictions on distribution of GNU software. See the GNU license at the root of the CD for more details.

Trial, demo, or *evaluation* versions of software are usually limited, either by the time they can run on this basis or by how much functionality they can offer (some, for example, may not let you save a project you create until you purchase and register the full version of the software).

Milestones Professional 2002 from Kidasa Software, Inc.

Kidasa Web Site: www.kidasa.com

Trial version for Windows.

Milestones Professional 2002's strength is in the way it allows you to communicate project information. Using Milestones Professional you can customize schedules to print out and distribute with a handy viewer for those who have neither Project nor Milestones, publish to the Internet with an easy-to-use feature, and generate color reports to add impact to project presentations. Milestones Professional also offers project scheduling and earned-value calculation features.

Milestones Project Companion from Kidasa Software, Inc.

Kidasa Web site: www.kidasa.com

Trial version for Windows.

Milestones Project Companion is something like Milestones Professional Lite, in that it offers most of the presentation and reporting features of Milestones Professional, without the project scheduling and earned value features. If you need a less robust and less expensive solution focused specifically on project presentations, choose this option.

PERT Chart Expert from Critical Tools, Inc.

Critical Tools Web site: www.criticaltools.com

Demo version for Windows.

The Network Diagram in Project has a kissing cousin — the PERT chart. PERT Chart Expert enhances the control you have over Network Diagrams in Project, allowing you to more easily view dependencies and the critical path in your project. When you install this software you get a Chart EXPERT toolbar in Project, which you can use to work with these added features.

With PERT Chart Expert you can work with existing MS Project files, or create projects from scratch.

PlanView Project Portfolio Management from Planview

PlanView Web site: www.planview.com

Media version for Windows.

PlanView Project Portfolio Management is a Web-based software that focuses on process models that help you maximize efficiency of your resources. Using these models you can work with budgeting, resource management, and time and expense billing tasks. PlanView also helps you work with your project team by offering collaboration tools based on specified roles in various process models. If you have significant resource-management challenges, check this one out.

PMP Certification Exam

For readers who are interested in taking the PMP Certification Exam, there is a practice test that contains over 200 questions similar to what you'll find on the exam. You can select questions from any of the content domains to focus on your weak areas, or you can take the entire test. You can also randomize the questions to keep it interesting!

Project KickStart from Experience in Software

Web site for Project KickStart: www.projectkickstart.com

Trial version for Windows.

Project KickStart is actually a neat way to brainstorm your project at the outset. Using it's tools you can begin to envision the structure of your project, creating "Knowledge Libraries" of phases with accompanying goals and objectives. Then drag and drop phase information into your project to build it. You can use the Project KickStart with ten levels of subtasks and even create industry-specific libraries of project data.

WBS Chart Pro from Critical Tools, Inc.

Critical Tools Web site: www.criticaltools.com

Demo version for Windows.

If you're a super-serious user of WBS codes, WBS Chart Pro is for you. You can customize WBS codes in a more refined way than Project alone allows. In addition, you can use WBS Chart Pro to create hierarchical views of tasks that help you analyze workflow with more accuracy. You can even create projects in WBS Chart Pro, and then transfer them to Project.

Troubleshooting

I tried my best to compile programs that work on most computers with the minimum system requirements. Alas, your computer may differ, and some programs may not work properly for some reason.

The two likeliest problems are that you don't have enough memory (RAM) for the programs you want to use, or you have other programs running that are affecting installation or running of a program. If you get an error message such as Not enough memory or Setup cannot continue, try one or more of the following suggestions and then try using the software again:

- ✔ **Turn off any antivirus software running on your computer.** Installation programs sometimes mimic virus activity and may make your computer incorrectly believe that it's being infected by a virus.

- ✔ **Close all running programs.** The more programs you have running, the less memory is available to other programs. Installation programs typically update files and programs; so if you keep other programs running, installation may not work properly.

- ✔ **Have your local computer store add more RAM to your computer.** This is, admittedly, a drastic and somewhat expensive step. However, if you have a Windows 95 PC computer with a PowerPC chip, adding more memory can really help the speed of your computer and allow more programs to run at the same time. This may include closing the CD interface and running a product's installation program from Windows Explorer.

If you still have trouble with the CD-ROM, please call the Wiley Product Technical Support phone number: (800) 762-2974. Outside the United States, call 1(317) 572-3994. You can also contact Wiley Product Technical Support through the internet at: http://www.wiley.com/techsupport. Wiley Publishing will provide technical support only for installation and other general quality control items; for technical support on the applications themselves, consult the program's vendor or author.

To place additional orders or to request information about other Wiley products, please call (800) 225-5945.

Appendix B

Glossary

- -

actual: The cost of the percentage of work that has been completed on a task.

ACWP (actual cost of work performed): Cost of the actual, real work done on a project to date, plus any fixed costs.

ALAP (as late as possible): A constraint put on a task's timing to make the task occur as late as possible in the project schedule, taking into account any dependency relationships. *See also* dependency.

ASAP (as soon as possible): A constraint put on a task's timing to make the task occur as early as possible in the project schedule, taking into account any dependency relationships. *See also* dependency.

BAC (budget at completion): The sum total of all costs involved in completing a task. *See also* baseline cost.

base calendar: The default calendar on which all new tasks are based, unless a resource or task-specific calendar is applied.

baseline: The detailed project plan against which actual work is tracked.

baseline cost: The total planned costs for a project's tasks, before any actual costs are incurred.

BCWP (budgeted cost of work performed): Also called earned value, this term refers to the value of work that has been completed. For example, a task with $1000 of costs accrues a baseline value of $750 when its 75 percent complete.

BCWS (budgeted cost of work scheduled): The percentage of the plan that's completed times the planned costs. This calculated value totals a task's completed work and its remaining planned costs.

calendar: The various settings for hours in a workday, days in a work week, holidays, and nonworking days on which a project schedule is based. You can set Project, Task, and Resource calendars.

circular dependency: A timing relationship among tasks that creates an endless loop that can't be resolved.

collapse: To close up a project outline to hide subtasks from view.

combination view: A Project view with task details appearing at the bottom of the screen.

constraint: A parameter that forces a task to fit a specific timing. For example, a task can be constrained to start as late as possible in a project. Constraints interact with dependency links to determine a task's timing.

cost: The amount of money associated with a project task when you assign resources, which are equipment, materials, or people with associated fees or hourly rates.

critical path: The series of tasks that must occur on time for the overall project to meet its deadline.

critical task: A task on the critical path. *See also* critical path.

crosstab: A report format that compares two intersecting sets of data. For example, you can generate a crosstab report showing the costs of critical tasks that are running late.

cumulative cost: The planned total cost to date for a resource's effort on a particular task. This calculation adds the costs already incurred on a task to any planned costs remaining for the uncompleted portion of the task.

cumulative work: The planned total work of a resource on a particular task. This calculation adds the work completed on a task to any planned work remaining for the uncompleted portion of the task.

current date line: The vertical line in a Gantt Chart indicating today's date and time. *See also* Gantt Chart.

CV (cost variance): The difference between the baseline costs and the combination of actual costs to date and estimated costs remaining (scheduled costs). The cost variance is either positive (over budget) or negative (under budget).

deadline date: A date you assign to a task that doesn't constrain the task's timing. However, if a deadline date is assigned, Project displays an indicator symbol if the task runs past the deadline.

dependency: A timing relationship between two tasks in a project. A dependency link causes a task to occur before or after another task or to begin or end at some point during the life of the other task.

detail task: *See* subtask.

duration: The amount of calendar time it takes to complete a task.

duration variance: The difference between the planned (baseline) task duration and the current estimated task duration, based on activity to date and any remaining activity still to be performed.

EAC (estimate at completion): The total planned cost for resource effort on a specific task. This calculation combines the costs incurred to date with costs estimated for a task's remaining work.

earned value: A reference to the value of work completed. A task with $1000 of associated costs has a baseline value of $750 when 75 percent complete. *See also* BCWP.

effort-driven: A type of task that requires an assigned amount of effort to be completed. When you add resources to an effort-driven task, the assigned effort is distributed among the task resources equally.

enterprise custom fields: Custom fields stored in a global file; these fields can be used to standardize Project plan content across an organization.

enterprise resources: A feature that allows you to save all resource information for resources used across an organization in one location.

estimated duration: A setting that indicates that you are using a best guess of a task's duration. When you enter an estimated duration for a task, you can then apply a filter to displays only tasks with estimated duration, which reflects the fact that they have questionable timing.

expand: To open up a project outline to reveal both summary tasks and subtasks.

expected duration: An estimate of the actual duration of a task, based on work performance to date.

external task: A task in another project. You can set links between tasks in your project and external tasks.

finish date: The date on which a project or task is estimated to be — or actually is — completed.

finish-to-finish relationship: A dependency relationship in which the finish of one task determines the finish of another task.

finish-to-start relationship: A dependency relationship in which the finish of one task determines the start of another task.

fixed duration: The length of time required to complete a task remains constant no matter how many resources are assigned to the task. A half-day seminar is an example of a fixed-duration task.

fixed-unit: A type of cost for which the resource units are constant; if you change the duration of the task, resource units don't change. This is the default task type.

fixed-work: A type of task for which the number of resource hours assigned to the task determine its length.

float: *See* slack.

Gantt Chart: A standard Project view that displays columns of task information alongside a chart that shows task timing in bar-chart format.

gap: *See* lag.

generic resources: A type of resource that allows you to make skill-based assignments based on a skill/code profile.

grouping: The organization of tasks by a customized field to summarize costs or other factors.

ID number: The number automatically assigned to a task by Project based on its vertical sequence in the project list.

indent: To move a task to a lower level of detail in the project's outline hierarchy.

lag: The amount of downtime that can occur between the end of one task and the beginning of another. Lag is built into a dependency relationship between tasks when you indicate that a certain amount of time must pass before the second task can begin.

leveling: A calculation used by Project that modifies resource work assignments for the purpose of resolving resource conflicts.

linking: (1) To establish a connection between tasks in separate schedules so that task changes in the first schedule are reflected in the second. (2) To establish dependencies among project tasks.

material resources: The supplies or other items used to complete a task (one of two resource categories; the other is work resources).

milestone: A task of zero duration, which marks a moment in time or an event in a schedule.

network diagram: An illustration that graphically represents workflow among a project's tasks; one of Microsoft Project's standard views.

node: In Network Diagram view, a box containing information about individual project tasks.

nonworking time: The time when a resource is not available to be assigned to work on any task in a project.

outdent: To move a task to a higher level in a project's outline hierarchy.

outline: The structure of summary and subtasks in a project.

overallocation: When a resource is assigned to spend more time on a single task or a combination of tasks occurring at the same than that resource's work calendar permits.

overtime: Any work scheduled beyond a resource's standard work hours. You can assign a different rate than a resource's regular rate to overtime work.

percent complete: The amount of work on a task that has already been accomplished, expressed as a percentage.

PERT chart: A standard project-management tracking form indicating workflow among project tasks. This is called a Network Diagram in Project. *See also* network diagram.

portfolio analyzer: A view that gives higher-level managers an overview of data across several projects to enable analysis and decision making.

portfolio modeler: A feature that allows you to model any changes to your project and see what impact those changes would have.

predecessor: In a dependency link, the task designated to occur before another task. *See also* dependency *and* successor.

priorities: A ranking of importance assigned to tasks. When you use resource leveling to resolve project conflicts, priority is a factor in the leveling calculation. A higher-priority task is less likely than a lower-priority task to incur a delay during the leveling process. *See also* resource leveling.

progress lines: Gantt Chart view bars that overlap the baseline taskbar and allow you to compare the baseline plan with a task's tracked progress.

project: A series of tasks that achieves a specific goal. A project seeks to meet the triple requirements of timeliness, quality, and budget.

Project Guide: A wizard-like help feature that takes Project users through various steps to build a Project schedule.

project management: The discipline that studies various methods, procedures, and concepts used to control the progress and outcome of projects.

Project Server: A Web-based companion product of Microsoft Project that enables team members to enter information about their tasks into an overall project schedule without having Project installed on their own computers.

recurring task: A task that will occur several times during the life of a project. Regular project-team meetings or quarterly inspections are examples of recurring tasks.

resource: A cost associated with a task. A resource can be a person, a piece of equipment, materials, or a fee.

resource-driven: A task whose timing is determined by the number of resources assigned to it.

resource leveling: A process used to modify resource assignments to resolve resource conflicts.

resource pool: (1) Resources that are assigned as a group to an individual task, such as a pool of administrative workers assigned to generate a report. (2) A group of resources created in a centralized location that multiple project managers can access and assign to their projects.

resource sharing: A feature that allows you to copy resources you've created in another project to your current plan.

Resource Substitution Wizard: A wizard that replaces an unavailable resource with another of similar skill and cost.

roll up: The calculation by which all subtask values are "rolled up," or summarized, in a single summary task.

Shared Workspace: A feature of Windows SharePoint Services in which you can share documents online that were created with various Microsoft Office 2003 applications.

slack: The amount of time you can delay a task before the task becomes critical. Slack is used up when any delay in a task will delay the overall project deadline. Also called float.

split tasks: Tasks that have one or more breaks in their timing. When you split a task, you stop it part way, and start it again at a later time.

start date: The date on which a project or task begins.

start-to-finish relationship: A dependency relationship in which the start of one task determines the finish of another task.

start-to-start relationship: A dependency relationship in which the start of one task determines the start of another task.

subproject: A copy of a second project inserted in a project. The inserted project becomes a phase of the project in which it is inserted.

subtask: A task detailing a specific step in a project phase. This detail is rolled up into a higher-level summary task. Also called a subordinate task. *See also* roll up.

successor: In a dependency relationship, the later of two tasks. *See also* dependency.

summary task: In a project outline, a task that has subordinate tasks. A summary task rolls up the details of its subtasks and has no timing of its own. *See also* roll up.

task: An individual step performed to reach a project's goal.

template: A format in which a file can be saved. The template saves elements such as calendar settings, formatting, and tasks. New project files can be based on a template to save the time involved in reentering settings.

timescale: The area of a Gantt Chart view that displays units of time; when placed against those units of time, taskbars graphically represent the timing of tasks.

tracking: To record the actual progress of work completed and the costs accrued on a project's tasks.

Value List: A customizable feature of Project that allows you to create a list of values in a field from which a user can choose, as an alternative to entering data manually.

variable rate: A shift in resource cost that can be set to occur at specific times during a project. For example, if a resource is expected to receive a raise or if equipment lease rates are scheduled to increase, you can assign variable rates for those resources.

WBS (work breakdown structure): Automatically assigned numbers that designate an outline structure for each project task. Government projects often require the use of WBS codes.

work breakdown structure: *See* WBS.

work resources: The people or equipment that perform work necessary to accomplish a task. *See also* material resources.

workload: The amount of work any resource is performing at any given time, taking into account all tasks to which the resource is assigned.

workspace: A set of files and project settings that you can save and reopen together, so that you pick up where you stopped on a set of projects.

Index

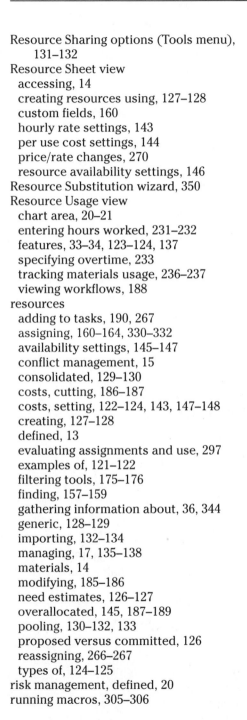

Wiley Publishing, Inc.
End-User License Agreement

READ THIS. You should carefully read these terms and conditions before opening the software packet(s) included with this book "Book". This is a license agreement "Agreement" between you and Wiley Publishing, Inc. "WPI". By opening the accompanying software packet(s), you acknowledge that you have read and accept the following terms and conditions. If you do not agree and do not want to be bound by such terms and conditions, promptly return the Book and the unopened software packet(s) to the place you obtained them for a full refund.

1. **License Grant.** WPI grants to you (either an individual or entity) a nonexclusive license to use one copy of the enclosed software program(s) (collectively, the "Software") solely for your own personal or business purposes on a single computer (whether a standard computer or a workstation component of a multi-user network). The Software is in use on a computer when it is loaded into temporary memory (RAM) or installed into permanent memory (hard disk, CD-ROM, or other storage device). WPI reserves all rights not expressly granted herein.

2. **Ownership.** WPI is the owner of all right, title, and interest, including copyright, in and to the compilation of the Software recorded on the disk(s) or CD-ROM "Software Media". Copyright to the individual programs recorded on the Software Media is owned by the author or other authorized copyright owner of each program. Ownership of the Software and all proprietary rights relating thereto remain with WPI and its licensers.

3. **Restrictions on Use and Transfer.**

   (a) You may only (i) make one copy of the Software for backup or archival purposes, or (ii) transfer the Software to a single hard disk, provided that you keep the original for backup or archival purposes. You may not (i) rent or lease the Software, (ii) copy or reproduce the Software through a LAN or other network system or through any computer subscriber system or bulletin-board system, or (iii) modify, adapt, or create derivative works based on the Software.

   (b) You may not reverse engineer, decompile, or disassemble the Software. You may transfer the Software and user documentation on a permanent basis, provided that the transferee agrees to accept the terms and conditions of this Agreement and you retain no copies. If the Software is an update or has been updated, any transfer must include the most recent update and all prior versions.

4. **Restrictions on Use of Individual Programs.** You must follow the individual requirements and restrictions detailed for each individual program in the About the CD-ROM appendix of this Book. These limitations are also contained in the individual license agreements recorded on the Software Media. These limitations may include a requirement that after using the program for a specified period of time, the user must pay a registration fee or discontinue use. By opening the Software packet(s), you will be agreeing to abide by the licenses and restrictions for these individual programs that are detailed in the About the CD-ROM appendix and on the Software Media. None of the material on this Software Media or listed in this Book may ever be redistributed, in original or modified form, for commercial purposes.